Dharma

IN
EARLY BRAHMANIC, BUDDHIST
AND JAIN TRADITIONS

Sri Garib Das Oriental Series No. 286

Dharma

IN EARLY BRAHMANIC, BUDDHIST AND JAIN TRADITIONS

VINCENT SEKHAR, S.J.

Sri Satguru Publications
A Division of
Indian Books Centre
Delhi, India

Published by
Sri Satguru Publications,
Indological and Oriental Publishers
A Division of
Indian Books Centre
40/5, Shakti Nagar,
Delhi-110007
India

Email: ibcindia@vsnl.com
Website: http://www.indianbookscentre.com

First Edition: Delhi, 2003

ISBN 81-7030-791-0

Printed at Chawla Offset Printers, Delhi 110 052

As

A mark of Respect and Reverence

To my Parents, Teachers, especially (Late) Dr. M.D. Vasantharaj,

and

To the Followers of Non-Violence

Acknowledgment

My sincere thanks to Dr. Michael Amaladoss, S.J., one of the acknowledged Asian Christain theologains, who wanted me to study the meaning of Dharma in depth, especially from the Śramaṇa point of view and to seek its contemporay relevance to the society at large. It was (Late) Dr. T.G. Kalghatgi who gave me firm footing in Jain Metaphysics and Ethics. His association and guidance helped me acquire an interest in all that concerns a Jain, in order to pick up a sense of being a Jain.

I am much indebted to (Late) Dr. M.D. Vasantharaj, former professor and Head of the Department of Jainology, University of Madras, my doctoral guide. He paid special attention to the reading of the material I had prepared, and guided me with much encouragement, provocations and reflections. Dr. Christopher Key Chapple, Professor of Theological Studies, Loyola Marymount University, Los Angeles, and Dr. A. Pushparajan, Head of the Department of Interreligious Relations, Madurai Kamaraj University, valued my doctoral thesis, and their suggestions have been duly incorporated in this print form. I feel honoured to have received compliments from Dr. Chapple and the veteran Jain Scholar Prof. Sagarmal Jain. I thank them for writing the Foreword and the Appraisal.

My sincere thanks to (Late) Fr. Lawrence Sundaram, S.J. of Loyola College, Fr. Vedanayanam, S.J. and Dr. N. Vasupal, Professor and Head of the Department of Jainology . University of Madras, for going thorugh this work, correcting mistakes, grammatical errors, etc. Thanks to Ms. Kavitha and Priya for preparing meticulously the index and bringing the manuscript in a presentable form. Thanks to the University of Madras for allowing me to publish my thesis. I am deeply indebted to the MISSION PROCURATOR of German Jesuit Province. Without their encouragement and support, it would be impossible to see this in book form.

Dr. Vincent Sekhar, S.J.
October 2, 2003
Gandhi Jayanthi

Foreword

The concept of dharma stands as the cornerstone of Indian religious and philosophical thought. Derived from the verbal root dhṛ (hold), it refers to the processes through which society finds coherence. On a personal level, it provides meaning and context for human action.

The Dharmaśāstra materials of the Brāhmaṇical traditions suggest specific life paths and offer rules and regulations for the maintenance of peace, harmony, and justice. Even today, these books help instruct individuals regarding their responsibilities and outline ideal patterns for behavior. In Buddhism, the term dharma refers both to the teachings of the Buddha and to the particular building blocks of the constructed world. For Jainism, dharma helps explain the continuity of movement in the universe; it also serves to underscore the need to observe correct and auspicious behaviors.

Dr. Vincent Sekhar, S.J., has written about dharma in all three traditions. Recognizing the underlying concern in dharma for the enhancement of proper action, he identifies and explicates key themes, including its relationship to ritual and meditation. From a Jaina perspective, he emphasizes teachings on right knowledge, the need to purify oneself of negative karmas, and the doctrines of nonviolence (ahiṁsā) and plurality (anekānta).

This work continues a long standing Jesuit tradition in respecting the religious ideas and philosophical ideas of all traditions. In this comprehensive survey of Dharma in Hinduism, Buddhism, and Jainism, Sekhar has articulated similarities and differences among these three important traditions. Appropriately, the book concludes with a discussion of Mahatma Gandhi's understanding, practice, and teaching of Dharma. Gandhi demonstrates that a concern for highest values, particularly nonviolence, takes precedence over theological differences. This book will help the reader appreciate the truths of dharma as an overarching theme throughout the history of Indian thought.

Christopher Key Chapple
Professor of Theological Studies
Loyola Marymount University
Los Angeles, U.S.A.

Appraisal

The Sanskrit word *dharma* is generally translated in English as *religion* but the word *religion* is equivalent to the term *yoga*, which means union of the *self* with the ultimate reality. Religion, we think, is to do only with faith, as faith in some dogmas or as performance of some rituals as prescribed in the religious texts without much understanding or critical investigation. Dr. Vincent Sekhar rightly observes that Dharma is both one's vision and the way of life. In Indian religious systems metaphysics, ethics and religion are treated as one unit. In India, to be religious to be a moral person. For an Indian thinker, religion is not a matter of mere faith in some belief or in some rituals but it is an art of living harmoniously and peacefully in the society and with nature. Further more, it is coexistence with the nature or reality. This was the case with the *śramaṇic* religions like Jainism and Buddhism. These religions critically analysed the beliefs and rituals of their context and proposed new theories and means of life.

Dr. Vincent Sekhar notes that religion gives meaning to life and society. It does not provide merely an abstract creed as a set of beliefs but offers at the level of behaviour certain ethical principles through which the believing community seeks to reach the proposed goals and ideals. It is the task of religion to orient the whole of life for the common good of humanity.

It is not untrue that the Śramaṇic traditions did develop the Kṣatriya wisdom embedded in the *Upaniṣads* laying much stress on non-passionate, detached way of life of a renouncer, and an ascetic for realising the full potential of oneself as mokṣa or Nirvāṇa. They were atheistic and fully believed in the law of karma. The author has highlighted the ascetic ideals of the *śramaṇas* in their right perspective. The main theme of the book, namely the understanding of *dharma* in its several meanings, is an exhaustive and a fair treatment. In Indian religious traditions the term *dharma* connotes variously as *ṛta* or cosmic Order, the *essential* nature of things (*vastu svabhāva*), objects of key experiences, duty, and a system of spritual quest or moral living.

In the section on *Jain dharma* the author says that Ahiṁsā is the core of Jain religion and without this ideal it is impossible for anyone to attain *nirvāṇa* or *mokṣa*. I would say that it is not the case with Jainism alone. All religions of higher spiritual quest accept *ahiṁsā* as constituent of their soterology. Mahāvīra in *Ācārāṅga Sūtra* mentions that non-violence is the pure and eternal form of religion. It is the universal religion. The author rightly points out that *ahiṁsā*, preached by the ancient mastes and seers, has a strong contemporary relevance in a multicultural and global society, tarnished and wounded by war and violence. The ideal of *ahiṁsā* is a fine invitation and a great task to be accomplished. It may not be an exaggeration to conclude that *ahiṁsā*, in other words, protection and preservation of life and environment is said to be the essence of the *śramaṇa dharma*. The last three chapters are devoted to this focus and stress.

The author is of the opinion that it is the *śramaṇic* ideals and values of *ahiṁsā* and *anekānta* that will enhance the pluralistic culture of India. He says that the *śramaṇa* ideals of non-injury to life and detachment in the procurement and use of wealth, etc. are the best means of remedy to the ills of the world. The author stresses that the simple life-style and generous attitude promoted by the śramaṇa sages and other spiritual masters are the sure step to meet the challenges of the contemporary world of consumerism and hoarding mentality, violence and their several manifestations.

Equality and fair treatment are possible where people respect one another as *sacred* human persons. Violence to life and environment can be averted if the language of love prevails in the human and cosmic domain. This would avoid narrow attitude that prompts peoples to selfishness and ghetto mentality, fossilised in their own world, never to accommodate any one for growth and good. It is only a sense of *sacredness of life* and a large *accommodative spirit* that would mediate relationships and help promoting and building a cosmic society of love and mutual trust, justice and peace.

Dr. Vincent Sekhar's work is a rich contribution to the unfathomable riches of Indian understanding of life and reality, particularly from the Hindu, Jain and Buddhist perspectives. He has portrayed the significance of the basic concepts of all these traditions with a view to find solutions to the present-day world problems, especially violence and war, fundamentalism and religious fanaticism, consumerism ane exploitation of every kind, and ecological imbalance. It is a great thing that the author, the first Christian from India to write anything on Jain philosophy and religion, has done this work in the field of religious studies with an intellectual honesty and unbiased manner. I am sure, the work will be received well by the intellectual world, particularly by those engaged in Comparative Study of Religion.

Prof. Sagarmal Jain
February 6, 2003 (Vasanth Panchami)
Shajapur–465001 (MP), India

Preface

The word *Dharma* has come to be known as *duty* in the course of history and human civilization. But it had different meanings at different times. Races and Religious traditions have given special connotations to the term Dharma at all levels. The Buddhist tradition, for instance, has understood this term to mean the ultimate constituent of reality. Technically speaking, Dharma and Adharma in Jainism are related to the movement dynamics of the world.

When two different traditions with their set-patterns of beliefs and practices encounter with each other, the social dynamics bring about a relation and change in the people's attitude, belief and even practices. The Āryan and the Non-Āryan encounter in ancient India is a typical example of this. The Indo-Aryan literature is an outcome of the dynamics of cultural and religious encounter and exchange of these two races. The dialogue between the robust, positive attitude of the Āryans with the negative and renunciatory spirit of the aborigines has resulted in the balancing of thought and ideals, seen expounded in the Āraṇyakas, Upaniṣads, and the Epics.

Down the centuries, we see a shift in emphasis of the objectives of life and the sādhana. In the Brāhmaṇic age, it was ritual performance (Yajña) that ensured a happier life in some svarga or heaven. In the process of encounter, the objectives of life gave way to newer ideas such as *Karma and Rebirth* and ideals like *Mokṣa* or getting rid of the cycle of births and deaths. And the path of attaining Mokṣa is not any longer through merely external performances like ritual sacrifices, etc. but through ardent meditative and austere processes. This change in emphasis came through an age-long religious, theological exchanges between the *Śramaṇa* and the *Vedic/Brāhmaṇa* traditions. Living religions like Jainism and Buddhism are representatives of Śramaṇa culture.

The less life-affirming attitude of the Śramaṇas, life as impermanent and full of suffering, etc., has motivated them towards a definite objective in life, namely, conquering of oneself and rising above the limited conditions of life. To this end in view, the Śramaṇas would appreciate and live an attitude of detachment and renunciation. Getting rid of Karma that binds one to the life cycle is their primary concern and the goal to be achieved. For this, one needs to understand *reality* in the right perspective. It is the Right Knowledge of the Reality (of existence, its consequences, of the environment, its destiny, etc.) that will bring about the desired End. Hence, Ātmavidyā (knowlege about the Self) and Mokṣadharma (gaining the ideal of Mokṣa) are the twin-face of their goal/vision of Life.

The social and cultural outcome of the Indo-Āryan encounter is the *Varnāśrama dharma*, a general scheme or stratification of life in society. Indian cultural history illustrates that it is the highly educated Āryan brain and genius that played a major role in giving a shape to the material content of the Non-Āryan resources.

The ascetic spirituality of India is mostly attributed to the Śramaṇa trend of thought. The idea of detachment and renunciation seem to be related to the ancient Indian asceticism, which may have a Śramaṇa origin. This is seen in the age-old religious culture of the Jains, the Buddhists and other Śramaṇic traditions like the Ājīvikas. These religious traditions emphasize the significance of ascetic practices for the purpose of attaining the goal of life. Though Karma can hardly be rid of by newer acts, yet all Śramaṇa traditions acknowledge the fruit of ascetic practices. Jainism and Buddhism as living Śramaṇa religions are models for a greater understanding of Indian asceticism as a way of life, though they may differ from one another in their shades of meaning and understanding of different aspects of life.

As it is indicated earlier, the differences between traditions are mainly due to their vision about *reality*, the way they raise questions concerning the phenomenon of life, nature and environment, and the conclusions they arrive at through such a reflective process. Briefly, it is due to their philosophy of life and existence. Each tradition has its peculiarities in the understanding of concepts, common to all. It is these differences that form the basis for their differences in practice. For example, the ethical practices may seem similar in all Śramaṇa traditons, but their rationale is closely bound to their belif system. Hence, sometimes one is tempted to link these two, namely *philosophy and ethics* to mean *Dharma.* Each tradition has its tenets, follows its great line of teachers, who themselves had, in their time, adhered to their predecessors' teachings or perhaps modified or added newer elements to it (e.g. compare *Pārśva* with *Mahāvīra* in Jain tradition). It is in this context that the manifold understanding of Dharma becomes evident and meaningul.

The Buddhist's ardent love to get rid of mundane existence and its consequent pain and suffering has brought about a mediative process, to reflect upon the root carse of suffering , and an ethics of detached living. Later Buddhist trends show the worth of virtues like compassion in the legendary *Bodhisattvas,* whose actions present a model for right social relationship and personal psychological satisfaction. The development of newer ideals in Buddhism hasd given way to its deep-rootendness in different cultures and mations. The Jain *saptatattvas* or the seven mataphysical catergories are the foundations for their ethical life. Right Knowledge of the nature of reality with a Right Faith or vision into the truth leads them to Right Conduct. Since nothing short of complete annihilation of Karma is the very ideal of life, whatever obstructs its path of achievement has to be eliminated. The attitude of equanimity and self-control, protection of life and comprehensive view of the multiple facets of reality are some of the Jain traits in the understanding of *Dharma.*

Hindu dharma has gone through an evolutionary process from Vedic time onwards, and the Brāhmaṇic brain and position has played a vital role in the formation of the present-day understanding of dharma, namely, *religion* or *Way of life* in the broad sense, and *duty* in the moral sense. But it also refers to a social order, specified by the *varṇa* and the related system of Labour, and a spiritual order marked by the *āśrama* system. Dharma has retained the latter identity despite large-scale assimilation from other traditions. While Hindu Dharma can not be conceived without a person's placement in society, *Śramaṇa* thought pays attention to how a person leads one's life in society. A person's worth is judged by one's action with all his intention, etc. To be a person is to be a moral person.

Although morality or ethics is upheld by all traditions, yet we see variations in their motives, their standard of judgement, etc. Special reference is made to the Jaina tradition to show how Dharma as a way of looking at *reality* finally precipitates into a system of moral behaviour for the laity and the clergy. The *two-tier* system of morality, seen from the absolute and the practical points of view, resolves the seeming conflict between two moral standards. It is also shown how Jaina ethics is firmly founded on its metaphysics. Jain dharma is both its *vision* and the *way of life*. Both metaphysics and ethics are treated as one unit.

The Śramaṇa idea of liberation (Mokṣa, Nirvāṇa, etc.) is closely linked to *Ahiṁsā* or *Non-violence*. No virtue is so valuable as *Ahiṁsā*. While Buddhism stresses the virtue of compassion or *Karuṇā* to all living beings, Jainism treats *Ahiṁsā* as the core of its religion. The Religion of *Ahiṁsā* preached by the ancient masters is relavant even today. *Ahiṁsā* is based on an animistic belied that all beings possess a *life-force* that cannot be destroyed. Any injury done to a living the elemental bodies, is sinful. Nirvāṇa or Mokṣa is an ideal impossible to reach without Ahiṁsā.

This important concept has newer interprtations in modern times. It has gained acceptance in the intellectual, social and political of life and nation building. For example, the *Anekānta* doctrine of plurality, a special contribution of the Jains to the intellectual works, origainates from *Ahiṁsā*. And it is this pluralistic attitude of life and reality (opposed to dogmatism) that help in the modern age to practice dialogue and to negotiate with one another to resolve conflicts. M.K. Gandhi and similar world leaders practised *Ahiṁsā* in their world mission. There is no doubt that in a multi-cultrual and global setting, and especially in a wounded and tarnished world, the ideal of *Ahiṁsā* is a fine invitation and a great task to accomplish. It may not be an exaggeratoin to conclude that *Ahiṁsā*, or in other words, protection and preservation of life and environment, is said to be the *Essence of Śramaṇa Dharma.*

In the course of developing this thesis, I had a chance to delve deep into the ocean of ancient Indian culture and tradition, religion and philosophy, in order to contextualize their unfathomable riches. Hence the approach or methodology had to be interdisciplinary and in comparative light. The method included an analytical study of the texts and their commentaries and make critical reflections and evaluations. But the work was never easy as I am neither a historian nor a sociologist in order to interpret the texts of different traditions in a multiple socio-cultural contexts. Since the original texts and their commentaries are quite ancient and sometimes obscure, the contemporary reading of them and interpreting them were quite tough, but immensely valuable. Since very little has been said on Jain religion from sociological persective, secondary sources with specific social thurst are hardly available. Yet, in a modest way, I have tried to present the material in a coherent manner, putting them in their contexts, and have drawn contemporary meaning for building up a society fitting to the future generations.

Dr. Vincent Sekhar, S.J.
Arrupe Illam
Arul Anandar College
Karumathur 625514
Madurai Dt. India.
E-mail : sekharsj@rediffmail.com

Abbreviations

Ācār Sūtra	-	Ācārāṅga Sūtra
Ait Br	-	Aitareya Brāhmaṇa
Amit SA	-	Amitagati Śrāvakācāra
Aṅg N	-	Aṅguttara Nikāya
Āp DS	-	Āpastambha Dharmasūtra
Aran Kāṇ	-	Araṇya Kāṇḍa
Aup Sūtra	-	Aupapātika Sūtra
Ayod Kāṇ	-	Ayodhya Kāṇḍa
Bāla Kāṇ	-	Bāla Kāṇḍa
Baudh DS	-	Baudhāyana Dharmasūtra
Bhag Ār	-	Bhagavatī Ārādhana
Bhag Sūtra	-	Bhagavatī Sūtra
Br Up	-	Bṛhadāraṇyaka Upaniṣad
Chānd Up	-	Chāhdogya Upaniṣad
CW	-	The Collected Works of Mahatma Gandhi
Das Sūtra	-	Daśavaikālika Sūtra
Dīg N	-	Dīgha Nikāya
ER	-	Encyclopaedia of Religion
ERE	-	Encyclopaedia of Religion and Ethics
Gaut DS	-	Gautama Dharmasūtra
Gom Sāra	-	Gommatasāra
IHQ	-	Indian Historical Quarterly
Kār Ap	-	Kartikeyānupreksā
Kathā Up	-	Kathā Upaniṣad
Kaus Up	-	Kauśītaki Upaniṣad
M Bh	-	Mahābhārata
Mai Up	-	Maitrāyaṇī Upaniṣad
Maj N	-	Majjhima Nikāya
Muṇḍ Up	-	Muṇḍaka Upaniṣad
Prav Sāra	-	Pravacanasāra

Pur Sid	-	Pumṣārthasiddhyupāya
RKSA	-	Ratnakaraṇḍaka Śrāvakācāra
Sāgār Dhar	-	Sāgāradharmāmṛta
Sar Sid	-	Sarvārtha Siddhi
Śat Br	-	Śatapata Brāhmaṇa
SBB	-	Sacred Books of the Buddhists
SBE	-	Sacred Books of the East
SBJ	-	Sacred Books of the Jains
Saṁ N	-	Saṁyutta Nikāya
Sthān Sūtra	-	Sthānāṅga Sūtra
Sum Vil	-	Sumaṅgala Vilāsinī
Sūt Kr	-	Sūtrakṛtāṅga
Śvet Up	-	Śvetāsvatāra Upaniṣad
Tait Br	-	Taittīriya Brāhmaṇa
Tait Up	-	Taittīriya Upaniṣad
Tat Sūtra	-	Tattvārtha Sūtra
Up Das	-	Upāsakadaśāṅga
Utt Sūtra	-	Uttarādhyayana Sūtra
Vaj Up	-	Vajrasuci Upaniṣad
Vas DS	-	Vaśiṣṭa Dharmasūtra
Vas SA	-	Vasunandin Śrāvakācāra
Yaj DS	-	Yājñavalkya Dharmasūtra
Yud Kāṇ	-	Yuddha kāṅḍa

Contents

ACKNOWLEDGMENT		vii
FOREWORD		ix
APPRAISAL		xi
PREFACE		xv
ABBREVIATIONS		xxi
CHAPTER I	Dharma in the Dialectic of Traditions	1
CHAPTER II	The Ascetic Path of the Śramaṇas	20
CHAPTER III	A Manifold Conception of the Meaning of Dharma	46
PART I	Dharma in Hindu Tradition	46
PART II	Dharma in Buddhist Tradition	61
PART III	Dharma in Jaina Tradition	72
CHAPTER IV	An Enquiry into Jaina Ethics	103
CHAPTER V	Technical Discussion of the term 'Dharma'	126
PART I	In Buddhist Abhidharma Tradition	126
PART II	Technical Understanding of Dharma and Adharma In Jaina Tradition	143
PART III	Comparative Analysis of Bauddha Dharma And Jaina Dharma and Adharma	149
CHAPTER VI	Contemporary Relevance of Śramaṇa Dharma	160
PART I	The Phenomenon of Violence: Evil and its Remedies	160

PART II	Is Non-violence still a Myth?: The Śramaṇa Vision of Ahiṁsā as applied To the Emergence of a Non-violent Society	183
CHAPTER VII	Insights into the Śramaṇic Traditions	206
BIBLIOGRAPHY		217
INDEX		
Word Index		235
Subject Index		239

CHAPTER I

DHARMA IN THE DIALECTIC OF TRADITIONS

1.1. The Dynamics of social relationship

Dharma is a term that defies any definition. But it is often understood as religion or moral code. Understood as religion, it functions in a class society and amidst concrete social classes with their different degrees of power and interests. It is not merely goodwill or good fortune of a group of believers or religious leaders that determines the development and the end product of their religious or moral activity. Otto Maduro[1] remarks that it is mainly the structure of the society that will define what forms of religious or moral activity that is beneficial for them to develop.

In a class structure, the dominant class develops and exercises its material power in the economic, political, military, moral, educational, literary, artistic and religious spheres. As power increases, it is exercised more and more over all dimensions of collective life, like the co-ordination of all the activities of the society. The dominant group will have the material means to achieve their interest with good chances of success. Thus, for instance, it will enunciate the specific orientations, rules and regulations; it will meticulously preserve them; it will either annihilate or subjugate all religious elements (rites, beliefs, behavioural norms, groups, leaders, etc.) that become dangerous or an obstacle to the preservation and consolidation of the group. It would plan out all strategies to fulfil this by disqualifying, converting, disparaging, replacing, competing or even by violently preventing other groups coming up with proposals, etc. It would, at the same time, create or develop all religious elements clearly helping its consolidation of power.

Similar dynamics were at work among the peoples of ancient India. The indigenous people belonging to various tribes co-existed with their specific cults and practices. Some of their cultures and civilizations were quite developed and far advanced in every respect. The remnants of *Mohenjadaro-Harappa*[2] are evidences to this. Such a people encountered another race, the Āryans, whose character was considerably different from the natives in many respects. As the encounter between two distinct cultures grew into a nature of class divisions as Brāhmaṇas, Kṣatriyas, etc., the pattern of relationship became a class-relationship, the dynamics of which has been put forward briefly.

The pattern of relationship was the same in both Race-to-Race and Class-to-Class encounters: hostility, self-preservation and consolidation, harmony and learning in the process of which assimilation, absorption, even forcible insertion and rejection of beliefs, practices, etc. began to take place. The present chapter describes the *dynamics of such a relationship between the Brāhmaṇic and the Śramaṇic traditions* in the context of their respective understanding of Dharma.

1.2. A Historical Overview

1.2.1. First phase of the Encounter: Race-to-Race or the Political Encounter

The incoming Āryans propitiated their gods with hymns and sacrifices and pleaded for cattle, strong children and long life. They were optimistic about life. They recognized this world to be the best of theirs and were satisfied with the pleasures of this world. They sought to affirm that there was a higher reality behind what they saw and believed and that was the ultimate value of their life and quest. Their mission was not to civilize the aborigines, not even to destroy them completely. But as they advanced along the Gangetic valley they fought against those who put an obstacle to their march, sometimes mingled freely with those who were as civilized as their own.

Among the Non-Āryan tribes, mention may be made of the Nāgas[3], so called because of their Nāga or snake-worship. They were known for their exhaustless treasures and beautiful women. The Nāgarājas were the ruling powers that succeeded in maintaining a prolonged struggle against the invading Āryans. References to the ancient Nāga empire abound in Hindu story: the clearance of the jungle of Indraprastha was effected by the expulsion of the Nāgas; One of the heroes of the Mahābhārata had an amour with the daughter of a Nāgarāja[4]; the Āryan conquest of Prayāga and other parts of India are mythically described as a *great sacrifice of serpents.*[5]

The snake-worship of the Nāgas was a powerful stimulus to Indian religious thought from ancient time. Pārśvanātha, the 23rd Jain Tīrthaṅkara, has 'snake' as his symbol. The serpent with its poisoned fang, its association with the phallus and its fabled homes in the under-world suggest all that is terrible, sensational and mysterious in humanity. The serpent is everywhere respected, and more or less propitiated as the deity of the tree, as the guardian of secret treasure, as the domestic god of the family, and as the symbol of the power of reproduction. The Dravidian in general worshipped guardian deities of the village and of the household. Snake was part of their worship.

One can not say definitely about the early phases of history. But historical memories of Āryan conquest and the life thereafter, etc. are buried under a jungle of legends. It was mythified as war between gods against demons. The invaders were Āryan gods, the deities of fire and light. The enemies against whom they contended were the earth-bom demons of ancient India. The dark-skinned aborigines of India were described with exaggerations of hatred as Dásyus, Daitya, Dānava, Piśāca, Rākṣasa, Barbara, etc. Many hymns of the Ṛgveda[6] are fervent appeals to the gods to annihilate the Dásyus: 'we are surrounded on all sides by Daśyus. They do not perform sacrifices. They are unbelievers. Their practices are all different, They are not men. O! Destroyer of foes! kill them, destroy the Dása race!'

The Āryan settlements felt that they were living amidst enemies and hence needed recruits into their ranks to safeguard themselves and to progress in war campaigns. And this recruitment was done chiefly in the Vrātya land of the East. It was a political necessity. And hence, without looking into the credentials of race, descent or even respectability, they absorbed outsiders into their community. For this purpose, they had to be smart proselytizers and this dynamics of proselytization continued during the Epic time too. The *Sṭoma Ritval* or the *Conversion Ceremony* is very well described in the Pañcaviṁśa Brāhmaṇa[7]:

1. This ceremony was necessary for taking into the Vedic Āryan fold and it transformed the subjects into Dvijā, not dvijā of this or that caste[8]. The objective was to attain prosperity.
2. It was for reinstating those who being base and censured lead a Vrātya life (signifies integration).
3. It was for initiating young persons bom of Āryan lineage who, for some reasons, missed their initiation at the very right time.
4. It was for those beyond the age of procreation.

Thus the *Sṭoma ceremony* raised manpower for the Āryan settlement. The Vrātyaṣtoma was performed (the great 61 days Sattra)[9] in the capital city of Magadha. It included the Anupadésa and extended up to the Vindhya forest in the South. Later, the missionary movement rolled westward where the converted Vrātyas go out to Pāñchāla and Kuru to proselytize and convert the Vrātyas of the principality. There is evidence in the Upaniṣads[10] and elsewhere of Devakiputra Kṛṣṇa taking lessons from Ghora Aṅgīrasa in the Neo-Āryanism. The story of Gaupalāyaṇa and Gandharvāyaṇa[11] are proofs of thc rigorous *proselytizing movement* in favour of the Neo-Āryanism. This proselytizing effort, although primarily for political motives, included in its dynamics the absorption of some of the non-Āryan elements in the Āryan thinking and practice.

1.2.2. Second phase of the Encounter: the Class or the Religious Encounter

Kṣatriyas, the military community of the Āryans, do not appear prominently under this name in the Vedic hymns but they are the heroes of the legends, preserved in the Mahābhārata and Rāmāyaṇa. Their ambitions and pursuits were different from the Vedic Ṛṣis and their culture was more military and political. They were intellectual in character just like the Ṛṣis.[12] The Kṣatriyas hailed the gods with attributes very different from those of the Ṛṣis. For instance, the Ṛṣis invoked the sun as the divine illuminator of the universe. The Kṣatriyas worshipped him as their own ancestral hero. While the Ṛṣis worshipped Indra as the deity of the firmament the Kṣatriyas saw in him a warrior and ruler of the universe and sovereign of the gods. He was the protector of the Vedic Āryans against the dark-skinned non-Vedic people. Their offering too at the worship differed greatly from one another: the Ṛṣis offered the portion of their daily food of grain and butter whereas the Kṣatriyas feasted the gods with flesh meat and strong wine. Among the most famous feasts were the Rājasūya, celebrated after the acquisition of a kingdom and the Aśvamedha, signifying the recognition of the sovereignty of the king over the others.

The class controversy between the Brāhmaṇas and the Kṣatriyas had not arisen yet. The formation of groups until then was on the basis of profession, given their interest and capacity. It is only in later times that we find a profound conflict between the Brāhmaṇa dharma and the Kṣatriya dharma (this is not the wisdom of the Ārya-kṣatriyas but of the pre-Vedic and non-Āryan Vrātya-kṣatriyas of the East whose thesophic ideas were carried later to the Vedic groups by the Ārya-brāhmans residing in the court of Vrātya Rājanyas or kings through ceremonies like *Vrātyaṣṭoma* and other missionary efforts).

It was only in the mature caste system (when the priesthood and mechanical sacerdotalism got institutionalized) that the Brāhmaṇas wanted to have a firm basis for their moral and intellectual hegemony opposed by the Kṣatriyas. The Brāhmaṇic profession influenced the general public, called the Vis, in the field mainly of education of the youth. They also enforced severe moral discipline upon themselves and on the members of other professions. But they submitted to the political domination of the Eastern Eka-vrātya. The struggle between the two distinct types of politics and cultures of the Āryan aristocracy is vividly seen in the feud between the Yādava confederacy and Jarāsandha[13] and also in Prithu-Vainya legend.[14] Sometimes the learned Brāhmans sought asylum in the court of great Vrātyas.

The Brāhmaṇas in the Vrātya land[15] were not esteemed so highly. The best of them lived in the court of the king and they were chiefly employed in composing and recounting the mighty deeds of the members of the Royal house and of the nobility on certain occasions. They also officiated as priests in the Gṛhya (house) ceremonies of their noble employers. The kings and nobles were however intelligent men and did not appreciate much of these ceremonies marked by superstitious beliefs and practices wherein incantation and witchcraft formed the main features. It is only slowly that the Brāhmaṇas impressed these Vrātya-kṣatriyas and converted them into the Āryan fold in order to receive favourable responses from the Āryan chieftains elsewhere. Thus the conversion was only nominal. But in reality the Brāhmans were the ones who got converted by the Vrātya-kṣatriyas' theosophical wisdom found in the Upaniṣads. It was these Brāhmans in the Vrātya courts that preached to the rest of the Ārya-brāhmans the theosophical faith and doctrines contained in the Āraṇyakas. They were evidently the wisdom of the Eastern Vrātya Rājanyas.[16]

It is the Brāhmans in the Vrātya Court who were responsible for the Atharvan literature. In fact they were the Vrātya literature, very different from the contents of the literature of the Āryans. For example, the Bhauma Sūkta of the Atharva Veda[17] portrays the world of the Eka-vrātya, which is so different from the Vedic Āryans' view of the world. The Vrātya book preached the theosophical doctrines of the Upaniṣads and brought all Vedic literature to subordination. The new doctrine preached by the Upaniṣads was nothing but the *Nivṛtti mārga*, a path of happiness with complete renunciation. This was different from *Saṁvṛtti mārga*, the perpetual hankering after the Vedic svarga or anything mundane or super-mundane. This pattern of thought governed the philosophical and the theological systems of India ever since the Vedic period.

1.3. The Theosophical character of the Kṣatriya Dharma

The Upaniṣads formed the sources to the Rājanya teachings. Sāṁkhya, Yoga and Vedānta systems represented the three conceptual framework of that single Upaniṣad-vedānta. Although Vedic-Āryanism had anything to do with the Upaniṣads, yet the Upaniṣads were made the 'Vedānta', summit of the Vedas. These doctrines were originally from the Vrātya-Rājanyas supported by the Eka-vrātya. These Eka-vrātya were known as *'Brahmavid'*[18], knower of Brahman. The kings and the nobles often held discussion on cosmo-theosophical subjects in their land. The Brāhman missionaries in their court later preached the Neo Āryanism to the rest of their fold through the Brāhman-made Āraṇyakas. Thus the faith of the Ārya-brāhmans [mantras and rituals] was subordinated to the theosophical wisdom of the Eastern Vrātya Rājanyas.

1.3.1. Karma and Rebirth

Janmāntaravāda or the doctrine of Karma and rebirth came from a non-Brāhmaṇic tradition. In the ancient Vedic period it had as yet no existence because of the keen delight in life. It originated from the aborigines of India with the idea of the 'continued' existence of men in animals and trees. But later this idea was absorbed into the Brāhmaṇic symbolism wherein birth and death became part of the cosmic sacrifice.

The Brāhmans from Kuru-Pāñcāla who had gathered at the court of Janaka generally did not know about the doctrine of Karma. At the court of Janaka, Jaratkārava Ārtabhāga asked Yājñavalkya about a person after his death. As an answer to this question they seemed to have discussed about Karma.[19] When a living being died there always remained a remnant of merit and guilt still unrewarded or unpunished from which derived the germ of a new existence. Actions, character and deeds of a person accompanied the one at the moment of departure. This idea was different from the older notion that a man hoped for a blessed end after life, which might be in the company of pitṛs or of the gods.[20] Those who performed sacrifices and liberality went *to pitṛloka* and those who practiced austerities living in the forest went to *devaloka.* While good men ascended to heaven to the companionship of gods and there led a painless existence, free from all earthly imperfections, the wicked were born as animals or Caṇḍālas and those without moral quality took birth as insects and such other lower beings.

But very unhappily even sacrifices could not do any more than secure temporary happiness in higher forms of existence and not completely free people from the cycle of existence.[21] Hence there occurred the distinction between true and false desires. False desires such as securing a better status in the next birth were to be shed and the true desires are to be fulfilled. Hence the supreme end of spiritual endeavour to find release is to be sought no more through Karma marga of sacrifice, etc. than through Jnana marga, the Way of Knowledge. Deliverance from the pressures of worldly existence can be found only in the knowledge of the essential nature of things. This 'saving knowledge' removes ignorance. And this is the doctrine of Jñāna, leading to Nivṛtti, in opposition to Karma, which is tied with Pravṛtti and transmigration.

1.3.2. Ātmavidyā and Mokṣadharma

It is only in this context that sections relating to Yājñavalkya in Bṛhadāraṇyakopaniṣad[22] have to be understood. The quest for immortality was quite different from the quest for wealth. Hence one needed to seek renunciation of homes, children, wealth and fame, etc. Chāndogyopaniṣad[23] points out that what is mortal is limited and that, unlike common opinion, cattle and wealth, wife and slaves, fields and houses are all merely limited things and they are contrasted with the infinity and self-sufficiency of the spirit. The fourth chapter brings out the legend of Jānaśruti and Raikva[24] in which the knowledge of Brahman is far superior to wealth and liberality.

The legend of Upakośalakāmalāyana speaks about human life as full of desires, transgressions and diseases. Satyakāma says that one who knows is never tainted by sin like the lotus leaf in water. In Bṛhadāraṇyakopaniṣad Janaka questions Yājñavalkya as to what leads one to vimokṣá. He replies that in deep sleep a man is freed from everything and enjoys a wholly innate bliss not dependent on anything external. He transcends all social and moral descriptions and all misery. This condition is explained as one of non-dual consciousness, as one of imperishable *self-knowledge*. This saving knowledge consists in the recognition of the unity of Brahman and the Ātman and the object of the Upaniṣads is to teach such a knowledge of Brahman.[25]

Vedic and allied knowledge were clearly recognized as insufficient for the attainment of salvation: Nārada[26] laments that he is not learned in the Ātman and hence to be led to the shore beyond sorrow. Śvetaketu[27] blames his father for his education because his father Āruṇi fails to answer his questions. Mere learning and book knowledge is not sufficient.[28] True knowledge is the knowledge of Brahman or the Ātman. The king's role in developing this philosophy is seen when the Brāhmins go to them to leam the secret of life: King Aśvapati Kaikeya[29] instructs five learned Brahmins concerning the nature of Ātman called Vaisvānara[30] after their fellow casteman Uddālaka Āruṇi had been unable to solve their perplexities. Pravāhaṇa Jaivali[31] teaches two Brāhmins about the nature of Ākaśa and also explains to Śvetaketu,[32] Uddālaka's son, about the nature of metem-psychosis (transmigration). Great Vedic scholar Gārgya Bālāki, after repeatedly failing to elucidate the nature of Brahman, receives the solution from King Ajātaśatru of Kāsi.[33] Considering these, we may well agree with P. Deussen[34] that the doctrine of Ātman was taken up and cultivated primarily in Kṣatriya circles, and the Brāhmins adopted it only later.

The aim of Upaniṣads was to gain emancipation (Mokṣa, Nirvāṇa, Kaivalya, Mukti, etc.) from the cycle of births and deaths. The awareness of 'emancipation' as such was not found in the earliest recorded expressions of the Indian mind. In Ṛg Veda gods were invoked to deliver the mortals from sin which 'clang to the body'[35] and that the enemies be ensnared and be slain.[36] The vocabulary of freedom was not yet born except ideas like 'may I be detached from death like a gourd from its stem, but not from the immortal amṛta.'[37] The idea of emancipation was not still mature in Taitirīya and Chāndogyopaniṣads.

We read these favourite similies[38] for deliverance: 'I shall only so long belong to this (system of birth and death) till I am emancipated (vimokṣaye); then I shall go home'; 'Freeing oneself from the body, as the moon frees himself from Rahu's jaws, I go into the world of Brahman'. From these the idea of liberty is seen as an important ideal. Bṛhadāraṇyakopaniṣad[39] talks about certain attainments as constituting liberty. Liberty does not stop with reaching the stainless sky, to the brighter worlds of heaven. Asked by a Kṣatriya 'to speak of the higher thing which avails for emancipation,' Yājñavalkya, the great Vedic teacher finally discourses on the soul and of beholding the soul as god.[40]

In order to achieve emancipation the Kṣatriya dharma believed not on works but on knowledge. Knowledge alone would bring the most desired freedom from the cycle of births. This end was higher than the one sought by the Brāhmans through sacrifices and other means pleasing to the gods. Some of the early Upaniṣads[41] reject works altogether as utterly inadequate, if not useless, for the attainment of salvation because they aim at worldly happiness only.

1.4. Śramaṇa features of Kṣatriya wisdom

1.4.1. Renunciation and Asceticism

It is important to note that the founders of Buddhism and Jainism, the living Śramaṇa religions, were Kṣatriyas by caste. Buddha, a yuvarāja, was the son of Suddhodana, King of the Sākya clan in Kapilavasthu and Mahāvīra, the twenty fourth Tīrthaṅkara of the Jains, was born to king Siddhārtha and Queen Triśala (Priyakāriṇī). Jainism traces its antiquity to Rṣabhadeva, the first Tīrthaṅkara, mentioned in the Ṛgveda.[42]

According to the Jain tradition, Rṣabha was the first king of the universe and he taught the two sciences, writing and arithmetic, the knowledge of omens, the 64 accomplishments for women and

1000 arts and three occupations for men.[43] Bhāgavata Purāṇa[44] recapitulates with respect the life history of Rṣabha as the founder of Jainism and the master of yoga. He renounced his kingdom entrusting it to Bharata his son. He performed hard penance, acquired various 'riddhies' and became an Arhant by destroying karma. After attaining Kevalajñāna, the fullness of knowledge, he advised the people to lead a holy life, to refrain from killing animals, etc. Kalpasūtra[45] gives number of his followers, both the ascetics and the laity. We hear similar stories with regard to other Jaina saints like Pārśvanātha,[46] the 23rd Tīrthaṅkara and Mahāvīra,[47] the 24th and the last of the Tīrthaṅkaras in the present age.

The Késī Sūkta of the Ṛg Veda[48] makes reference to the Vedic poets expressing awe at the sight of naked ascetics with long hair. Such a tradition was little known during the Vedic period and it was generally treated with contempt.[49] The Vedic Āryans called the Śramaṇa sages Siśnadevas and exhorted Indra to protect them from their obstruction of animal sacrifices.[50] These sages engaged themselves in the fight for their *Religion of Ahiṁsā*. The Tirthaṅkara of the Jain tradition renounced the world at some stage in their life and preached dharma to the world establishing the Tīrtha or the community. It was true also of Buddha who renounced the kingdom in order to be enlightened.

1.4.2. Jñānamārga and the Śramaṇa traditions:

The Jñānamārga of the Upaniṣads emphasized that work as such was essential to purify the mind. But every action unfailingly brings its own reward or punishment and the cause of action is desire. Desire is due to ignorance, which mistakes the real nature of things. It is this that causes the cycle of births and deaths. Such an idea generates a firm conviction on the misery of the mundane existence. Both Jainism and Buddhism share in this thought.

Buddhism maintains that mundane existence is full of suffering and desire to enjoy the apparent delights of this world is its root cause. The cause of this attachment is ignorance. Ignorance and all that follows will be dissipated when attachment to this world is renounced. Jainism says that the innate nature of the Soul is pure and due to passionate attachment or aversion the karmic matter flows in it and obscures the natural beauty or the original status of it just like that one is not able to see one's face in the mirror because of the dust formed on it. Through discriminate knowledge accomplished by right vision and right conduct the original nature of the soul can be restored.

The role of Sāṁkhya-yoga[51] was significant in the formation of such theories. Matter was real in Sāṁkhya and not illusory as in the Upaniṣads. Prakṛti -the three guṇas united in dissimilar and unstable proportions- exhibits different qualities of Sattva, rajas and tamas. Material universe evolves as a result of a disturbance of equilibrium by the mere presence of Puruṣa, the soul (it excites matter to activity and development). The soul (Puruṣa) is eternally unchangeable but the matter (Prakṛti) is changeable through evolution. Its aim is to set the soul free from the sufferings of earthly existence.

Both Sāṁkhya and Buddhism share in the pessimistic view of the universe: all conscious existence is suffering and even pleasure conceals pain in its womb and leads infallibly to suffering. The soul of Sāṁkhya brings pain to consciousness through the body and the inner organs. The link between the Puruṣa (soul) and Prakṛti (matter) is due to 'want of discrimination,' that is, the non-recognition of the essential distinctness of soul from matter. This want is common to all living beings inherited from their last existence. The sole means of deliverance, therefore, is 'discriminatory knowledge,' by virtue of which, one discerns the absolute difference between the soul and the matter. The soul in the state of emancipation continues to exist individually, that is, in final separation from matter.

The Jñānamārga of deliverance seen in Sāṁkhya-yoga has similarity with the path of deliverance propounded by the great founders of Śramaṇa. For example the dualism of matter and soul, innumerable souls, souls characterized by intelligence, the indefinite nature of matter is the same in both Sāṁkhya and Jainism. Though Sāṁkhya considers the evolution of the material universe through the contact of puruṣa and prakṛti, both prakrti in Sāṁkhya and pudgala in Jainism uphold the 'primeval disposition' (lokasthiti) of the material world.[52]

Sāṁkhya, owing to its allegiance to the Brāhmins, adopted Brāhmaṇical ideas and modes of thought, whereas Jainism, being distinctly non-Brāhmaṇical, had worked upon popular notions of a more primitive and cruder character, like for instance, animistic ideas, and concepts like dharma and adharmāstikāya. But all of them - Sāṁkhya, Buddhism, Jainism - share a pessimistic view on life and advocate a hard ascetic path to secure the final liberation.

1.4.3. Atheism and anti-Vedic sentiments

From the very beginning, the Śramaṇa thought carried an anti-Vedic and anti-Brāhmaṇic sentiment. While the Vedic religion had propitiated several gods of natural powers with simple sacrifices for the welfare and the happiness of the community, the ascetic traditions of the Śramaṇas, especially Jainism, concentrated on the self or the person and its purification.

Both Buddhism and Jainism were atheistic in their conception. They did not believe in any supreme God, personal or impersonal as the Creator or Sustainer or Destroyer or even Lord of all things. They admitted innumerable gods at various degrees of perfection. But none of these gods was eternal. However long be their life, it must come to an end when the merit of the god in question is exhausted. The longest life of a celestial being in Jain Cosmology is the life in the highest heaven called 'Sarvārthasiddhi', which lasts 33 sāgaropamas (ocean of years). Those liberated souls go up to the top of the universe and remain there for ever in the state of absolute perfection. Accordingly, the functions of a supreme God as Lord and Ruler of the world cannot be attributed to liberated souls. Syādvādamañjarī[53] and the commentary on Ṣaḍdarśanasamuccaya[54] bring out a refutation of the existence of an eternal, omniscient-god.

But the Jains recognize a highest deity (parama devatā) as the object of veneration, namely, the Jina who teaches the Sacred

Law. Being absolutely free from karma, from all passion and delusion, the Jina is Omniscient. Jina is utterly indifferent to all that belongs to the world, and is entirely free from all emotions. Jina does not reward the adorers or satisfy their wishes, but instead, the gods who watch and control true discipline (Śāsanādhiṣṭhāyika devatas) hear their prayers. For, the practice of the discipline taught by the Jina is the best mode of worshipping the deity.[55]

Similarly Buddhism does not accept the theory of God as a 'personal being' nor any substantial reality. All that can be said of a being is a part of a succession of impermanent phenomena called dhammas. The world is a flux of phenomena and it could never have been the effect of a single, ultimate cause. Retribution for deeds is believed to operate automatically by reason of an energy called the 'indestructible'. The idea of god to this way of thinking is clearly out of place and the system is, therefore, atheistic. Brahma is considered inferior to Buddha and Brahma himself is born again and again and it is imaginary that he creates the world, etc.[56]

The Śramaṇic opposition to the idea of God as creator arises essentially from their belief in the autonomy and centrality of the doctrine of Karma. The working of human minds is due to direct or through the unseen force of karma. Hence no prayers and worship are of any avail against the force of Karma. Hence the path stresses on 'self-reliance' in the quest for salvation. Man needs to improve himself by a patient training of the will and the purification of feelings. This leads to an inward illumination of which the power is inside or innate in the soul or in the mind. This thinking is different from the Vedic view where illumination comes from outside, either from the grace of god or from an eternally revealed Veda or the Word. Buddhists and the Jains believe in authentic revelation but not necessarily, the Vedas. They accept 'Omniscient human teachers' not necessarily, a god. Jain works like Tattvasaṅgraha and Prabhācandra's Nyāyakumudacandra deal at length with the Mīmāṁsakā's orthodoxy of the Vedas.[57]

1.5. The Response of the great Śramaṇas–Buddha and Mahāvīra

Monasticism was a protest against the tyranny of caste. The ascetic life became a refuge from the burden of caste rules and ostracism because an ascetic surpassed caste and every other institution of the mundane life. He became casteless and went beyond the restrictions of a society, which the ordinary man might not transgress.[58] In the then prevailing anti-caste attitude and especially against the bṛahmaṇic hegemony, the Kṣatriyas placed themselves above the Brāhmaṇas in the social hierarchy and decried the caste hierarchy in favour of spiritual learning and achievement. They gave new definitions to Brāhmanhood and declared that Brāhmanhood depended on conduct: By one's actions one becomes a Brāhmaṇa, a Kṣatriya, or a Vaiśya or a Śūdra ... him who is exempt from all karma we call him a Brāhmaṇa.[59] And the main conduct prescribed by the Śramaṇas was Ahiṁsā especially against animal sacrifice.

Buddha and Mahāvīra founded monastic orders. Mahāvīra's Saṅgha included both clergy and laity, which in their administration and functioning followed any tribal organization. Admission into the Saṅgha was open to all, unlike the call to priesthood and scriptural study, which was the monopoly of the Brāhmins in the Āryan class society. Rhys Davids observes that the percentage of low-bom members of the Saṅgha was probably a fair proportion to the percentage belonging to the despised jatis and sippas when compared with the rest of the population. We have lot more evidences to show that the people of mean origin occupied important places in the Buddhist Saṅgha.[60]

Ancient Indian history witnessed a process of assimilation and rejection of views and way of life between different groups (between the Āryans and the aborigines, between Brāhmanas and Kṣatriyas, etc.) and mellowing down of antagonistic feelings between them. While the Kṣatriyas of the Northeast regions were nearer to the original Śramaṇa legacy, the rulers of the Northwest and the Western regions like Pravāhaṇa Jaivali or Vasudeva Kṛṣṇa being nearer to the home of Vedic orthodoxy, sought to reconcile the doctrines of saṁsāra with the world of ritualism. Action or Ritual might not be abandoned completely. One must seek to live a hundred years, all the time engaged in work. But one should not look for reward for the actions, as enunciated by the Gītā. This was an alternative prescribed to the total renunciation of life upheld by the Śramaṇas. Even within the Vedic orthodoxy there was a clear transition from the Vedic way of life to the Śramaṇic ideal of renunciation and freedom from the cycle of births and deaths.

In the course of time, Bhakti cult of Hinduism made an impact on both Buddhism and Jainism. Jainism reached nearer and nearer to Hinduism and introduced practically all forms of Bhakti and saṁskāras into Jain religious way of life. Bodhisattva in Buddhism brought about great changes in the religious life of the Buddhists. Jains and Buddhists began to worship gods and goddesses within their temples in order to be rid of all worldly pleasure. But their tradition summarily rejected some of the ideas and ideals valued most in the Brāhmaṇic tradition, like the worship of the Vedic gods, the rituals and sacrifices to these gods as a sign of propitiation, Vedic authority, caste claims, and so on.

Thus a definite change had taken place in the religious thinking of India by a process of assimilation and rejection. The Āraṇyakas portray the philosophical and religious encounter of these two great Śramaṇa and Brāhmaṇa traditions and the resultant of which has until now had a considerable influence of the Indian mind. The following Chapter focuses on the Śramaṇa path of Asceticism recognized as 'the Path' of achieving their Great Ideal.

Notes

1. Otto Maduro: p. 41-43, 66-67, 75-77.
2. The Cultural Heritage of India, Vol. I, PP. 113-120
3. Saletore, R.N., Vol.III, pp.1006-1008
4. Wheeler, p 57
5. Ibid. p.57, Foot note, 31
6. Ṛg Veda V.I. 100-108
7. Pañcavimsa Brāhmaṇa, XVII, 1-17. The texts and notes are included in the Appendix B of Ghose, pp 217f
8. Lātyāyaṇa Vrātyaṣtoma texts, VIII, 6.29 ref. Ghose, p224f

9. Pañcavimsa Brāhmaṇa, XXIV, 18
10. Chānd Up III, 17.6
11. Baudhāyana śtrauta Sūtra, XVII, 26, ref. Ghose, PP; for the text see Ghose, pp. 222-223
12. The supremacy of the Kṣatriyas is lauded in Br Up VI.2.8: King Pravāhaṇa Jaivali tells Brāhmaṇa Gautama, "Before this, this knowldege did not reside in any Brāhmaṇa" and a similar statement in Chānd Up V.3.7
13. As described by Kṛṣṇa in Sabhā parva of Mahābhārata; also see Ghose, pp. 19-20; for the description of the feud, see pp. 176-178
14. Ghose, pp 20-23
15. There is an contention that these Rājanyas represented an earlier wave of immigration and that they had little part of share in Vedic Āryan customs and mode.
16. The Atharaveda :narked the Brahmacāri Vedic student the subject of a psalmody in the 5th sūkta of the XI Book. The Brahmacāri Vedic student is exalted to heights which might arouse envy in the heart even of the great vrātya of the vrātya book(Atharva Veda XV). But it is not the Vedic student as such who is exalted but it is the Brahmavid in the Vedic student. The theosophical wisdom of the vrātya had spell-bound the Ārya Brāhman to the extent that he wanted his student to learn the right knowledge, namely Brahman from the beginning. See Ghose p160.
17. Atharva Veda, XII.1
18. Macdonell and Keith, Vol.2, p.79
19. Br Up III 2.12-13, ref.SBE, Vol. 15, 126-127
20. Naciketāgni in Karthopaniṣad portrays Yama's immortal status through the impermanent means of ritual; ref.SBE Vol.XV, pp 1-24, also see Chānd. Up.5.10.If
21. The doctrine of karma and rebirth are fully accepted in Ch VIII of Chānd Up; the doctrine of Saṁsāra is becoming more and more clear in later Upaniṣad like Kathopaniṣad and Muṇḍakopaniṣad. The second section of the first Muṇḍaka condemns the sacrifices as 'frail boats' those who follow the ritualistic path or engage in charitable works keep on revolving in the cycle of existence. For the first time, a clear rejection of vedic ritualism is seen here.
22. Br UpII.4
23. Chānd Up Ch VII 23-25; also see SBE Vol. I pp 123-125
24. Chānd Up Ch IV4, 3
25. In Ṛg Veda, Brahman denotes 'a mysterious power which can be called forth by various ceremonies: it also denotes a magical force derived from the orderly co-opertation of the hymns, chants and the sacrifical gifts; it is purely a spiritual force (Ṛg viii 3.9; ii 2.10; vi.75.19 etc.) In the Śatapata Brāhmaṇa we find the neuter Brahman exalted as the supreme principle, moving behind the gods. This is taken up in the Upaniṣads.

Their aim is search out the Brahman and to impart the Knowledge of it (Brahmavidyā-expounding the doctrine of Brahman). The Vedic Experience provides us with innumerable quotes from the principal Upaniṣads concerning the true meaning of Ātman realization, the supreme ideal. See Sekhar, Vincent, 'The Way of the Spirit-A Jain Journey: (Studies in Jaina Spirituality)', in Journal of Dharma, Vol. XIII, No. 3, September 1988, pp-218-219

26. Chand Up VII 10
27. Br Up vi 2, also Chānd Up. V.3-10
28. Kathā Up I ii.23
29. Aśvapati Kaikeya, SBE Vol.I.p 85-91; Macdonnel and Keith, Vol.1, pp. 205-206
30. Chānd Up VII -24 or Śat Br X Vi.1
31. ibid.18f;, Macdonnel and Keith, Vol. 1, p. 290
32. ibid.V.3-10;vi.2 also Kaus, UP 1, p. 290
33. Br Up ii.1; Kaus Up IV
34. P. Deussan, ERE Vol.7, p. 721
35. Ṛg Veda vi.24. 3; cf.i.24.9, viii.18.12 muñchatam
36. ibid.vii.9.8
37. Ṛg Veda vii.9.12
38. Chānd.Up VI.XIV.2; I.iii.15 same simile in Kathā Up 'freed from the jaws of death'
39. Br Up III i.3f
40. ibid. IV.iv 7-8
41. He is not exalted by good works; he is not degraded by evil work (Br Up VI. 4, 22)
42. One who worships Rṣabha with devotion must get laksmi (Ṛg Veda Ast 5, Adh, I, varga 22); Rṣabha gives infinite knowledge, power and bliss (Ast 4, adh 6 varga 8); The prayer and worship of Rṣabha destroys all pains, sufferings, ignorance and enemies (Ast 8, adh 8, varga 24); Rṣabha to be seet -worded, most learned and worshipful (Maṇḍala 1, sūkta 190, mantral); Rṣabha got full, complete, infinite, supreme, unobstructed, unabating, all-seeing and all - knowing knowledge Omniscience (Maṇḍala 2, Sūkta 33, Mantra 5); Rsabha praised as the care-taker of the world (Maṇḍala 6, Sūkta 1, Mantra 8); Advises for the prayer and worship of Rṣabha (Maṇḍala 10, Sūkta 187).
43. SBE Vol. XXII, p 282
44. Bhāgavata Purāṇa, Skandha I,II,V and VII; For details about Rṣabha's life see two articles by the author on Rṣabha in Certificate Course in Jainology through Correspondence, University of Madras, 1991, Paper II pp. 20-42
45. SBE, Vol. XXII, p. 284
46. Bloomfield, Maurice, Saraga 5 to 8 describes his life in detail; also see the story of Pārśvanātha in Kalpasūtra, SBE, Vol. XXII

47. The story of Mahāvīra in Kalpasūtra, SBE, Vol. XXII
48. Ṛg Veda x.136 of the vrātya book of the Atharva Veda (Book XV). According to some scholars, the vrātyas were ecstatics of the Kṣatriya class and forerunners of the yogin.
49. In the Bhāgavata, one royal sage became an avadhūta with uses of such phrases as 'keśa bhūri-bhāraḥ'
50. Ṛg Veda vii.22.5
51. A brief presentation of the philosophy of Sāṁkhya-Yoga is take from ERE, Vol. 11, p 190
52. Tat. Sūtra iii 6. Com
53. Syādvādamañjarī, p.29f
54. Ṣaḍdarśanasamuccaya, 45 f
55. For more details see the author's article "Jaina Religious consciousness: a paradigm for a socio-secular involvement" in Jinamañjarī, Vol.V.No. 11, October 1992
56. Rhys Davids, Dialogues of the Buddha, p. 30, 280
57. The Mīmāṁsakas argue the validity of the Vedas on (i) the Svatapramāṇyavāda ('Self-validating' character of Knowledge) (ii) Sabdanityatvavāda (doctrine of the 'eternity of the word') and (iii) Apauruṣeyātvavāda 'impersonal' character of the Vedas, i.e. no personal authorship).
58. When the Brāhman Sundarika of the Bharatvaja Gotra asked the Blessed One (Buddha) a question regarding his gotra, the latter replied: I am not a brahman, or the son of a king... houseless with my hair shorn, tranquil not consorting with men in this world. Importunately, O Brahman, does thou make enquiry of me regarding my gotra " (Sutta Nipāta iii 4). Also see SBE. Vol. X, pp. 74-75.
59. SBE. Vol. XLV, pp. 130-140
60. Upāli, a barber, was the chief authority after Gautama himself; Sati, son of fisherfolk; Nanda, a cowherd; Capa, born of a deer-stalker; Punna and Punnika, slave girls; Śubhā, daughter of a smith, etc.

CHAPTER II

THE ASCETIC PATH OF THE ŚRAMAṆAS

Asceticism is derived from the Greek word 'askesis' which means 'exercise' or 'practice' or 'training'. This was used in the context of an athlete who trained himself in certain practices or exercises for acquiring the necessary conditions for sports. It was a physical discipline. But in religious context it meant a voluntary, sustained, systematic programme of self-discipline and self-denial. It also meant renunciation of immediate, sensual or profane gratification of the senses in order to attain higher spiritual state.[1]

2.1. Objectives and Basis of Asceticism

Ascetic practices are universal in all world religions. In primitive society these practices were sought in order to escape from the demonic powers and to restore oneself to normal health and behaviour. Through such practices they penetrated the sacred realms (like that of Shāmāns or the medicine men) of the gods, or to be one with the spirit-world or to generate visions. Further, major ascetic practices like fasting, sexual continence and seclusion were undertaken to keep one pure to approach the gods. Gradually an 'inner asceticism' developed which was more spiritual in nature. The spirituality of 'being in the world and yet untouched by it' or 'renunciation of the reward of action' is a good illustration to inner asceticism.

Scholars like Brunton and Oman suggest that climatic conditions of a place could play an important role in the growth of the attitude of its people. Indian climate has an effect on its people in evoking a sort of pessimism and life-denying tendency. But modern philosophers like Swami Vivekānanda, A. L. Basham and others hold that the very same climate of India has produced a sense of balance in the people's attitude towards life: neither attachment nor rejection.[2] Asceticism is often justified by well-articulated philosophical and theological systems. Theistic traditions develop a sort of mystical union with the personal god through ascetic activity. Asceticism is the meritorious type of behaviour for salvation or, at the least, a better condition to obtain after death. Hence self-denial is rewarded and the reward is attributed to the deity. Ascetic activities can also be a penance for misdeeds, a sort of atonement for all transgressions. They become expressions of true repentance, which earn sympathy, mercy and forgiveness of the personal god.

In the non-theistic traditions, it is the thirst for the Ultimate that justifies ascetic activities. In Jainism, it is the path of realization of the essential nature of one's self or the True Self. In Buddhism, it is the means of liberation from the cycle of births and deaths or from the wheel of suffering. This realization itself is identified with Salvation, or Mokṣa, Nirvāṇa, Kaivalya, etc.

In the non-theistic system there is no personal god or deity to bless with graces or to pardon the sins of human persons. Hence knowledge becomes the key instrument for realization. Divorced from knowledge, realization can never generate salvation but only a lesser objective[3] like magical powers. In Jainism the ascetic practices undertaken without right vision and right knowledge cannot free one from the bondage of Karma. Similarly, the importance of right knowledge is stressed in the very First Sermon of the Buddha on the Eight-fold path. It is for this very reason that meditation or Dhyāna is upheld as one of the significant ascetic practices in Jainism and Buddhism. Meditation brings about physical discipline, realization of total freedom (Kaivalya) according to Sāṁkhya, true nature of the Self in Jainism, emptiness of the Self in Buddhism, and realization of Brahman in the Upaniṣads.

The objectives of ascetic practices vary from tradition to tradition. They are secular as well as religious. Ascetics engaged in such practices cultivate magical and miraculous powers and thus they become popular among the masses. Jain canonical texts condemn those ascetics who are after powers of divination, soothsaying, etc.[4] The Tāntric traditions are well known in this context. On the other hand, ascetic practices are prescribed with a view to attain certain religious ends and goals. Asceticism is a means to attain such religious ideals. It is, as Prof. Nathmal Tatia puts it, an integral part of holy life and not merely a condition of higher spiritual life.[5]

Ascetic practice is based on the general belief in the dualism of body and soul, spirit and matter and the idea that the Soul or the Spirit higher than the body or the matter. Hence from ancient times there has been a tendency to deny the world and what is material, including the body, and to uphold ideals like renunciation, embracing the life of a mendicant, etc. It is only because of certain liberal traditions in Buddhism that we see a reversal of extreme ascetic tendencies and affirm positively world and life as in the early Vedic tradition.

Since the end of asceticism lie beyond this phenomenal world, any ascetic act does not seem normal. An ascetic seeks to transcend the normal or the natural.[6] In Yoga, it is referred to as 'going against the current'. The yogi takes to postures and activities like breathing which are not the ordinary posture or the activity of a normal human being. Similarly, one can notice other abnormal practices of the ascetics: constant wandering, shutting oneself in cells, being absolutely silent or continuous recitation and chanting, neglect of body or abuse of body through mutilation, flagellation etc, abstinence from sex or engage in sexual intercourse in an abnormal way as practiced in Tāntric tradition, etc. Outward signs of an ascetic indicate similar abnormalities: pulling out the hairs, shaving of heads as practiced by Jain and Buddhist monks, growing long hair, distinctive clothes or no clothing at all as in the case of the Digambara Jain monks, etc.

2.2. Śramaṇa roots of Indian Asceticism

The seals available at the Indus Valley Civilization evidence that ascetic practices like yogic meditation, etc. are non-Āryan and indigenous in their origin. Indian Asceticism can be discerned for the first time in Indian Śramanism. The Ṛg Vedic word 'Vātasrana munyo' in the Muni-sūkta[7] is synonymous with the Upaniṣadic Śramaṇas. The characteristics of the Muni[8] or the Keśin is described in it. The Vedic Āryans called the Śramaṇa sages 'Siśnadevas' and pleaded with Indra to protect them from their obstructing efforts in violating animal sacrifices.[9]

The Śramaṇa sages engaged themselves in the fight for their Religion of Ahiṁsā. They were the wandering monks called 'Parivrājakas' who sought particular form of conduct that would free them from suffering. Some of them were gnostics or contemplatives who sought ecstatic experiences through power of knowledge and insight. They were known as ganācaryo, titthakaro, sādhusammato, cirappabajito, etc. in the Buddhist scriptures.[10]

This itinerancy or wandering is borrowed most probably by the Śramaṇas from the wandering teachers of Brahmavidyā, Uddālaka Āruṇi, the first known teacher.[11] Similar conclusions are drawn by Barua[12] and Sukumar Dutt.[13] Dr. D. N. Bhargava contends that Śramaṇa is a combination of the Brahmacāri and the wandering master (Brahmavādi) of the Brahman knowledge. Hence many of the rules of the Śramaṇas can be traced back to the rules and habits of both these types of men.[14] Several scholars unanimously declare that the Brahmacāri was the model and the origin of the Śramaṇas.[15] But this Brahmacāri is not the Brahmacāri of the Vedas (the Vedic student). He is of the great Vrātya of the East whose interest was not just memorizing the old texts and mantras of the Vedas in the house of his preceptor but the one who would generate within himself the Brahman (knowledge of the holy power), who would want to know and attain Brahman. The Atharva Vedic Brahmacāri is very different from the Brahmacāri of the rest of the Vedas.

Nagendranath Ghose[16] in his doctoral dissertation on the origins of the Indo-Āryan literature and culture shows that Atharva Veda was the first to be composed even before the other Vedas and it has its origin in the East in the Vrātya-rājanya milieu. Thus ideas like the Brahmavid and efforts to attain Brahman, etc. had their origin rather in the Śramaṇa culture of the East than in Brāhmanism. That these Śramaṇas had cherished anti-Vedic sentiments came into light with the Atharva Veda. Later on, this was discovered in the isolated passages of the Āraṇyakas and the Upaniṣads.

2.3. Evolution of Sannyāsa as the Fourth Āśrama

Chāndogyopaniṣad gives us instances of a clear change over to ascetic ideals. Vedic knowledge becomes secondary and the enquiry into the self takes the upper hand.[17] There are hostile references to sacrifice[18] and a rival method of holiness, namely asceticism, is suggested. From then onwards learning and teaching becomes important in the life of a Brāhmaṇa.[19] Knowledge can be gained from other than the Brāhmins. Brāhmins themselves seek the kings like Janaka, Pravāhaṇa Jaivali, Aśvapati Kaikeya, Ajātaśatru and so on. Women taking part in the discussion becomes a new feature. It was not in the case of the Dharmaśāstras, which did not allow women to enter into the ascetic Order, nor to perform sacrifices.[20] On the other hand, the Śramaṇa tradition allows the Order of nuns, subject to the same general rules of life as the monks. Attempts at reconciling the claims of the study of the Veda and the performance of sacrifice with asceticism were made.[21]

Muṇḍakopaniṣad makes a unique reference to mendicancy *bhaikṣācarya.* The very name carries the Śramaṇa flavour. It is rather an adaptation of a passage from Chāṅdogyopaniṣad where it had referred only to the 'anchorites' in the forests. For the first time the text gives a clear picture about emancipation, its nature and the process.[22] The second section of the first Muṇḍaka condemns sacrifices *as frail boats.* Those who follow the ritual path or engage in charitable works keep on moving in the cycle of existence. This is the first time wherein a clear rejection of Vedic ritualism is noticed. The third Muṇḍaka refers to *Yatis,* who abandon inner evil (ksīnadoṣaḥ) and practice truth, austerities (tapas), brahmacarya and right knowledge (saṁyag jñāna). They adopt the vow of renunciation and are thus purified (Sannyāsa yogat yatāyaḥ śuddhasattvaḥ). There is a unique reference to 'ignorance' (avidyāgranthi) whose knot can be resolved only by the essence of meditation. Pāṇini's Aṣṭādhyāyī[23] refers to 'Bhikṣu-sūtra' and some earlier Dharma sūtras mean 'Samana sūtra'[24] and hence there must have existed some specific ascetic literature in India even before the Sūtra period. But generally the Dharma sūtras stressed Gṛhasthāṣrama[25] more than Sannyāsa and brought asceticism in the rigid Āśrama system.

The word Āśrama is not found in the Ṛg Veda. The Vedic view on life was positive, active and robust. It never denied life as unreal or rejected it as evil but sought to affirm that there was a higher reality behind all they saw and which gave ultimate value to human life and quest. Quite opposed was the Śramaṇa view, which was obsessive with the miserable conditions of human life, subject to passions and actions, births and deaths. It tried to transcend the realm of the phenomenal world and realize the soul in its original nature, far from the sphere of sorrow.

Hence even the Kṣatriyas, kings and nobles, who were entitled to govern and protect the people with their might and power sought a mendicant way of life. Both the Epics and the Upaniṣads illustrate this feature so vividly: 'where are the arms or where is the forest? Where is Kṣatriya Dharma and where is asceticism? They are opposed.'[26] Similar events are described in the life of Buddha. Bimbisāra (or King Śreṇika) pleads with Buddha[27] : 'O Samana, thy hands are fit to grasp the reigns of an empire and should not hold a beggar's bowl... Believing that thou art of royal descent, I invite thee to join me in the government of my country and share my royal power. Desire for power is becoming to the noble minded, and wealth should not be despised...'

In the Brāhmaṇic tradition[28] the life of every Brāhmaṇa (even other ref. in Manu VI) has to pass through four Āśramas: the Brahmacāri in the house of a teacher, the Gṛhastha performing the duty of founding a family, the Vānaprastha or the hermit in the forests devoting himself to gradually increasing austerities and the Sannyāsi, moving about without a home or property, living merely on alms, free from all earthly ties and awaiting his end. Every person desirous of salvation must pass through these four stages of life one after the other (kramasaḥ), and live as prescribed in order to obtain the End.[29] The Dharmāśastras have condemned those who seek Mokṣa without fulfilling the duties in the first three Āśramas: 'they will sink low in damnation.'[30]

Although Āpastambha would not prefer to place one stage before the other,[31] he, Manu and others have praised the stage of the Gṛhastha, because the householder is the source of these four Orders and the others do not produce offspring[32]: 'In thy offspring thou art born again that mortal is thy immortality. These sons... increase the fame and heavenly bliss of their departed ancestors.'[33] But there are passages that disparage the order of the Householders: 'Sages who desired offspring went to burial-grounds. Sages who did not desire offspring went to immortality.'[34] While the vow of celibacy was much praised, the Dharmaśāstras cursed those who praised other duties (the order of ascetics and the like). They would 'becomes dust and perish.'[35]

Even the Epic-author Vālmīki believed in an active life motivated by Dharma and not in any such idea like emancipation from karma. He praised the Householder's life to be the highest and the best stage in all the four schemes of life.[36] The threefold scheme of the Rāmāyaṇa age is another proof in support of the contention that Vālmīkian ethics was social in nature. Even the hermits are depicted with social responsibility. They entertained their guests and showed hospitality to the strangers.[37] Prof. Khan[38] says that there was very little difference between the householder and the forest-dweller and all these hermits acquired heaven by performing penance and following the path of Dharma constituted mainly by such social virtues as hospitality, non-violence, tapas, Vedic study, asceticism, self-mortification, worshipping the ancestors and performing sacrifices.

All these show that there was a mutual encounter between the Brāhmaṇic and the Śramaṇic traditions regarding the ideal of renunciation and the mendicant way of life and the subsequent recognition of Sannyāsa as the fourth and final stage of life. While the Brāhmaṇas adhered strictly to the scheme of life as enunciated by the Dharmaśāstras, the Śramaṇas did not care for such an order. It was this breaking with the tradition prescribed by the laws related to the Āśramas that was the chief contention of the orthodox Brāhmaṇas against Buddhists and their predecessors. A Brāhmin may take to Sannyāsa only if he had first passed through the three stages of a student, householder, and a Vānaprastha. But to become a Bhikṣu without these previous stages of life was a heresy in the eyes of the Brāhmaṇas and it was exactly that heresy which the Buddhists preached and practised.[39]

One need not conclude that the fourth Āśrama originated with the Śramaṇa sages alone but we can say that the Śramaṇa ascetic and monastic practices did influence the growth of the fourth Āśrama in the Brāhmaṇic tradition. In the older Upaniṣads the theory of the four Āśramas is seen in the course of formation: there is mention of only Brāhmin student and Householder;[40] tapas along with other practices are mentioned as third 'branch of duty';[41] after studies some take to Gṛhastha Dharma and some to Vānaprastha, mentioned side by side.[42] But in classical times the doctrines of Saṁsāra, Karma, and the ascetic way of life became the common repertoire of both Śramaṇism and Brāhmaṇism. Sannyāsa came to be considered the highest of all Āśramas.

Solitary life in the forest existed as a special branch of vocation (dharmaskandha) side by side with the position of the Householder. For example Yājñavalkya retires to the forest at the end of Gṛhastha life[43] and there is a sort of abstinence from the desire for children, etc.[44] A distinguished fourth stage is seen in the example of King Brihadratha,[45] surrendering his kingdom and retiring to the forest to lead a mortified life. He devotes his time to ascetic practices and meditation[46] but has not yet attained the highest goal: He who without knowing the Ātman practises austerities for many thousand years earns only a finite reward.[47] Asceticism, in this case, only leads one to Pitṛyāṇa, the 'way of the fathers.'[48] Hence Chāndogyopaniṣad talks about 'faith in asceticism or faith as asceticism'[49] through penance and fasting. Through these 'one will seek to know the Ātman (vividiśanti).'[50] Thus tapas becomes an indispensable means to the knowledge of Ātman.[51]

Until the post-Vedic age the separation between the third and the fourth Āśrama was not strictly carried out. The fourth Āśrama was not yet settled in the early Dharmaśāstras either. The four-fold number is afforded by the words of Muṇḍakopaniṣad: Mortification, truth, and the life of a Brāhmin, instruction.[52] And the oldest passage indicating the four-fold division is given in Jābāla Upaniṣad.[53]

If emancipation is the discovery of one's self as the Ātman, and if that discovery is possible at any stage of life, not necessarily at the end of a prescribed Order, then asceticism of the Vānaprastha becomes superfluous, just like the Gṛhastha's sacrifice and the Brahmacāri's study of the Veda.[54] It was precisely this understanding that deviated the Śramaṇas from the usual, Brāhmaṇical scheme of life. The acceptance of Sannyāsa as the fourth separate Āśrama was a revolution, which changed the significance of the other three. Thereafter it attains an exalted position: He who knows the Ātman is 'atyāsramin' (exalted above the three Āśramas).[55] He has attained release from his individuality and all that pertains to it as family, possessions, and the world.[56] He is called Sannyāsi because he 'casts off everything from himself (Sam-ni-as)'. He is called 'pravrājaka' because he has given up everything. He is called a 'bhiksu' because he lives only as a beggar without possessions.

In the later Upaniṣads, especially in the Brahma, Sannyāsa, Āruṇeya, Kanthaśruti, Paramahaṁsa, Jābāla, Āśrama Upaniṣads, the fourth stage becomes the means of attaining the knowledge of Ātman. These Upaniṣads depict the full account with numerous contradictions in details of the preliminary conditions imposed upon the Sannyāsin, of his departure from life, of his dress and equipment, of his food, place of abode, and occupation.[57]

Despite the Śramaṇic influence on the Brāhmaṇical scheme of life in the formation of the fourth Āśrama, the Brāhmaṇic hegemony claimed the right and privilege of asceticism in the beginning.[58] It was then extended to all the twice born and finally all restrictions were removed and admission into the ranks of the ascetics was accorded to men of every position and degree.[59] Prof. Hoernle notes that it was due to the reaction against such claims of the Brāhmins to a monopoly of admission into the ascetic orders the contemporaneous movements like Jainism and Buddhism arose.[60]

2.4. The Ascetic ideals and practices of the Śramaṇas

On the outset we can make a bold assertion that it was asceticism in practice that brought all different heretical philosophers together. Jainism represented the extreme of world denial and asceticism. Buddhism sought the middle way between the extreme pleasure of the Cārvāka and the extreme ascetic mortification of the Jains.[61] The Ājīvikas, again, taught the extreme form of asceticism based on fatalistic doctrines. Despite the differences among these Śramaṇic traditions, they all agree on the fundamental experience of life as pain and suffering. All the three traditions resorted to different methods of alleviating suffering.

2.4.1. The Middle-Path of the Buddha

Although Buddhism does not accept a substantial permanent entity called Self or Ātman, it believed in the power of Karma and in the doctrine of transmigration. Hence Nirvāṇa consisted in getting rid of the cycle of births and deaths and from the Wheel of Existence. The ultimate cause of bondage was *taṇhā or* thirst or desire and hence the spiritual discipline stressed putting an end to desire or thirst. Buddhism accepted every spiritual practice that helped in this process and kept away or even condemned certain practices, which would harm this process. The reason for avoiding and even condemning extreme ascetic practices like self-inflicted pain, etc. was that instead of achieving the purpose or the End, they increased more pain and hence they were considered 'dukkha.'[62] In Buddhism any austerity which is likely to weaken the body or the mind is forbidden.

When almost worn out by his austerities Buddha said, 'Not by this bitter cause of painful hardship shall I arrive at that separate and supreme vision of all-sufficing, noble (Āryan) knowledge, passing human ken. Might there not be another path of enlightenment.'[63] Where upon he took reasonable care of the body[64] and chose meditation spots[65] where the natural environment was of a kind to sooth and braces the spirit. Once having achieved the enlightenment, he is reported to have soliloquized, 'Ah, Free am I from that toil so hard to achieve.'[66] Now Māra the evil one approached him and said: 'Those penitential task abandoning/ whereby the sons of men are purified/ the impure fancieth that he is pure/ when he hath strayed from path of purity.' Then the Exalted one, discerning that this was Māra the evil one, replied: 'I understand full well how any rites/austere aimed at the over throw of death/ belong to matters useless for our good/ Yea, nothing good they bring along with them/ like oar and rudder in a ship on land/but morals, concentration and insight, the path to Enlightenment-these were my task/that path creating and developing/ "Have I attained the purity of supreme." Then, Māra the evil one thought: 'The Exalted one knows me!/ The blessed one knows me!' Sad and sorrowful, he vanished.[67]

For Buddha 'affectionate moral conduct, noble (Ārya) views, are commended as securing Phasuvihāra, i. e. easeful serene living.'[68] Consequently it could not well sanction any deliberate infliction of pain, or dis-ease as such on oneself or on others.

The Canonical books of the Buddhists delight to divide humanity into classes of men as self-tormentors, tormentors of others, tormentors of both self and others, tormentors neither of self nor of other.[69] Under the fourth category came those who left the world and the home for the career of a recluse. These are, or should be, filled with charity and compassion for all living beings; they own no property in animals or in personal service. They harm no one, molest no one, and have thrown off the ties and the cares that torment the world. And, as it were in antithesis to the word 'burning' (tap), they are said to have 'become cool' (Śitibhūto).

Hence monastic life is an institutional alternative to prepare men and women who would 'torment neither themselves nor others.' Within monastic discipline two important rites are crucial to the survival of Saṅgha, namely the Ordination (Upasaṁpada) and the communal recitation of the Disciplinary Code (Pātimokkha) after the confession of faults.[70] All these three are expressions of morality that lead the person to the realization of Bodhi and the essence of Buddhahood.

At the root of these rules lie the ethical pre-supposition of the renouncer tradition. The word Vinaya is that which separates or leads away from the householder's way of life.[71] It is precisely the unanimous adherence to the Disciplinary Code that gives the doctrinal stability,[72] that keeps the unity of the Saṅgha on the one hand, and the progress in the path of perfection, on the other. Since Vinaya itself is formed because of the suggestion made by the Bhikkhus and Bhikkhunis,[73] (and sometimes by the public) the monastic community was sensitive to the popular opinion and public comments. The public noticed slightest mishap or shortcoming of the Bhikkhus.[74] Hence fortnightly recitation of the Disciplinary Code after the confession of faults forms an important practice in the monastic Saṅgha. Serious, slightest and even trivial slips are recorded.

The consciousness of sin and reconciliatory and purificatory processes become significant to a Buddhist monk as well as a lay person. The idea of sin will be equated to every kind of collision, individual and social, with the cosmic moral law. It is a folly and a result of ignorance or delusion that amount to egoism and thirst or passion and greed.[75] The sole origin of sin and ills is sought not in the objective world, but in the person's mind and the person's acts. It throws back an individual in one's long and painful pilgrimage of existence. Sin is not an offence against a personal deity and hence he cannot help.[76] There is no forgiveness of sins by a deity. It must work out to the bitter end, and of itself, its own fruit. No one can escape from this. Hence the need for purification or reconciliation. This substitutes what is called penance.

The path of purification is not an easy path. To the question of Milinda, 'whether Nibbāna is śukha or dukkha,' the sage Nagasena replies that Nibbāna is Śukha, yet the way of attaining it is dukkha (painful).[77] It requires certain amount of asceticism in the sense of 'abstinence from physical pleasures, etc.' This asceticism is necessarily associated with the final uprooting of fundamental vice. It is an inward spiritual grace. So ritualistic purification has hardly anything to do with Buddhist asceticism.[78] Buddhism is opposed to any outward and non-moral conception of purity.[79] It has rather condemned austerity measures for purification,[80] fire-rituals for purification,[81] water oblutions for purification.[82] Buddha advocates ethical purity unaided by external symbols and emphasized the inward purifying fire.[83]

In this context, earnest intention of realizing Buddhahood takes the form of solemn vows. It has a social implication too. Acceptance of the vows (Vyākaraṇa) by the presiding Buddha and the enthusiasm on the part of the vowant serve to impress the believers with the grandeur of the start, the merits accumulated by the vowant, and to stimulate the followers to the similar practice of praṇidhāna or parinamaṇa (contraction of the mind upon a certain object or idea).[84]

Vows are in the form of prayers addressed to Buddha. A specimen of the vow is as follows: 'There shall never be any being who, having heard the truth of Buddha, shall not attain Buddhahood. For the vow taken by Buddha is this: 'Let me lead them to Bodhi, by accomplishing my works.' Throughout future days Buddhas will expound many billions the threads of truth. They shall reveal this unique road (eka-yāna) and approach thereby the truth for the Tathāgataship.[85]

Mahāyāna tradition made the Bodhisattva as the object to which vows were addressed. The four-essential vows[86] of a monk are: (1) the vow to save the world (like a Bodhi-sattva); (2) the vow to destroy in oneself all evil and the passions that produce evil; (3) the vow to study and practice the dharma; and (4) the vow to attain wisdom and virtue. Among several other vows a lay person takes the vow of avoiding illicit love (kāma mithyācāra) and illicit intercourse with neighbour's wife or nun or illicit intercourse with his own wife. Perseverence till the end is stressed in several texts[87] and there are number of prayers for endurance to emulate the zeal and effort of their predecessors and to endure hardships.[88]

Buddhas and Bodhisattvas become great models to the followers of Buddhism. They show the way by first taking the vows and living them to the core. We could see the 'prime vow' of a Buddha as a redeeming power: twelve vows of Buddha the Bhai-sajya-guru (the medicine master), saving the people from diseases, etc. and the vow of Buddha Amitābha (the infinite light) the vicarious Saviour (developed into pietism almost like Christianity within Buddhism). Great personages and men of pure character, firm will and full of religious zeal are seen in the great Sāriputta, Moggallona, Mahākassapa, Rāhula, Upāli, etc. These and others are worshipped in order to realize the excellent qualities found in them. It amounts to the elevation of self to Buddhahood and the discovery of Bodhi itself. They stand a symbol and manifestation to their faith and inspiration of Buddhist Ideals.

2.4.2. Ascetic path of the Jains

The true objective of Jaina asceticism is to stop the inflow of Karma (Saṁvara) and to eradicate the already accumulated Karma (Nirjarā). The latter can be done only by penance: 'Tapasā nirjarā ca' i.e. previously accumulated Karma are to be annihilated by penance. Karma generally exhausts itself automatically after yielding its fruits (savipāka nirjarā) but an ardent aspirant cannot wait such a long period.

Several canonical texts of the Jains marvel at the significance of penance in moral life as means of annihilation of previous Karma.[89] It means extirpation of desire in order to strengthen the three jewels of right faith, right knowledge and right conduct.[90] It is on account of penance that a man is called a Brāhmaṇa or a respectable person (Ārya). The Jain masters warn that penance should be devoid of any desire pertaining to this world or to the next world[91] and make clear its true objective. Penance, though it could be physical mortification, is performed for the sake of self-control, exterminating attachment, annihilating Karma, performing meditation and acquiring scriptural knowledge and not for any worldly purpose.

Another important objective of Jain asceticism is to be reconciled unto oneself and to the universe. Sūtrakṛtāṇga points out that the root cause of sin (*pāpa* karma) lies in deceit, greed, anger and pride.[92] For the sake of splendour, honour and glory of this life, for the sake of birth, death and final liberation, for the removal of pain, man acts sinfully towards the earth, or causes others to act so, or allows others to act so[93] and a wise man should desist from them. It is attachment and aversion (rāga and dveṣa) that procure sins[94] in the mind and hearts of people. Jain teachers are emphatic in saying that those who procure themselves pleasures by sinful acts will not get rid of misery.[95] All creatures who have committed sins wail, suffer and tremble.[96] It is only the purity of heart that leads one to Mokṣa.[97]

In this context, the Jain religious texts distinguish between the wise and the fool: He who does not practise cessation (from sin) is called a foolish man; he who practises cessation (from sin) is called a wise man.[98] Unworthy Śramaṇas contemplate the pursuit of pleasures; (they are) sinful and very low,[99] whereas the Heroes (of faith) desist (from sins) and exert themselves aright, subdue wrath, fear and are entirely happy.[100] Knowing that life cannot be prolonged... a sage is not conceited[101] but rather he becomes awakened and turns away from sin[102] guarding his self and subduing his senses.[103] Ācārāṅgasūtra warns a person who does not comprehend and renounce the causes of sin would be bom again and again in manifold births and experience all painful feelings.[104]

Jainism enumerates the characteristics of a True monk: First of all he has a desire for discipline for the sake of acquiring righteousness.[105] He possesses virtuous conduct and life, practises the best self-control and keeps himself from sinful influences (nirāsrava).[106] He becomes equanimous by neither too elevated by pride nor too humble, does not care for respectful treatment nor blame, etc.[107] A bad Śramana lays stress on the outward signs of his calling as a means of living.[108] He follows heretical teachings, slights his teachers and despises the learning and discipline.[109]

The characteristics of a Nirgrantha is also enumerated in Sūtrakṛtāṅga:[110] He has no worldly ties, is instructed in the creed, practises chastity, exerts himself, obeys the command of the teacher, avoids carelessness, is not influenced by sounds and colour, controls his self, is rid of doubts, is free from passions, protects himself in three ways (of thought, word and deed), desires the highest good, practises austerities and silences, does not desire fame, etc., is engaged in learning the sacred texts. A great sage is one who is well instructed in the law and leads a life of abstinence. He is always a destroyer of the effects of Karma.[111] He gives up all his possessions[112] and relations and all undertakings, thinking that nothing belongs to him.[113]

Dr. D. N. Bhargava[114] has treated the ascetic life of the Jains in his book *Jaina Ethics.* He mentions in his concluding remarks[115] that ascetic practices must be characterized by spiritual awakening. Or else, it will become a mere torture of the body which is said to be 'bālatapas' or childish austerity. Jainism prescribes two types of austerities, external and internal.[116] The former consists in temporary fasting or fasting until death. It is abstinence with respect to substance, place, time, state of mind and development, collecting of alms - the seven modes of begging and other self-imposed restrictions and mortification of the flesh. The latter comprises of practices like expiation of sins, service, polite behaviour, study of texts, religious discourses, meditation and abandonment of the body. Each of these varieties is described in great detail in the several Jain ethical literature like Mūlācāra, Bhagavatī Ārādhana, Ṣaḍkhaṇḍāgama, Tattvārthasūtra, Anagāradharmāmṛta, Prāyaścittasamuccaya and so on.

One of the significant contributions of Jain asceticism is its meditational practice. Although meditation is common to all religions yet the way it has been conceived in terms of its meaning, varieties, objectives, results, signs, etc. and practised, it makes a big difference. Jain meditation is popular and practical. For instance, in Ārta dhyāna the mental condition of the person is over laid with agony and anguish when the person is to get rid of an undesirable object, or when he is attached to some object or when he is confronted with an ailment, etc. The person suffers from agony and anguish. In Raudra dhyāna the mental condition of the person is over laid with cruel, sinful indulgences. He constantly indulges in injurious, violent acts, lying, stealing, etc. In Dharma dhyāna the mental condition of the person is absorbed in matters of Dharma, i. e. what is not antagonistic to the scriptural knowledge and the moral conduct,[117] where a person is encouraged and strengthened in religious faith and moral discipline. Finally in Śukla dhyāna the mental condition of the person is the result of freedom from Karma, from attachment. It is known as equanimity, a state mind, where a person enjoys absence of fear and agitation and he is not deluded. He sees things with Viveka or discrimination and rests content with absolute detachment. The Jain meditation rightly points out the role of self-effort in all its processes and evokes confidence in the individual to believe that independent of outside help a person can reach the highest perfection possible.

2.4.3. Ājīvikas, the hard-core ascetics

Ājīvikism got developed from groups of wandering monks who did not accept the popular interpretation of the doctrines of the soul, the existence of god and the future of life. Sāmannaphalasutta testifies that the teachers of such a sect were the contemporaries of Buddha and Mahāvīra. Ājīvikism was considered a third heretical sect[118] besides those of Buddhism and Jainism. The founder of the Ājīvika sect was Makkhaliputta Gośāla,[119] a mankha or a bard from Magadha. Tamil sources rename him as Mārkali. He was associated with Mahāvīra for six years according to Bhagavatīsūtra[120] and there occurred a rift between Mahāvīra and the Ājīvika leader probably on account of jealousy of the latter over the ascetic power of the former. Makkhaliputta Gośāla considered himself as 24th Tīrthaṅkara of the current Avasarpini age[121] two years before that of Mahāvīra.[122] He was in good terms with the six disācaras (the wandering ascetic philosophers) and they shared Gośāla's doctrines. The latter, in the 24th year of his career, codified the Ājīvika Scriptures[123] in consultation with the disciples at Sāvatthi in the workshop of the potter-woman Hālāhala.

Ājīvikas had earlier teachers who spread the true doctrine, taught in the Caityas outside various cities of the Ganges basin. Even some of the six heretical teachers[124] seemed to have been influenced by Ājīvika doctrines. For instance, Pūraṇa Kassapa believed in the Ājīvika theory of the six classes of men (Chatabhijātīya).[125] The cardinal doctrine of the Ājīvikas was Niyati, the only determining factor of all phenomena in the universe. They left no room for human volition. Niyati may have had a non-Āryan ancestry, according to Dr. A. L. Basham[126] because rigid determinism was not natural to the thought of Indian religions. Although there was the theory of karma, yet man, by his free will, can alter his future by choosing the right course of action. Probably the climate of India too contributed to the doctrine of Niyati, encouraged a fatalistic attitude to life,[127] namely, 'Human effort is ineffectual' (N'atthi purisakāre).[128]

The story of Marīci in Mahābhārata[129] who became a fatalist after the accidental loss of two bulls betrays the influence of Ājīvikism: there is no valour in force (name naiva pauruṣam).[130] In another place, Bhīma struggles with the python and he exclaims: 'who can conquer fate by human effort (puruṣakareṇa). I consider fate to be supreme, but human effort (pauruṣam) useless.'[131] Ājīvika doctrine of Niyati or fate thus comforted both the warrior who was fighting a losing war and to the peasant who sat with grief because of the failure of his crops or death of his herds. Buddha seems to have given a forcible opinion on the value of Makkhali's teaching: 'Just as a hair blanket (keśakambala) is the worst of all fabrics in texture, appearance and utility, so of all unorthodox doctrines (Samanappavadanam) that of Makkhali is the worst.'[132]

Based on a strict deterministic theory the Ājīvikas developed a complicated and fanciful cosmology incorporating an 'atomic' theory, which was probably the earliest in India. They also believed in the reanimation theory:[133] 'First as an uprooted seasamum plant may revive after rain, so a dead body may, given certain favourable conditions, be reanimated.' Just like the other two heretical systems, namely Buddhism and Jainism, the Ājīvikas too rejected sacrificial polytheism of the Āryans and the monistic theories of the Upaniṣad mystics. They practised an asceticism of a severe type, which often ended in death by starvation. They had classified the ascetic career in eight stages (purisabhūmi or stages of human existence):[134] the last three are monkhood (samana), enlightenment (jina) and the stage of highest cognition when he does not speak at all (panna-bhūmi).

The story of Jambuka[135] occurring in the Dhammapada commentary is a good illustration for the severest ascetic life of an Ājīvika: the boy Jambuka was initiated into the Ājīvika Order because his parents found him quite abnormal in the food habits. After initiation, the Ājīvika ascetics themselves found his asceticism too loathsome and expelled him from the community. Whereas he attained great reputation among people for his sanctity as a 'wind eater' (Vāta-bhakkho) and led a life as 'wind eater' for 55 years.

The word Ājīvika is derived from the word 'ājīvat' which means 'as long as life'. It denotes the life-long character of the vows undertaken by an Ājīvika ascetic in contrast to the temporary vows of the Buddha Saṅgha. At the time of initiation[136] itself the novice was to grasp a heated lump and burned his hands.[137] Initiatory ordeals resulted in mutilation and deformity as though naked and crippled. They pulled out their hair by the roots with a piece of the rib of a palm leaf.[138] Some of the Buddhist Jātakas give us a picture of Ājīvika penances: 'exerting themselves in a squatting posture (kukkutikappadhana), the bat penance (vagguli-vāta),[139] lying on beds of thorns (kantakappasaya) and the penance of five-fires (pañca-tapana)...' We have references to the 'penance-ground' (āyavaṇa-bhūmi) of Gośāla.[140] The Ājīvikas entered large earthen pots for doing penance.[141]

Sthānāṅga declares that they made varieties of penances called severe penances, terrible penances, the abstention from liquids, indifference to the sense of taste, etc.[142] Dr. Barua[143] writes that an Ājīvika 'never incurred the guilt of obeying another's command. He refused to accept food, which had been specially prepared for him. He did not accept food from people when they were eating, lest they should go short of food or be disturbed. He did not accept food collected in time of drought. He did not accept food where a dog was standing near or if flies were swarming round it.' Not only did they undertake severe penances, they prescribed great suffering to all souls as a necessary means of salvation.[144]

The final penance consisted of austerity of the extreme type. Bhagavatīsūtra[145] mentions about the eight finalities and the four drinks (and four substitutes for drink) declared by Gośāla. These are series of rules regulating the final penance of the Ājīvika ascetic, regulating the successive stages of religious death, a death undertaken for the sake of his spiritual welfare.

As the physical power was weaning the ascetic would undertake the six-month's course of austerities. At some stage he would refrain from all drinks except the four drinks (Panagaim):[146] 'that which has fallen from a cow's back; that which is soiled by the hand such as the water used in a pottery; that heated by the sun and that fallen from a rock.' At the final stage he would only allow himself the four substitutes for drinks (apanagaim):[147] 'taking a metal pot as though a drink to soothe fever - by implication holding an earthenware pot also; holding an unripe mango or other fruit in the mouth without drinking the juice; holding unripe simbali-beans or certain other seeds in the mouth in the same way, and the penance of the 'pure drink' (Śuddha-panae).' The last item is described in this way: 'On the last night of his six months' penance he submits to two mighty gods who soothe his fevered body. If he does not submit, a mass of fire arises in his body and he burns up his body with his own heat. Then he is saved and makes an end. That is the pure drink.'[148]

The Ājīvika ascetics practised nudity. Even their leader Gośāla lived in the state of nakedness.[149] Mahāvīra too was habitually naked and yet he permitted his followers to wear minimum of covering. The early Jaina monks were not completely naked but wore a loincloth.[150] The Ājīvikas classified men in six ways:[151] the white class consisted of Ājīvikas and Ājīvinis. The red class, which was two stages below Ājīvikas, were Jains or Nirgranthas who wore one cloth. From this it is clear that the Ājīvikas considered those who did not wear cloth to be in the first rung of perfection. Even some Jātakas[152] refer to Bodhisattvas becoming an Ājīvika, naked and solitary, ate refuse, small fish and dung.

Though the Ājīvika doctrine of Niyati denied free will or action, it did not mean the denial of the power of Karma as the determinant of destiny. This was the main reason why the whole ascetic community was engaged in severest of penances. Though they were hard-core ascetics of the extreme type, they had definite rules of ascetic conduct. They were a religious body with a normal corporate and social life, a Saṅgha, in fact.[153] It was not merely for religious ceremonies alone but for secular meetings too. This is evidenced by their common use of singing religious songs and the use of music for religious purposes.

Notes

1. ER, Vol. I p.441
2. Bhagat, M.G., pp.7-7
3. ER, Vol. I. 1
4. Condemnation of ascetics engaged in Divination, sooth-saying etc. Utt. Sut., 15. 7 f.
5. Tatia, Nathmal, p.18
6. ER, Vol.I, p.444
7. Rg Veda, x.16.-7
8. Bhagat, M.G., p.108
9. Ṛg Veda, vii. 22.5
10. Dīg N, I p.41-52
11. Śat Br, SBE, XI.4,1
12. Barua, B.M., p.61
13. Sukumar Dutt, p.69
14. Bhagaval, D.N., p.17
15. Kern, p.73; Humer, p.374; Rhys Davids, Buddhist India, p.247; Dialogues of Buddha, II, P.247; Eastern Monachism p.74
16. Ghose, Nagendranath, pp. 83, 96-97, 107-108, 116 etc.
17. Narada, Chānd. Up. VII.1; Śvetaketu, Chānd Up.VI. 1
18. Br Up. 11V.10; III.IX.6,21; Chānd.Up. 1.10 f
19. Best form of austerity for a Brāhmaṇa is the recitaition and study of the Veda (Manu II, 166-67); Recitation of the Veda kept in par with other austerities (iv.148); The austerity (must be understood to apply) to (the observance of) the rules (of studentship) Āp. DS. 1.2.5 (The daily recitation (of the Veda) is austerity) (I.4.12)
20. Sacrifices not to be performed by fools, infants and women (Manu II, 171-72, IV.205-6, XI 36-37)
21. Br Up. Theory of the four Āśramas IV. iv 22, Chand.Up II xxiii. 1 Kena 33, Katha I. ii.15
22. It is parallel to Buddhist Sutta Nipāta: "Just as the flowing rivers reach home in the sea by abandoming name and form so does the man who knows, freed from name, attain to the divine person who is higher than

the higest". Compare with another verse in Upasira-manva Puccha: "Just as the flame struck by the breeze disappeas and cannot be discoverd, so the muni, freed from the name, and body disappears and connot be discovered". Also see in Śāntiparvan of Mahābhārata:"Yatharnavagata nadyo-grhya-mane ca."

23. Pānini, Aṣtādhayāyī, IV.3 110
24. Gaut DS. 13.26; Baudh. DS. II. 6, 14, 15; Vas. DS. IX 10-11
25. Gaut. DS.III.26; Baudh.DS.II.6,15
26. M Bh., Aran Kān, 9.27
27. Cares, Aran Kān, 9.27
28. Br Up.11.4
29. Manu VI 88; Gaut. DS III; Ap DS II 21.2
30. Manu VII.35,37; Yaj DS. III. 56; Ap DS II 24
31. Ap DS. II. 9.24
32. Gaut DS.III 3; Manu VI 87-90
33. Ap DS. II. 9.24
34. Ap DS. II 9.23
35. Ap DS. II 9.24
36. M Bh., Ayod Kān, 106/22.24
37. Anusuya, Wife of Atri, gives Sita robe, gems and balsam; M B h., Araṇya Kāṇḍa 12/26, 27: 46/31
38. Khan, B., P. 127.
39. Maxmuller, SBE, Vol.XV, Part II, P.11
40. Chānd. Up. 8-15
41. Ibid, 2.23. 1
42. Ibid,5.10
43. Br Up. 4.5.1-2
44. Ibid, 3.5.1
45. Mait Up. 1.2
46. Chānd Up.2.23.1
47. Br Up. 38. 10
48. Br Up., 6.2.16
49. Chānd Up.5.10.1
50. Br Up. 4..4. 22
51. Mait Up 4.3; Jābāla Up. 4
52. Muṇḍ Up. 21.7
53. Jābāla Up. 4
54. Br Up 3.5, 4.4.21
55. Śvet Up. 6.21; Kaivalya Up.24
56. Br Up. 4.4.22
57. Deussen, P., P. 374-82
58. Manu VI, 1, 27, 29-30, 37, 40, 70, 85, 88, 91, 93-94, 97
59. Rāmāyaṇa, Uttara Kāṇḍa, 74.9f Manu i.86; In the Kṛta age the chief (virtue) is declared to be tapas.

60. Hoernle, JASB 1898, P, 39f
61. Both are denounced as ignoble (unāryan) and unprofitable SBE XI 146; Maj iii 230
62. Dukkha is evil and must be removed. Excess is Dukkha. Tapas is a form of excess and multiplies Dukkha. It does not even lead suffering to any gain; it is unprofitable. The futility of tapas and not any shrinking from pain, was the moral of Buddha's own strenuous efforts in austerities (Maj Nik. ii 93, ii 212; i.237)
63. Maj N i 307
64. For the earnest (Sekha) the body was something to be analytically studied and kept in cleanliness and good health. Clothing for it, regular and frequent baths, massage, shelters, regular food, rest and medicines were prescibed (Dhamma sāṅgani 1348)
65. Sam N. i 103
66. ibid,. i 128
67. ibid., i 128-129
68. Ang N iii 132
69. Maj N i 341, 411; ii 159; Ang N ii 205; Puggala 55
70. Hardy, F., P.728
71. ER, Vol. 15, p. 265.
72. Samantapāsādikā, I p 13
73. Admissioin of women into the Saṅgha through Ānanda (Cullavagga X. 1); Acceptance of Upasotha meetings because of Bimbisāra (Mahāvagga II. I.) Sanctioning of silk robes from Mendaka (VI.34); Acceptance of dinner invitatiions from Mendaka (VI.34); Rainy season robes provided by Visakha (VIII.15, 11); Accepting land for Saṅgha from Anāthapiṇḍika (Cullavagga VI.4); Influence of Gotami on the bathing rules for Bhikkuni (Vinaya. IV. p. 262)
74. Dispensation of bowls and accepting alms in hands (Mahavagga 1.70, 1): no donning or robes (1.70, 5); not keeping vassa (III, 1, 1); storing unnecessary things (VI 15,9); secular enjoyments (Cullavagga V.2.6), etc.
75. Maj N 13. Dukkha-khandha
76. Sam N ii.105 (Terms C.A.F. Rhys Davids also in Buddhism, P. 83 f)
77. Milindapanha 313, SBE, Vol XXXVI, p. 181 f.
78. Warren, H.C., P. 164 f
79. Dhammapada, XXVI
80. Sam N i. 103
81. Sam N i. 169, also tapas of the 5 fires, Dīg 165 f
82. Sam N i. 183, also Maj N i.39
83. Three applications of this 'inward purification' arc (1) the 5 purities: Vinaya, V.132; 132; SBE, XIII, i. 15, 5, etc. (2) 4 applications of mindfulness: Dialogues ii 22; (3) insight into impermanence, suffering and non-existence of soul: 'The path of purity " Dhammapada, 20: 277-279

84. Saṁ N vii. 10
85. SBE, XXI p.53
86. In other places they have stated as ten precepts: ERE, VII 320 a. A lay person follows the first five of these precepts.
87. SBE, XXI Lotus Truth, XXII
88. SBE, XXI, p.261
89. Tat Sūtra 9.3
90. Vīrasenacārya on Ṣaḍkhaṇḍāgama 5.4.26 Vol 13 p.55
91. Sthān Sūtra 9.19. The belief and the preaching of Achelakas, Ājīvikas, Nirigaṇthas, etc. is quoted by Buddha in Maj ii. 214f; i.238. The way in which Tapas held to guarantee the End was not as in sacrifical rites by the propitiation of gods, by satisfying as a system of act and abstinence, the Law of Karma.
92. Sūt Kr. 1.9.11
93. Ācār Sūtra 1.1.2.3
94. Sūt Kr. 1.8.8
95. Ibid., 1.9.3
96. Sūt Kr. 1.7.20
97. Sūt Kr. 1.1.3.26-27
98. Sūt Kr. II. 2.78
99. Sūt Kr. I. 11.28
100. Sūt Kr. I. 1.2.1.12
101. Sūt Kr. 1.2.2.21
102. Sūt Kr. I. 10.21
103. Sūt Kr. 1.18.21
104. Ācar Sūtra I.1.1.1.6-7
105. Utt Sūtra 1.7
106. Utt Sūtra 20.52
107. Utt Sūtra 21.20
108. Utt Sūtra 20.43:A Śramana is forbidden to practise divination from bodily marks and dreams augury and superstitious rites, magic skills, etc. (Utt Sūtra 20.45)
109. Utt Sūtra 17.3-18
110. Sūt Kr 1.14
111. Ācār.Sūtra 1.6.3.1
112. It should be noted here there are Jaina texts debating and discussing on the spiritual liberation of women. While the Digambaras hold that total renunciation of clothes is a prerequisit to attain Mokṣa, the Śvetambara do not think so. But both the Jaina sects admit that giving up clothes or nudity is not permitted for women. Hence for the Digambaras a woman cannot attain Moksa, while for the Śvetāmbars she can. Find texts and explanations for such debate in Jaini, P.S. Gender and Salvation: Collected papers on Jaina Studies, pp. 163 -198; in V.N. Jha, Ch. 14 Is

there Salvation for Women by Nrmala Kulkarni, PP. 145-154; and in Dr. Jag 'ishchandra Jain, PP. 164-171

113. Sūt Kr 1.2.1 21-22; Ācār Sutra 1.6.2.2 Sūt Kr 1.10.9; 019 Ācār Sūtra 1.7.3.2
114. Bhargava, D.N., PP152-178
115. Ibid., p 204
116. Utt Sūtra 30 8-28; 30.30-36
117. Sthānāṅgavṛtti, p. 118; Śrutacaraṇadharmādana - petam dharmyam (as quoted in prof Nathmal Tatia p.46)
118. Basham, A L.P3
119. The name and the titles of Makkhali Gośāla: Bsham, A. L. Ibiid. pp. 78-79
120. Bhag Sūtra XV, Sūtra 541, fol 663; Jinadāsa's Āvaśyka Cūrṇi epitomes the journeys of Mahāvīra and Gośāla.
121. Bhag. Sūtra Xv, Sūtra 554, fol. 679
122. Up Das, ii P, 108
123. Ājīvīka Scriptures: The Mahānimittas, the Maggas and the Onpatu-katir. The Mahānimittas are listed in Sthān Sūtra viii, 608; the two maggas are said to be those of song and dance: Tathamargau gitamarga-nrtya marga-laksanam sambhavyate-Bhag Sūtra 659. The Onpatu-katir is mentioned in the Tamil Source Nilakeśī, 671
124. Pūraṇa Kassapa, Makkhali Gośāla, Pakkuda Katyāyana, Ajīta Keśakambali, Nigantha Nātaputta, and Sañjay Belatthiputta: these six heretical teacher were known as the leader of an Order (ganācariyo), the founder of a sect (tithakaro), respected as a saint (sādhu-sammato), revered by many people, homeless wanderer of long standing (cirapabbajio) and advanced in years. The Sāmannaphalasutta of the Digha Nikāya contains their teachings Dīg No. i. pp. 47 ff. sec Basham, A. L., 11-18
125. Aṅg N.iii p. 383
126. Basham, A. L., p.8
127. Sāmannaphalasutta and Bhagavatīsūtra give ample evidences to the fatalistic doctrines of India
128. Dīg N i. p.53-54
129. M Bh., Śāntiparva, 176V.5ff
130. Ibid., 176, 12
131. M Bh, Vanaparvan, 176, 27
132. Aṅg Ni.p.286
133. The story of Gośāla and the Seasamum plant, See Basham, A.L., pp. 47-49
134. Sumaṅgalavilāsinī, pp. 163-164
135. Dhammapada Comm.ii, pp.52f
136. See Basham, A. L., 104-107
137. Tittira Jātaka, iii. p. 542
138. Ibid; also Civañāna Cittiyār, p. 255

139. Jātaka, i. p. 307
140. Bhag Sūtra, 546 fol. 666-67
141. Aup Sūtra, 41, fol. 196.
142. Sthān Sūtra iv. 309
143. Barua, B.M., pp. 167-168; Also see Basham, A.L., pp. 118 f
144. Civañāna Cittiyar, p. 255
145. Bhag Sūtra XV Sūtra 554 fol. 679.
146. Basham, A.L, p. 128
147. ibid.
148. Bhag Sūtra, XV, Sūtra, fol. 680
149. Ibid., fol. 662.; also see Basham, A.L., p. 37-40, 87
150. Ācār Sūtra i. 7.7.1
151. Sum Vil i. p. 162; The six abhijātis or classes of humanity described in detail in Aṅg N iii. p. 383; Similar to Jaina leśyas: Utt Sūtra 34
152. Lomahaṁsa jātaka, i. p. 390
153. Basham, A. L., p. 115

CHAPTER III

A MANIFOLD CONCEPTION OF THE MEANING OF DHARMA

PART I -DHARMA IN HINDU TRADITION

3.1.1. Evolution of the Meaning of Dharma in Hindu Tradition

Life in its entirety is beyond comprehension. Experience shows that manifoldness is fundamental to life. As one perceives so does one respond. Reality manifests itself in variety of ways. The underlying unity flows from an attitude of Anekānta, a typical Jain approach to life. It recognizes and admires the multifarious nuances of life.

The word *dharma* has many meanings. The term suggests the composite nature of life and of the universe. The meaning varies from age to age and from circumstance to circumstance. In the Stone Age the meaning of *dharma* referred to the 'World Order' or Ṛta, when man discovered, for the first time, the seasons. When he started making an enquiry into the nature of reality, the word acquired a philosophical meaning. At the advent of the Āryans in India and as they encountered the numerous indigenous groups of people the meaning of *dharma* was a resultant of a dialogue between them, a meaning that gained momentum in the process of assimilation, rejection, etc. by different groups. Such was a historical necessity.

Hence to arrive at one, comprehensive definition of the term *dharma* is not only impossible but also not valid. What one needs to know is how a particular group seeks to understand the meaning of the term given its particular context.

3.1.2. Meaning and Sources of Hindu Dharma

The general meaning of the *dharma* is from the root 'dhṛ'[1] to sustain, to support, to uphold, etc. It is the essential foundation of something or of things in general. It is the way things are: factual, authentic, actual and which signifies truth: It is that which is established, customary and proper and therefore traditional or ceremonial. It refers to one's duty and responsibility and hence imperative and everyone is morally obliged to follow. It is that which is right, virtuous, meritorious and, therefore, ethical. It is that which is required, precepted or permitted through religious authority and thus legal.[2] In a descriptive sense, dharma would mean 'the way things are' and in a prescriptive sense it would refer to 'the way things ought to be.'

Historically three categories of meaning have been given to *dharma:* (1) It is the law governing the natural order; hence it may mean the natural law or the universal Order; (2) It is the normative principle on which the moral and social Orders are established and by which the ethical quality of human actions (Karma) is to be determined and evaluated; and (3) It is the body of injunctions and prohibitions governing religious life, primarily the performance of sacramental rites. It originates from the hoary past and spread through the Vedic and post-Vedic period.

Most orthodox Hindu traditions affirm three sources (mūla) for ethical and legal decisions: divine revelation, sacred tradition and the practice of the wise. Some texts add a fourth, namely, conscience. According to the orthodox thought, the primary source for all knowledge, legal and otherwise, lies in the Vedic canon comprised of the Mantra Saṁhitas (liturgical hymns of the Ṛg Veda, Yajur Veda, Sāma Veda and Atharva Veda), ceremonial instructions (Brāhmaṇas), and philosophical treatises (Āraṇyakas and Upaniṣads). All these texts together constitute *Śruti* or revealed eternal truths. In all orthodox traditions Sruti is the primary source of normative guidance.

Dharma may also be discerned by the tradition, by the examples given by the time-honoured members of its society. It is known as *Smṛti.* One could have recourse to the actions of great people who are right in their conduct (sadācāra) and who generally are believed to be acting according to the Vedic instruction (siṣṭācāra) if Śruti and Smṛti fail to clarify a problem. These are characterized as the virtuous, learned, slow to anger, free of jealously, contented, modest, etc. by the *Dharmaśāstras.*

Manu and a few other Dharmaśāstras identify A fourth source. It is referred to as *conscience* in modern language: that which satisfies the self or 'ātmanus tuṣir'[3] or that which pleases the self, "priyaṁ ātmanaḥ'[4] But generally the source is primarily traced to Śruti, Smṛti and Sadācāra.

3.1.3. Hindu Dharma: A Literary Survey

Hindu tradition is broadly classified into several periods: (1) the early Ṛg Vedic period; (2) the time of the composition of the other Vedas and their respective Brāhmaṇas or the period of the Brāhmaṇas; (3) the period of the Āraṇyakas and the Upaniṣads and (4) the period of the Dharmaśāstras, of the Epics and the Purāṇas.

Ṛg Vedic Literature is said to be the earliest form of Vedic akin to Avestic literature. The tenth book of Ṛg Veda is deemed to be a composition of a later date. The largely prose text, known as the Brāhmaṇas, is written with ritualistic purpose and the age of which one can discern the growth of the caste structure. The *Āraṇyakas* are forest treatises related to the forest dweller, the *Vānaprastha,* and they form part of the Brāhmaṇas and are different in their nature and content from the earlier portion of the Brāhmaṇas. The *Upaniṣads* form the end of Brāhmaṇas. They betray the influence of the Śramaṇa tradition whose world-view was, to a great extent, different from that of the Brāhmaṇa ethos. To these we may add the Sūtra period which characterized by the prose, poetry and drama written in Classical Sanskrit.

3.1.3.1. Vedic meaning of Dharma[5]*:* **Ṛta** *or Cosmic Law*

The early Vedic period or the Ṛg Vedic period highlights the concept of Ṛta, an unchanging Order that prevailed in nature. The gods were believed to maintain this Order. They were all personifications of the phenomenon of nature suclfas Sun, Dawn, Fire, Wind, etc. Ṛta stands a Vedic parallel for the notion of dharma, the established Order of things, proper behaviour, and fitting truth, etc. Though it sounds like an impersonal force that harmonizes and keeps everything in its proper place, it has an ethical rolc to play in society.

At the conceptual level, Ṛta is a cognitive representation of universal Order. At the practical level it is the basis for any normative judgement or moral action. Hence 'anṛta' (disorder) would mean 'asatya' (untruth) and it suggests improper action that would lead to the fall of the universe and to non-being. This is also seen in the performance of the ritual. The improper or in-correct performance of the ritual would signal the collapse of cosmic Order as though the sun were not to rise in the East and the rivers run up the hill.[6] Ṛta, in this case, would mean a system of activity that guides the world in such a way that its Order is maintained.

There were two realms of Vedic dharma, one belonged to the celestial and the other to the human realm. The former consisted of a mysterious, hidden, even magical power (ṛta) and the gods Varuṇa and Mitra were associated with it. The physical power of the world Order was associated with god Indra. The human realm comprised of the social structure of the community, which was a power. For instance, the Brāhmin caste wielded Varuṇa's power in their knowledge of the rites of sacrifice and as mediators of sovereign sacred power, etc.

The sacerdotal class of Ṛg Vedic age addressed these gods by way of hymnals, praising them for their greatness and mighty deeds and begged them for wealth in cattle, numerous offspring, prosperity, long life, and victory. They performed simpler rituals like the Soma oblation and the Fire sacrifice of melting butter, which became an elaborate system in the Brāhmaṇic period. And as a result, the various gods on earth, air and heaven performed their actions, maintaining the universe.

These gods had a beginning and their physical aspect was anthropomorophic. Some of them were imagined as warriors wearing coats of mail and helmets, etc. and armed with spears, axes, bows and arrows. The only deity in whom injurious features were prominent was Rudra. The evils proceeded from the demons, big and small. Evils such as disease, etc. which are linked to human life came from minor demons while the greater ones such as draught, etc. were produced by demons like Vṛtra. Once they were appeased, they manifested their overwhelming, beneficient nature. Though the gods were moral in their nature as guardian of honesty and virtue, their power and greatness were held more prominent. Their power got manifested especially when they were offered with hymns of praises and request and sacrifices, especially the offerings of Soma.

Some gods like Indra and Agni became more prominent in the course of time. The sacerdotal class engaged itself in the Agni or 'fire' cult on its many manifestations as fire on earth, as fire in the atmosphere in the form of lightning and as celestial fire seen as sun, moon, etc. Such mystical speculation on the nature of Agni gave birth first to pantheism in which a single individual deity was considered as the manifestation of several others and then to henotheism in which the individual gods were regarded as the highest.[7]

The important feature of Atharva Veda was sorcery and it was mainly directed against hostile elements such as diseases, noxious animals, demons, foes, oppressors, etc. The auspicious elements contained in them secured harmony in the family and village life, reconciliation of enemies, lay life, health and prosperity, besides prayers for protection on journeys and for luck in gambling. It took some time for the book to be recognized as a canonical literature. For instance, the Āpastambha Dhramasūtra rated it as inferior in quality. Arthaśāstra classified those who recited the deadly incantations from the Atharva among the seven kinds of assassins. Physicians and astrologers were considered impure and sorcerers were severely punished.

But its importance and canonical character were recognized in the Mahābhārata. The Purāṇas assigned an advanced position to it. For instance, Brahman, the Atharvan priest, was required of the knowledge of the other three Vedas and of the sacrificial application. He acted as superintendent or Brahma of the sacrificial ceremonial.

3.1.3.2. Dharma at the age of the Brāhmaṇas: **Yajña** *or Sacrifice*

The sacerdotal element was already seen in the early Vedic age and in the Śukla Yajur Veda where the Brāhmins had gods in their power owing to their knowledge of the ritual sacrifice and the place of each god in it. The Brāhmaṇas went a step further to say that there were two kinds of gods, the Devas and the Brāhmins, of whom the latter were held as deities among men.

Among the three later Vedas, the Sāma Veda was in close link with the Ṛg Veda. The Udgātṛ priests employed this book chiefly at the soma sacrifice with its special chants. The Saṁhita or the mantra portion of the Yajur Veda dealt with Soma as well as with new and full moon sacrifices on the one hand, and with the construction of the fire-altar on the other. All these applied only to sacrificial rites.

The Yajur Veda brought about a new age in socio-religious life in India. The centre of Vedic civilization had by then moved from the West to the East. It was here that the religion of the Brāhmaṇas and the social system got developed and from where they spread to the rest of India. The new features introduced in the religion of the Yajur Veda were: (1) Rudra of the Ṛg Veda, appeared on the scene as Śiva along with other epithets like Śaṅkara and Mahādeva. Viṣṇu occupied a prominent position than in the Ṛg Veda; (2) the demons were regularly called Asuras as the group of evil beings opposed to the gods as seen in the myths of the Yajur Veda. Asuras were represented as a section of Eastern people who had the cult of Bhāgavatism (worship of Śiva, Viṣṇu, etc.). They were opposed to Vedic polytheism. Yoga or meditation was their spiritual sustenance; (3) the word *Brahma,* which simply meant *devotion* in the Ṛg Veda, came to be signified as the essence of prayer and holiness. It was a foretaste of the later development in the Upaniṣads; (4) snake worship which was unknown to the Ṛg Veda, now appeared as an element in Indian religion and more interestingly (5) the gods who were the object of devotion in the Ṛg Veda became secondary to Sacrifice itself. Thus its correct performance became all-important.

Its power was so great that it compelled the gods to do the will of the officiating priest. Thus the Brāhmins became more powerful than the gods. Verily there were only two kinds of gods the gods themselves who were assuredly gods, and the priests who had studied the Vedic lore.[8]

Thus the simple Ṛg Vedic devotion like the adoration of the power and the benevolence of these gods, consciousness of one's guilt, etc. could not survive in the Brāhmaṇa period. The ritual became a mystery to the commoners other than the Brāhmaṇa caste. It was believed to have a magical effect on the audience and at every ceremony the priest's presence was imminent. As complex rituals got developed, the place of the priest secured a high religious as well as social status. In the Vedic and the Brāhmaṇic period, a transpersonal, universal Law or cosmic Order soon got linked with the social structure of the community and to the specific actions of a specialized group, supervised and protected by various deities like Mitra and Varuṇa. As Prof. B.K. Ghosh rightly pointed out, the Brāhmaṇic literature became an arid desert of puerile speculations as religious ceremonies marking the lowest ebb of Vedic culture[9]. But the chief human interest of these Brāhmaṇa literature lay in the numerous myths and legends and the several interesting information concerning the geographical data, Indian tribes, Āryanization (Vrātya ṣtomas),[10] etc.

3.1.3.4. Dharma in the Āraṇyakas and the Upaniṣads: Jñāna *or Liberating Knowledge*

The Āraṇyakas were a particular class of Vedic writings attached to the Brāhmaṇas. While the Brāhmaṇas were known as the Karma kāṇḍa related to ritual action, the Upaniṣads were called the Jñāna kāṇḍa related to knowledge. It was only in the Upaniṣads that one came across elements that were contrary to the sacrificial and priestly cult of the Brāhmaṇas. The writings were characterised by the total absence of any Brāhmin exclusiveness. They dealt with themes like nature of god and the soul, of man and the world, and the relation between them. They also expounded the nature and purpose of existence, the ultimate reality and its nature. They spoke about the relationship between the body, the mind and the senses, about worship and meditation and the various means of salvation and other eschatological principle, and how men could attain what they wanted.

The essence and the goal of life according to the Upaniṣads was to realize the inner most self, the Ātman and its identity or sharing with the universal Self, the Brahman. Both these terms signified different things in the course of religious history. For instance, Ātman in the Ṛg Veda meant only the 'breath' (ātman of varuṇa). In the Brāhmaṇa it came to be known as soul or self. Later, it was attributed to the universe as pervading the universe. The term Brahman in the Ṛg Veda signified 'devotion' or 'prayer.' In the oldest Brāhmaṇas it had the sense of 'universal holiness' as manifested in prayer, priest and sacrifice. In the Upaniṣads it signified the holy principle that animated nature. The fundamental doctrine of the Upaniṣads explained the identity of the individual soul with the universal Soul or Brahman.[11]

The meditative philosophy reflected in the Upanisads portrayed a shift in the means of salvation. Dharma in the Upaniṣads became the soul-searching process of realizing the essence of the Ātman. The Ṛg Vedic robust view of life through accumulation of wealth, cattle, etc. and the Brāhmaṇic sacrificial and ritual means of attaining better heavens were but the *way of the Fathers* or Pitṛyāna. Their result would only bring people to fall into the age-old rut of birth and death cycle. But the aim proposed by the Upaniṣads was the *way of the gods* or Devayāna,[12] the realization of the Atman and its identity with the universal Brahman.

Meditative and Yogic reflection was a special contribution of the Śramaṇa culture. The doctrine of Karma, the realization of Self and the path of renunciation got assimilated in the Brāhmaṇic soteriology only later as supported by the several Upaniṣadic passages at later time.[13] For instance, most of the Upaniṣads attributed to the Atharva Veda represented the theosophic, mystic, ascetic or sectarian views. The fundamental doctrine common to all of them got developed in various special directions: the first group studied the nature of the Ātman; the second treated the absorption into the Ātman through ascetic means like meditation (Yoga); the third recommended the life of a religious mendicant (sannyāsin) as necessary condition for realization. The oldest of them, namely, the Muṇḍaka the Praśna and, to a less degree, the Māṇḍūkyopaniṣad represented the Vedānta doctrine most faithfully.

3.1.3.5. Dharma of the Sūtra Period: Varṇa and Āśrama

The Sūtra period (500-200 BC) abounded in the sacrificial and other manuals like the Śrauta Sūtras, Gṛhya Sūtras and Dharma Sūtras. Sacrifices were performed for the benefit of the individual, the Yajamāna. The Śrauta sūtras were indispensable for the understanding of the sacrificial ritual such as the Agnihotra, the Daśapūrṇamāsa, the Chaturmāsa, the various kinds of Soma sacrifices and the building of the altar, etc. The Gṛhya manuals dealt with sacrifices performed at the domestic level for the domestic life of a person and the family from birth to death, and even after death. They described a number of saṁskāras or sacraments performed at various important stages in the life of the individual. The Dharma understood in these rituals was nothing more than that of the Brāhmaṇas. Sacrifice was the comer stone of life, and heaven was the reward or the result of sacrifice.

As Dharma was the Order of the universe, it validated the rules pertaining to it, namely, the prohibitions and injunctions found in the Dharmasūtras. The Āpastamba Dharmasūtra (400 BC according to Bühler) depicted the performance of sacrifices and the duties of the three upper classes. The Baudāyāna Dharmasūtra spoke about the duties of the four religious stages or the Āśramas, the mixed castes, etc. The Gautama Dharmasūtra, the Vaśiṣṭa Dharmasūtra and the Manu Dharmasūtra were similar in nature and content. They all spoke about the performance of duties according to the social stratification or caste structure and the different stages of life of the Brāhmaṇic social order. Anything outside this structure was forbidden or, at the least, reviled.

For instance, Manu said that it was for the sake of prosperity and protection of the world that castes were originated.[14] Manu contended that a Brāhmin was a great divinity whether he was learned or not,[15] and a Brāhmin was more respectable among the various classes of man.[16] Any connection with the outcastes, like the Vrātyas, was forbidden.[17]

Although the ideal of Mokṣa and Sannyāsa were completely recognised at the time of the Dharmaśāstras,[18] the fourth stage of life was either disparaged when compared to the order of the Gṛhastha[19] or it was claimed only by the Brāhmins.[20] All the Dharmaśāstras described elaborately the duties of each caste and the characteristics of each stage of life.[21]

Despite the commentaries and legal digests to the Dharmaśāstras, the purpose of certain rules were not understood. Acceptance of a rule did not always mean that its purpose was clearly understood. Dharma had both a visible purpose (dṛṣṭārtha) as well as an invisible purpose (adṛṣṭārtha) purpose and the rules for that which had the invisible purpose was deemed greater in importance to those that had a visible purpose. Thus dharma was *mysticized.*

Prof. Arthur Macdonnel[22] says that the progress of research in Dharmasūtras tends to show that the basis even of the sacerdotal ritual of the Brāhmins was popular religious observances. From this he concludes that Brāhminism acquired and retained such a hold on the population of India because they could exploit these popular religious observances and devotion and were intelligent enough to make them systematic.

3.1.3.6. Dharma of the Nītiśāstras: Harmony and Legal justice

The main objective of Dharma in the Nītiśāstras such as *Arthaśāstra* of Viṣṇusharma was to bring justice in society (personal and social) and to enforce harmony. The Nītiśāstras covered the whole field of political ethics and moral behaviour, administration and state welfare, livelihood, trade and commerce, agriculture and cattle breeding, wealth or profit, kingcraft, laws governing kingship, administration,force or coercion (daṇḍa Nīti, etc.)

It was both a religious concern and a political affair to administer law courts and to take care of the enforcement of law. The political, legal and religious aspects of Indian legal tradition were all intertwined. Dharma was both law and religion. The main objective of the legal system was to ensure that people followed the duties and obligations of dharma. It was believed that the whole world was organized according to the rational and moral Order of Dharma and hence the legal observances were right and valid. It followed, then, that those who gave the law, especially the kings and monarchs, were implicitly accepted and they were the protectors of dharma.[23] King Yudhisthira was addressed as *dharmaputra* or the 'son of cosmic (or moral) law' and the protector and preserver of that law. Kings were supposed to execute and be the regents of dharma just as Rāma, the embodiment of dharma, was. People needed kings for their own well being. The king punished those who violated dharma and the punishment was considered as purification.[24] It was linked with the concept of penance.[25]

3.1.3.7. Dharma of the Epics: Moral Order

Mahābhārata and the *Rāmāyaṇa,* the great Epics, were written during the classical Sānskrit period (500-50 BC). Mahābhārata contained a vast anthology of pre-Āryan and Āryan material, mostly episodical comprising cosmology, theogony, statecraft, and the science of war, ethics, legendary history, mythology, fairy tales, several digressions and philosophical interludes detailing the political, social and religious life of the times. It is a mirror of life showing effectively the strong passions of the human person, Duryodana's greed and jealousy, Draupadi's grim determination, Yudisthira's steadfast devotion to duty, compelled with love of gambling and the like.

Brāhmaṇical redaction seemed to have taken place at the close of its final state. They incorporated didactic matter calculated to impress the people, especially on kings, with the doctrines of the priestly class. It thus assumed the character of a vast treatise on duty (Dharma) in which the divine origin and immutability of

Brāhmin institution, the eternity of the caste system, and the subordination of all to the priests were laid down.[26]

Dharma in Vālmīki Rāmāyaṇa referred to spiritual and moral perfection and it was a means to obtain svarga or heaven.[27] Although Lakṣmaṇa expanded pragmatic and realistic approach to life,[28] Vālmīki asserted the supremacy of Dharma over the other ideals of life. Vālmīki said that Artha and Kāma were to be grounded in Dharma. A person who went after lust devoid of Dharma suffered from infancy and he was not admired by any.[29] Artha and Kāma sprang from righteousness.[30] Vālmīki accepted Dharma more as the reflective principle of conscience or the inner voice of a person or the 'inner moral order' than a mass of external rituals preserved and observed by people. It was almost the End of human life.[31] The ideal of Mokṣa was yet unknown to Vālmīki and Dharma was never a means but an end in itself.[32]

Dharma also stood for a principle or duties, fixed, unalterable and absolute having its source in the Vedas, Dharmaśāstras, customs, traditions and the usages of the community.[33] Rāma was said to tread the path approved and followed by the predecessors.[34] Gṛhastha Dharma was praised as the foremost among the four modes of life[35] and ascetic life was ridiculed for a Kṣatriya.[36] Vālmīkiyan ethics was social in nature. Even the hermits were depicted as sociable beings.[37] Rāma's character was portrayed as an ethically perfect person, devoted to the welfare of the subject and who did not injure any one.[38] Service to mankind, service to parents and love for enemies were some of the main principles of Vālmīkian. Perfection of the individual and that of the social order was the basis of moral life, according to Vālmīki.

3.1.3.8. Dharma in Bhagavad Gītā: Do thy duty

Dharma, in the Bhagavad Gītā, became the manifestation of god. This was not so in the Ṛg Vedic time. The Vedic view was that gods were seen as the offspring of Ṛta. In the Gītā the doctrine of Bhakti (faith) was exalted and one has to listen deeply to the call of God and be attached to him. For instance. God himself (Kṛṣṇa) created the normative social order and hence it had a divine origin. Hence the duties of caste had to be upheld above all other obligations. One hears the call of Kṛṣṇa to follow the action appropriate to one's birth, moral constitution and social status or caste position[39] and to perform actions according to one's own dharma (svadharma). One had to perform all beneficial and meritorious human deeds in strict compliance with Dharma. It was nothing but caste duties. The virtuous and the self-abnegating[40] would maintain Dharma. And whenever Dharma declined, Kṛṣṇa would take a birth in order to restore it.[41] Thus one wonders whether adhering to caste duties itself became the yardstick for Dharma, as the rights and responsibilities of an individual in today's classical Hindu society are determined by caste.

Bhagavad Gītā tried to synthesize the two different views of Brāhmaṇic and Śramaṇic traditions. On the one hand it advocated the pursuit of Yoga and dwelt on the advantages of self-mortification and asceticism, on the need for the annihilation of self and the virtue of seeing god in everything. In the place of complete renunciation of action, which was a Śramaṇa trend of thought, the Gītā propounded selfless-action, action that looked for no reward (Karma-phala tyāga).

A new path of Devotion or Bhakti transcended the social order and caste structure. And yet Dharma in the Gītā paid more attention to *svadharmạ*. Kṛṣṇa advised Arjuna to *'do thy duty'*. Though the Gītā expounded a manifold method of attaining perfection, some by way of meditation, others by knowledge, others by invitation, action or worship,[42] yet the Brāhmaṇical social order was thoroughly maintained and caste duties or *svadharma* still played a vital role in the life of people. Duty was essentially work and, work, according to the dictates of caste.

3.1.3.9. Dharma in the Purāṇas: the 'status quo' retained

Purāṇas provided a great deal of religious teaching. They spoke about deeds, good and evil, and their consequences through stories and events. Good deed would take one to svarga or heaven and evil deeds, to hell. The doctrine of sin and punishment was vibrant in the Purāṇas. So much so, the Purāṇas were known as the 'Vedas of the common folk.' They propagated many forms of Bhakti, belief in miracles, spurious legends of gods and Ṛṣis, devout exercises like pilgrimages to some sacred places (Tīrthas), etc. They also expressly declared that the above were available to women and the lowest classes, thus disregarding caste and personal limitations. Observing such exercises as efforts in bringing the lower strata of people into the mainstream, Caterina Conio says that by the time of the Purāṇas religious festivals and pilgrimages had increasingly become occasions ofinter-caste fraternity and a sort of model of a return to an original unity.[43]

3.1.3.10. Dharma of Poetic Literature: Puruṣārtha

Vast literature were written during the Kāvya period (200 BC-1100 AD) in the form of drama (like that of Śākuntala of Kālidāsa), poetry (Siśupālavadha of Māgha), prose romance (Kādambarī of Bāṇa), Campu lyrics. Gnomic verses, popular tales, fables, etc. They depicted the theme of love, valour, truth, duty, etc. Problems of life and destiny form part of the Dharma preached in and through this literature. For instance, in Act IV of Śākuntala the theme of destiny foreshadowed life almost at very step both positively and negatively. When King Duśyanta proposed to take Śākuntala away by the end of the third day. Fate completely altered this plan by interposing the curse of sage Durvāsa even before Duṣyanta could reach his capital. It was only with the sight of the ring that he could revive his memory.

Several religious literatures like Buddhacarita of Aśvaghosa, Yāśastilaka of Jain Somadeva and Gīta Govinda of Jeyadeva taught the didactic tenets of that religion. In all these such sentiments as Bhakti or prapatti or Śaranāgati or complete dedication were delineated. The Gnomic verses like Sṛṅgāra, Nīti and Vairāgyaśataka of Bartṛhari emphasized the evanescent nature of things and the vanity of human wishes.

The vast literature on popular tales and fables such as the Śatakas and other story books of the Buddhists and the Jains were written in Pāli and Prākrit for the purpose of religious edification, worldly wisdom, etc. Stories such as Bṛhatkathā of Guṇāḍhya in

Prākrit, Śūkasaptati in Sānskrit for the purpose of amusement. The didactic fables like the Pañcatantra and Hitopadeśa had a rich moral content. In most of these literature the Puruṣārthas or the Life-values such as Dharma, Artha, Kāma and Mokṣa were studied, the ways of attaining them were discussed and the Āśrama and Varṇa dharma were taught and practised. Thus Dharma embraced the whole gamut of moral and social life as means to the final liberation.

Thus, in the post-Vedic period the term Dharma assumed very many meanings. It referred to law, ordinances, customary observances, etc. and was recognized as what was established and firm with regard to both the rational as well as socio-ethical Order. It meant what was dutiful, what was right and just, what was virtuous, etc. Finally that by which one fitted in the social Order became normative to Dharma. Thus Dharma got linked to duties determined by one's social class (Varṇa) and stages of life (Āśrama). These two ensured the well being of the cosmic and the social Order.[44] The priest and others had to attend to their class duties; similarly one had to adhere to the life-style of the stage of life one lived. Any imperfect observance of one's duty and responsibility would harm society. No one could shift responsibility or assume another place in society.[45] Svadharma or particular duty with responsibility was determined by one's place in society.

And still there was a provision given by Āpaddharma or 'duty determined by emergency.' It was meant to suspend the norms determined by Varṇa and Āśrama in order to survive the society from stress. But at no time could a person who is not a Priest earn a living by teaching the Veda or by performing Vedic ceremonies. Human life was organized in terms of the four social classes (Varṇas), the four goals (Arthas) and the four stages (Āśramas) and obedience to the caste rules was the very essence of Dharma.

To remark briefly, Hindu Dharma in its nature and import was never univocal or static. It had undergone several changes in the socio-religious history of nearly thousand years and come to mean what could be seen as moral and social order of humankind.

Hindu Dharma was mainly Brāhmaṇical in its character. The Śramaṇa ethos did shape the understanding of Dharma in the course if time due to encounters between races and group cultures, especially during the time of the Epics and the Upaniṣads. The encounter between the Vedic and non-Vedic traditions was obvious in the evolution of the meaning of Hindu Dharma. The coming chapters will portray in detail the characteristic of Śramaṇa Dharma as lived by the Buddhist and Jain traditions.

PART-II DHARMA IN BUDDHIST TRADITION

3.2.1. Historical survey

Dharma, one of the three refuges in the Buddhist tradition, was originally meant to denote the teachings of Buddha in general. But in the very first council at Rājagriha immediately after the death of Buddha, the whole teachings of Buddha was recited and categorised into the three pitakas.[46] While the Sutta Piṭaka contained the discourses, stories, anecdotes of Buddha, the Vinaya Piṭaka exclusively dealt with the disciplinary codes of the community of followers. The Abhidhamma Piṭaka dealt with the philosophical teachings.[47] Although Buddha was silent about discussing metaphysical problems[48] like the existence of the soul, its continuation after death, etc., later Buddhism, especially the Mahāyāna tradition speculated philosophical issues such as discussions on the existence of the Tathāgata after death, the nature of the Buddhas and Bodhisattvas, etc. almost leading the Buddhist trend in a similar path to that of the Upaniṣads. Abhidhamma Piṭaka served as the source material, which was interpreted in different ways which, in subsequent times, got formed into various sects within Buddhism.

3.2.1.1. Metaphysical Considerations

The original teaching of the Buddha known as Dharma consisted of the Four Ārya Satya or the Four Noble Truth[49] regarding suffering, and the Eight-Fold path[50] regarding the way of getting rid of sufferings. There were only few important conceptions which were fundamental to the Buddhist thoughts:

1. The doctrine of Anatta or non-soul in the sense of a permanent, unitary entity. What we ordinarily call a self is a compound of material and mental qualities, called Khandas.
2. The doctrine of Karma is not original with Buddhism. It appears in the Upaniṣads though apparently as an esoteric doctrine. The Jains also knew it. The Jatilas, ascetics, who joined the Buddha's Order already believed in Karma. To Buddha, the doctrine of Karma was wholly a *moral conception* unlike the metaphysical soul-theory as in the Upaniṣads or the materialistic conception as in Jainism. It was the *law of the deed as* impersonal, universal principle of moral cause and effect.
3. The doctrine of Nirvāṇa: its primary meaning metaphorically signifies the extinction of the desire and attachment, which leads to rebirth.

3.2.1.2. Monastic-Lay discipline

The early monastic order was not either original with Buddha. It was common for religious teachers with many disciples to organize them into regulated communities. Such Saṅgha or Order was a convenient structure to uphold the general teaching of the master and a visible sign of the path towards perfection. Besides the routine activities such as recitation and prayers begging of alms, partaking in the daily meal and meditation, regular instruction to the junior monks and the lay people, observing the bimonthly upasotha days of abstinence and fasting, confession of sin etc. were other activities in the monastery.

A less strict discipline than that of the monks was provided to the lay Buddhists. They were to abstain from taking life, drinking intoxicants, lying, stealing and unchastity. Further certain virtues were stressed like kindness, compassion, temperance etc., and practices like alms-giving, religious conversation were encouraged, mutual duties were enjoined in relations of parents and children, pupils and teachers, husband and wife, friend and friend, masters and servants, laity and clergy.[51] The middle path was upheld, a path between the extremes of asceticism and luxury.[52] Although the individual monks were poor (their equipment was alms bowl, vestments, staff razor, toothpick, water-strainer, etc.), the rules of poverty did not apply to monasteries in their corporate capacity. The monasteries were wealthy and influential through gifts of land, revenues from estates or villages, etc.

3.2.1.3. The religious revolution within Buddhism

A great change came over Buddhism in North India after Ashoka's time, especially during the first and second centuries A. D. The simple understanding of the truth of suffering and the moral discipline in order to overcome suffering were overshadowed by speculative and imaginative processes. The ideal of Arhat who finds Nirvāṇa by a strenuous discipline was replaced by the Bodhisattva who reaches release by means of a devotion to others in a long career reaching through endless lives; he foregoes Nirvana for the sake of others.[53] Buddhas and Bodhisattvas came to be regarded as supernatural beings worshipped as deities. Gotama was regarded as simply one earthly manifestation of a cosmic Buddha, an essence that has incarnated itself countless times in the past and will do so yet countless times in the future; and that reveals itself also in heavenly Buddhas who rule paradises in other worlds. Emphasis came to be placed on salvation by faith in some Bodhisattva like the invocation of the name of Amitabha secures rebirth in his paradise, etc.[54]

The causes of these changes could be traced in the continued growth of Indian thought: the interest in metaphysics kept developing beyond the limits; secondly the influence of the other Indian religious thought and practice like the Sāṁkhya philosophy, the polytheistic Hinduism, the monism of Vedānta, Yoga, etc.; thirdly the need of the people for a more emotional morality and more personal, sympathetic deities and fourthly the foreign converts naturally brought in other ideas which mixed with those of Buddhism. For instance, Mahāyāna was largely of foreign origin, and its development was the result of the complex interaction of Indian, Zoroastrian, Gnostic and Hellenistic elements.[55]

3.2.1.4. The scholastic tendency in the Mahāyāna tradition

Scholasticism in Buddhism arose in the interest of perpetuating this teaching and not to allow any dissension to mar its unity.[56] In the process of selecting and enumerating these basic doctrines a distinction was made between the discourses (suttānta) and the scholastic treatises (Abhidhamma). The former was considered as popular teachings (vohāra desana) and the latter as discourses on ultimate reality (paramattha desana).[57] This led to the emphasis on the difference between dhamma and Abhidhamma, the latter being defined as *special dhamma* (abhivisittho dhammo). While the discourses were looked upon as dealing with dhamma, the Abhidhamma treated dhamma as special and ultimate reality (paramatta).

The period 200-500 AD was a time when all the great religious movements in India sought to give philosophical expression to their ideas. This was made possible in part by the peace and prosperity of North India under the Gupta period, which lasted from 320 until 647 A.D.[58] Two main schools came to be differentiated in the Mahāyāna:

(1) ***The Mādhyāmika School:***

Mādhyāmika founded by Nāgārjuna (flourished 2nd century A.D.): This system grew from the germs of Buddha's original teachings such as the doctrine that'there is no permanent soul and that every individual is made of elements (dhammas) which are momentary and perishing though real while they last. The Mādhyāmikas taught that everything was void; it said that the dhammas as well as the individual are unreal. Existence is a continuous procession of illusory, unreal dhammas and our acceptance of them as real is due to ignorance. The only knowledge that can arrest the renewal of dhammas is knowledge of their radical and fundamental unreality.

The Mādhyāmika interpreted Nirvāṇa as the end of the

production of these phenomena. Impurity is attachment to phenomena conceived as pleasant; purity is complete detachment from phenomena. Ignorance is a clinging to the substantiality of phenomena, which induces attachment. Wisdom is the real truth, which is the knowledge of the vacuity of things.[59] The extreme positions held that the object described, the description and the person describing are all similarly non-existent and *Absolute truth is silence.*

(2) ***The Yogācāra School:***

Yogācāra (or Vijñānavāda) school founded by Asaṅga and Vasubandhu (4th Century A. D.): They agreed with the Mādhyāmika teachings[60] that all the dhammas are but the constructions of ignorant minds and that there is no movement in the external world for it does not exist. We construct it ourselves and then are deluded that it exists by itself. All our phenomenal knowledge is without any essence or truth and is but a creation of *māyā,* a mirage or a dream. There are distinctive conceptions of Yogācāra school. All phenomena, both material and non-material, originate in mind. Mind according to its action reveals eight functions of consciousness including the Ālayavijñana or receptacle consciousness. The seeds or possibilities of all phenomena are contained in it. When they grow and unfold there springs up the distinction of subject and object and the illusory multiplicity of an objective world. In consequence of this we are disturbed and move about in search of peace, suffering the pain of attachment to this or that transient thing. If we once fully understand that nothing else exists but mind then the objective world ceases to exist for us and all types of consciousness are turned into enlightened wisdom by means of which we can unite with the ultimate which transcends speech and thought. The Ālayavijñāna is the ocean; the whole phenomenal world is but the waves resulting from its operations.

In the awakening of faith (ascribed to Aśvaghoṣa) there is a special form of the Vijñānavāda. Three main conceptions[61] got developed in the process:

1. *Suchness* (bhūtatathatā): it is a universal soul, which is the oneness of the totality of things,[62] the absolute spiritual reality. In its own essence this spiritual absolute is pure and at rest. But aroused by ignorance its activity produces the illusory multiplicity of the phenomenal world; it is then called *defiled mind,* the recognition that *Suchness* is the only true reality, i.e.. Nirvāṇa.
2. The theory of Triple personality: Dharmakāya or the body of the law, the absolute in itself, Nirmāṇakāya or the Body of transformation, the absolute as embodied in earthly Buddhas and Sambhogakāya or the Body of Bliss, the absolute as embodied in heavenly Buddhas.
3. Salvation by faith[63] i.e. if you believe in Amitābha Buddha, you will then be born in his paradise.

3.2.2. Buddhist Dharma - its shades of meaning

3.2.2.1. As cosmic and moral Law

Within the Buddhist context, Dharma as the universal Order of. cosmic law is co-ordinated in the doctrine of dependent origination[64] (Pratītya Samutpāda), the fundamental constituents of the universe (dhammadhātu), the reality of existence (dhammatā), the essence of reality (dhammadhātu), suchness (tathatā) and emptiness (śūnyata)[65], store-consciousness (ālayavijñāna), three marks of all existence (Tilakkhana: anātma, anitya and dukhha),[66] the five aggregate (skandhas), etc.

As a moral law or the law of righteousness, Dharma in Buddhism includes the whole system of moral and spiritual discipline[67] or the system of right conduct or the path of virtue. It would mean Buddha's proclamation of the path towards deliverance such as the vinaya or monastic discipline, the rules and regulations for the application and practice of dharma, the prātimokṣa (the monastic code) which contains rules of conduct, called Dharma.

The first preaching of Buddha known as the 'First turning of the wheel of Dharma'[68] (the Four Noble Truth and Eight fold path) flows from the experience of awakening (bodhi) and the resultant state of freedom from passion, suffering and rebirth called Nirvāṇa.[69] This was taken to be the sphere of knowledge of the eternal Buddhas (bodhisattvas, tathāgatas).[70] The Mahāyānists symbolized Dharma in the concepts of the eternal body of the Buddha[71] (the dharmakāya) and the nature of Buddha or Buddhahood (Tathāgata garbha or the womb of Buddhas).[72]

Vinaya is regarded as the affective expression or pragmatic implementation of the Buddha's Dharma. It is precept put into practice. The successful cultivation of discipline (Vinaya) is understood to be a process of mental and spiritual purification whereby a bhikṣu (a mendicant) is increasingly capable of resisting the power of the āsravas (passion, hatred and delusion) to affect his internal volitions. Actions not motivated by the influence of asravas, which are in turn rooted in the indulgent sense of I-ness (ahaṁkāra), are the mark of one in whom Vinaya as been installed. Historically, Vinaya has not only been the charter for the Buddhist monastic experience, but it has continued as a legitimising device for reform within the saṅgha as well.

The responsibility of the lay Buddhist is to make sure that Vinaya remains a primary concern especially when monks have tended to interfere in the secular affairs of society. Their objective is to see that Saṅgha truly functions as a spiritual refuge and a worthy object of meritorious action necessary for the positive fruition of karmic efficacy.

3.2.2.2. Dharma as a system of ethics

The following remarks can be made on Buddhist Dharma as a system of Ethics and morality:

1. The doctrine of the Dependent Origination (Pratītya Samutpāda) or the law of Causation explains the order of the Universe and the existence of human reality. There is no 'being' but becoming. The continuous chain or flow of experiences explains the cycle of birth and rebirth. Buddhism traces the origin of existence to desire or *taṇhā*.

2. The root or seed of Dharma is in every being and it has to be realized *as such*.
3. There is no entity which is not subject to anicca or anitya and there is no conscious entity which is not subject to dukkha. The state of impermanence and disease will always be there as long as one is caught up in the *wheel of life*.
4. The practice of the noble path of Buddha (the acceptance of the 4 noble truth and the following of the 8 fold path) is mainly to attain the state of ultimate freedom and the organization (Saṅgha) is to facilitate in attaining this goal. The infinite possibilities of the innate nature of Buddha is in every being and the state of Nirvāṇa or Nibbāna is the supreme goal of Buddhist endeavour and it is available to all. The concept of past and future Buddhas forms a 'respectable rationale' for popular cult among ordinary mortals.
5. The three levels of the manifestation of Buddha (as the absolute Dharma of Dharmakāya; the Sambhogakāya of the wise and the Nirmāṇakāya of historical incarnation) mark the levels of attainment of the wisdom or the levels of spirituality. They trace from the accessible to the absolute path in the whole endeavour. In the social and political order, important personages (Lāma in Tibet, for instance) are considered to be the manifestation of future Buddhas like Avalokiteśvara.
6. The middle path is the fundamental principle of Buddhist ethics and morality realizing the Ideal in accordance with thc Truth. It is thc solid way (Khema) in contrast with the crooked (Kumma); the holy or noble (Āriya) in contrast with the false (miccha) or base (un-Āriya); and it leads to the perfect enlightenment (Sambodhigami).[73]
7. The basis of the content of enlightenment, namely, denial of the phenomenal, of human weakness, illusions and passions and the teaching of non-ego (anatta), extinction (nirodha) of pains and the well known Nibbāna is found in the stability of Truths (dhamma-tthiti)[74] and all virtuous acts flow from this metaphysical source.

8. Morality is in vain unless it is well founded on profound knowledge and high attainments. Buddha asks his disciple to realize the profound things through wisdom comprehended by the wise.[75]
9. Buddhist dharma is closely linked with the ideal of universal salvation. Every being is a Buddha in his essential quality and on this account the standard of a perfect Buddhist was transferred from an Arhat to a Bodhisattva. Hence it is essential for everyone to touch the immortal region with the body i.e. by personal experience and actual realization.
10. The origin of ills is traced to the one root of thirst (taṇhā) and the source of all vices is traced in passion and greed (kāma and rāga).[76] This is the *original sin,* so to say, and the root of all evils. The sole origin of sin and ills is sought not in the objective world but in our own mind and acts. It is by up-rooting this fundamental vice one can realize the holy way (Āriya magga) and the attainment of enlightenment (Bodhi).
11. The ideal of Buddhist dharma consists in the imbibing of the personal qualities of the Buddha who is both moral and intellectual perfection. The different schools of Buddhism aimed towards the perfection of an Arhat or to become a Bodhisattva preparing one's own Buddhahood.
12. Morality associated with wisdom and mental training is the way to the realization of the essence of Buddhahood and it is the way of being in communion with the Buddhas. Morality itself is possible only when there is this substantial identity of our own mind with them.
13. The mind is the root of all actions although body and speech have great influence upon one another for the acceleration of the good and for the repression of the bad. The classification of vice and virtue[77] reveal the scope of Buddhist morality and their mental training
14. The organization for the promotion of morality is established in the Order (Saṅgha). It includes the monks and the laity. The Buddha in the rules of obedience (Vinaya) laid down the guidance of morality in the Saṅgha.[78] It includes

prohibitions and commandments and rules to carry them out. Householders can attain the moral ideal of Buddhism with less difficulty by means of homeless life than. Hence Buddhist Dharma is pre-eminently monastic in character and hence the duty of the lay followers is to pay a special respect to the monks. Similar consideration occurs when applied to the relations between the sexes. Female ascetics have to pay special respect to those members of the male sex.[79] But we also see many excellent women playing their role as Buddha's disciples.[80]

15. The Bodhisattva ethics has exalted the lay life and of the female sex. Yet the life of nobles or householders are in no way compatible with the practice of the pāramitas and the attainment of Bodhi. Hence communion in Buddhist term consists of all kinds of beings, both human and angelic, and among them there are various Bodhisattvas side by side with monks and ascetics.

3.2.2.3. Newer interpretations

But the recent trends in Buddhist ethics show that there are attempts to bring about Buddhist forms of contemporary social and political ideologies. For instance, the Buddhists have started interpreting nationalism and national responsibility. There have been recent developments in the world to justify democracy and socialistic trends. For example, Burmese Buddhists worked towards a theoretical and practical synthesis between Buddhism and Marxist social theory. There are several literature that interprets Buddhism, its doctrine and practice, in a social, Marxist perspective.[81] There are attempts in some parts of the world (e.g. Tibet) to actualize a Dharmic social order in the symbol of a monk (ruling line of lāmas).[82] Buddhist social ideals are modified as filiality, social and moral hierarchy and unitary political authority (in China and Japan).

Buddhist social ideas were articulated in two ways: (i) by those who were integrated into the established regimes (conservative social visions) and (ii) by those who sought to overthrow established authorities (revolutionary version). Many of the anti-establishment expressions of Buddhist social ideal were connected with expectation of the coming of the future Buddha Maitreya. Bodisattva often identified with the leaders of revolutionary groups committed to political change to establish on earth a new social order in which prosperity, justice and opportunity would abound for all classes of people.

3.2.3. An evaluation of the Buddhist Dharma:

Buddha had attained the solution of his mental struggles in the enlightenment of the 4 Noble Truths. The keynote of Buddhist Dharma was the infusion of practical needs with theoretical knowledge. Stress was laid upon the ascetic life against worldly life. Though Buddhist Dharma clearly betrays the Hindu mental disposition especially with ascetic aspects, yet it exhibits a fundamental contrast with Brāhmaṇic morality in not adhering to the social institutions and traditions.[83] But it seeks the basis of morality in the universal truth which are to be realized in everyone's wisdom and attainment. Practical morality in both the religions was founded on the Dharmas but it had different meanings to Brāhminism and Buddhism. To the former it meant the Divine ordinances incorporated in the legal codes and it is to be realized in every one's wisdom.

The fundamental feature of Buddhist Dharma consisted in its autonomic and personal principle in contrast with the legal and social principle of Brāhmanism. The significance of Buddha's personality[84] is seen from this angle. He is revered as the founder of the religion and as the revealer of final truths and guide of all beings to the same attainment as his own.

The prominence of personality is closely linked with the glorification of individual liberty, spirit of toleration and liberalism. This is seen in the Master's last sermon where he advises his disciple to leave off minor precepts and be light unto themselves. This liberal spirit stands in close connection with the esteem shown for the *middle path* between extreme pleasure and extreme asceticism. This remained the leading spirit, which led to the manifestation of newer forms in the history of Buddhism.

The Buddhist associated ethical theories and moral practice in such a way that the latter was founded on the former. Thus the whole discipline (sikkhā) is divided into the three branches which are to be taken care of mutually: morality (sīlā), mental training (samādhi or chitta) and wisdom (prajñā).[85] In other places, too, the inseparable connection is shows between morality and wisdom and super natural or mystic attainment.[86] Buddhist morality forms part of the religious ideal of complete enlightenment. It is not merely a means to attain perfection; it is an integral part of the perfection. One has to abound both in wisdom and goodness. Thus Buddhist ethics is never a system of theoretical discussions or speculation on ethical problems; it is always associated with enlightenment. It is the moral and intellectual perfection of a personality that is the highest aim in Buddhist Dharma.

PART - III DHARMA IN JAINA TRADITION

3.3.1. Levels of meaning of Dharma

Dharma in Jainism has two levels of meaning: one is generic and broad and the other is technical and specific to the term. Dharma in the latter usage is the basis for movement or motion as it is opposed to adharma or stillness and rest. Dharma and adharma are the medium of motion and rest respectively.[87] They are said to occupy the whole inhabited space of the universe (Lokākāśa).[88] No other system of philosophy has conceived these two in such a way as it is peculiar to Jaina philosophical system.

The general usage of the term Dharma has again two levels of meaning: one is metaphysical and, the other, ethical or moral. Our behaviour cannot be isolated from our metaphysical beliefs. Ācārya Samantabhadra goes to the extent of saying that without knowing the real nature of things which is *permanency in transitoriness,* all moral distinction between the antithesis of bondage and liberation, puṇya and pāpa, heaven and hell, pleasure and pain will be blurred.[89] If, for instance, the nature of things is absolutely transitory, as in the case of the Buddhist metaphysics, it would be impossible to carry on any financial transaction or to explain the fact of memory (pratyabhijñā) or to have any relation like that of husband and wife.[90] Hence the ultimate aim of philosophy is the realization of this relation between metaphysics and ethics.

To signify such a relation, the word *Dharma* is used. It means the essential nature of things (vastusvabhāvaḥ) on the one hand, and *moral duties* on the other. The seven fundamentals of Jainism, which are known as the *Saptatattva,* are only corollaries to the doctrine of Karma. It is on the foundation of Jīva and the concept of Karma that the edifice of Jaina ethics is built. 'As you sow, so shall you reap' is the basis for Jaina ethics.

Metaphysics and ethics could very well said to be the Jaina vision and way of life. It is this that binds an individual with society. Religion can be understood in this way. Hence Dharma in Jainism would mean seeing the vision and translation of it to life. This vision has been seen by the Jains, lived by them and taught by them (scripture); it is accepted and followed by a community (tradition); the same is urged by the community (normative and legal) and freely accepted by the followers (personal and social).

Thus, Jaina Dharma is seen as:

1. A *system of belief* (a) belief in the truth about *reality* expressed in the seven fundamental principles (Saptatattva) and, (b) truth about *karma,* the foundation of all metaphysics and ethics.
2. A vision of great *Jaina ideals of Right Faith, Right Knowledge and Right Conduct*
3. An attitude of pluralism seen as *Anekānta*
4. An ethical precept especially *Ahiṁsā* and respect for life expressed in vegetarianism, etc.
5. A ladder of spiritual formation called *Guṇasthānas* or the stages of spiritual formation
6. A system of discipline, the *ascetic* and *householder* way of life
7. And finally, as a *system of Religion,* Dharma pervades the whole gamut of topics such as the Tīrthaṅkara and the holy

pentad (Pañ caparameṣtin) and the idea of god (Paramātma); grace, merit, sin, penance, heaven, hell, etc.; cult and worship and spiritual exercise like prayer, fast, festivals, pilgrimage, etc. (Sāmāyika Dharma); authoritative teachings of the Tīrthaṅkaras in the Āgamas (sacred texts); and the tradition of the Jaina community, the four holy orders or Tīrtha.

3.3.2. Jaina Dharma as a system of Reality

One has to be conversant with the 'essence' of reality[91] in order to attain the goal of life. Daśavaikālika sūtra says: 'one who does not know the self and the non-self, how can he know the path to self-control (saṁyama).'[92] The metaphysical background to Jaina ethics is described in the seven fundamental principles: Self (Jīva), non self (Ajīva) the inflow of karmic matter (āsrava), bondage (bandha), Checking (saṁvara), shedding (Nirjarā) of karmic matter and liberation (Mokṣa).[93]

Jīva or the Self is the fundamental principle of Jaina metaphysics. It is so because the basic problem of ethics, namely, the removal of misery can be solved only by self-realization. Nemicandra Siddhānta Cakravarti summarizes the Jaina view of self: Self (Jīva) is the conscious entity endowed with apprehension and knowledge. It is an intangible entity and the agent of actions. It remains co-extensive with the body[94], which is animated by it. It is the enjoy er of the fruit of its actions and passes through births and deaths and gets liberation from karma and takes the upward motion, which is natural to it. Samayasāra of Kundakundācārya makes a clear distinction between the empirical and the transcendental self.[95] From the empirical point of view, the self (Jīva) is associated with non-self (Ajīva), becomes the agent of actions Experiencing pain and pleasure. From the transcendental point of view the self is nothing to do with matter. What distinguishes the self (Jīva) from the non-self (Ajīva) is the quality of consciousness.[96] This first metaphysical concept namely Jīva comprises all the living beings in the universe including the elemental bodied[97] and souls having one to five sense. That is why the Jaina Concept of non-violence is not confined only to men and animals but to all these elements bodied as well, meaning to say that all souls are equal in their transcendental form.

Regarding matter the idealists say that it is only the projection of the mind. The realists reject this and say that the mind is an image of the real outside world. Jainism is a realistic system and affirms the reality of matter which consist of atoms. The Jain atomic theory is subtler than the Nyāya-Vaiśeṣika atomism. Matter, composed of atoms, forms the basis of body, speech, mind, and vital airs.[98] Wordily enjoyment, pain, life, death are also caused by matter.[99] Another important idea in Jaina Metaphysics is that the six substances (dravyas) namely the self (Jīva), the matter (Pudgala), dharma and adharma (movement and rest), the space (Ākāśa) and Kāla (time) are characterised by permanence and change.[100] Substance is both substratum and its changing modes.[101] The essence of a substance (dravya) is never annihilated when we say that the object is permanent.[102] Both the substance in its essence (dravya) as well as modifications (paryāya) is equally real. We can't reject anyone of the two, neither continuity nor change.

Jīva due to contact with Ajīva has its activity. Due to the activity of the soul (yoga) Karma particles flow (Āsrava) into the soul. Bhāvāsrava refers to the psychic impediments responsible for the creation of the conditions of the influx and dravyasrava refers to the corpus of the karmic particles flowing into the soul causing bondage. Bandha or the union of soul with matter is a beginningless relation.[103] The soul though intangible in the pure sense gets obliterated under the influence of karma particles and becomes tangible.[104] The cause of misery as well as happiness is due to the inflow of karmic matter. Man's activities cause the inflow of karmic matter and cause bondage.[105] Karma can be meritorious or harmful. The former leads to happiness and the latter to misery. From a practical point of view man prefers good actions because they lead to happiness and he avoids bad ones; but from the real point of view all activities whether they are good or bad the soul with karmic matter and hence liberation is not possible. Hence one needs to rise above good as well as bad Karma.

Bandha has been distinguished into four types:

1. *Prakṛtibandha* refers to the nature of karma that has entered the soul
2. *Sthitibandha* refers to the state and the limitation of karmic particles in the soul
3. *Anubhāgabandha* refers to the intensity of experience of karma which leads to the intensity of the bondage, and
4. *Pradeśabandha* is concerned with the extensiveness and the aggragates of the karmic particles associated with the soul.

Basically there are 8 types of Karma[106]: knowledge, perception-obscuring, deluding and hindering karma; Feeling breeding, family-body determining karma. Tattvartha Sūtra enumerates the number of moral lapses that cause these 8 types of karma. A single scheme is presented here:

Activities	Type of Karma
Condemning the learned Concealing the knowledge Obstructing knowledge, its progress, Envy	Knowledge-obscuring
Denying proclaimed truths Refuting them purposely	Perception-obscuring[107]
Defaming the liberated person Defaming the scripture Defaming the church Defaming the religion	Right belief-deluding
Intense passionate feelings	Right conduct-deluding[108]
Disturbing others in their activity of charity, gain, enjoyment of goods and making use of their power	Hindering[109]

N.B: These above mentioned 4 types of karma are known as the Ghāti Karma. They tend to obscure the real nature of the self and also retard the moral progress of the aspirant.

Pain, sorrow, remorse, weeping, killing, pathetic mourning	Base-feeling-breeding
Compassion for living beings, charity, self control, equanimity austerities (initial), contemplation, forgiveness, contentment breeding[110]	Good feeling-
Self-praise, speaking ill others, concealing the good qualities of others, proclaiming what one does not possess	Low-Family-determining
Humility to the superiors, not being proud of one's achievements	High-family-determining[111]
Too much of sinful activity or attachment	Age-determining, and leading to hell
Deceitfulness	Age-determining, and leading to subhuman birth
Less of wordily activity and attachment, humble disposition	Age-determining, and leading to human birth
Self-control, equanimity austerities	Age-determining, and leading to heavenly birth.[112]
Crookedness of the mind body. and speech, disintegrity	Bad-body determining
Opposite of them leads to excellent moral character	Good-body determining[113] Tīrthaṅkara-body determining[114]

N.B: The above mentioned 4 types of Karma are known as Aghāti Karma and these do not retard the moral progress of a person.

The force holding the soul bound to Karma is due to four basic passions (kasaya) namely, krodha (anger), māna (pride), māyā (deceit) and lobha (greed).[115] It is this bondage due to passions which leads one to births and rebirths. Pūjyapāda enumerates 39 ways by which the flow ofkarmic matter (āsrava) takes place.[116] Any type of such activity is the cause of inflow of karmic matter. Bondage is said to take place when karmic matter clings to the soul affected by passion.[117] Bhatta Akalankadeva and Pūjyapāda have elaborately commented on the causes of such bondage. They are wrong belief (mithyādarśana),[118] vowlessness (avirati),[119] negligence (pramāda),[120] passion (kaṣāya)[121] and yoga or activities (mental, vocal and physical activities).

But this does not deprive man of his freedom. Human efforts have found ways and means to achieve Mokṣa. The Jain Ācāryas have shown the way to stop the inflow of Karma and also to annihilate the accumulated Karma through self-effort. These are called Saṁvara[122] and Nirjarā, the checking of the inflow of fresh karmic matter and annihilation of the already acquired karmic matter.

The means of checking the inflow of Karma (Saṁvara) are as follows:

1. Three fold self discipline (Trigupti)[123]
2. Five fold path of vigilance (Pañcasamiti)[124]
3. Ten categorical qualities (deśalakṣana dharmas)[125]
4. Twelve fold reflections on the nature of the universe (dvādaśānuprekṣā)[126]
5. Equanimous fortitude achieved through twenty two hardships (dvaviṁśati parīsahājaya)[127] and
6. Five types of conduct[128], each of which is further enumerated and explained in detail by the Jaina ācāryas are as follows: It is through austerity measures that one can shed the accumulated karmic matter (Nirjarā) achieve this. Performance of both external and internal penance (tapas)[129] is a voluntary infliction on oneself to break with old habits that lead to further births.

Liberation or Mokṣa according to Tattvārthasūtra is a state free from all Karma due to shedding of the Karma.[130] The force of karma can be destroyed through a slow process as one climbs the ladder of the stages of spiritual formation, as explained in the Guṇasthānas (stages of spiritual formation). At the end of the 12th stage the aspirant gets perfect knowledge, perception, potency and bliss (anantacatuṣṭaya).[131] After liberation the self who has the natural upward motion goes right to the top of the universe (lokākāśa)[132] beyond which it cannot proceed due to the absence of dharmastikaya, the medium of motion.[133]

The *Saptatattva,* so far discussed, forms the basic truth in Jain Dharma. All else like ethics and morality, ecclesial communion, etc. are founded on this. This metaphysical belief in the 7 fundamental principles has larger implications. It throws light upon the truth about pain, sorrow, sinfulness, non-injury, renunciation, knowledge, etc.

3.3.2.1. Implications of Jaina Tattvas

Hence, the following are the implications of Jaina Tattvas:

1. Jivas in Jaina Dharma are qualitatively alike, but quantitatively different and they inhabit the whole universe. The quantitative difference is due to the Karma bandha (bondage of karma). Jīva from the Niścaya point of view is the basis for the fundamental respect for all living beings. As the nature of this (i.e. man) is to be born and to grow old, so is the nature of that (i.e. plants) to be born and to grow old (Ācārāṅga 1.1.5.6). This is based on the animistic belief in the plurality of spirits and ghosts, a spiritualistic attitude at the beginning of human culture.[134]
2. Every living being is concerned about its liberation. Hence the cause of bondage and the means of liberation from it is a common concern for all living beings. It has to be apprehended that especially sinful acts towards one another put a block to the achievement of such liberation. For the sake of the splendour, honour, glory of this life, for the sake

of birth, death and final liberation for the removal of pain, man acts sinfully towards earth, or causes others to act so, or allows others to act so. This deprives him of happiness and perfect wisdom.[135] A man that does not comprehend and renounce the cause of sin... is born again and again in manifold births, experiences all painful feelings.[136]

3. The Jaina Āgamas are very particular in expounding the truth about the phenomenon of life and living beings, especially about suffering: 'beings torment beings; See the great danger in this world; many pains (are the lot) of creatures.'[137] 'The (living) world is afflicted, miserable, difficult to instruct and without discrimination. In this world full of pain, suffering caused by their different acts, see the benighted ones cause great pain.'[138] The Ācāryas point out another basis and important truth about life: 'All beings are fond of life, (they) like pleasure, dislike pain, shuns destruction, like life, long to live. To all life is dear.'[139]
4. Though life is dear to all living beings there cannot be undue attachment to it. Attachment to life itself creates a block to the goal to be achieved. The spirit of renunciation and non-attachment is the gateway to liberation: 'Life is dear to many that own fields and houses. Having acquired dyed and coloured (clothes), jewels, earnings, gold, women, they become attached to these things. And a fool who longs for life and is worldly minded, laments that (for these worldly goals) penance, self restraint and control do not avail will ignorantly come to grief.'[140]

Taking 'wealth' into consideration the Jaina Āgamas instruct about the path of grief: 'Having acquired it (wealth) employing bipeds (mānuṣya) and quadrupeds (animals), gathering riches in the three ways (3 modes of activity or yoga) he will desire to enjoy it. Then at one time, has manifold savings are a large treasure. Then at another time, his heirs divide it or those who are without a living steal it or the king takes it away, or it is ruined in some way or other or it is consumed in the conflagration of the house. Thus a fool who does cruel deeds, which benefit another, will ignorantly come thereof to grief.'[141] Such passages hint indirectly at the blessings of renunciation and religious life.

5. The equality and plurality of beings suggest the *principle of reciprocity:* what happens to me and in me will happen to you and in them. This principle unites life and the environment. 'Knowing what is bad, he who knows it with regard to himself, knows it with regard to (the world) outside; and he who knows it with regard to (the world) outside, knows it with regard to himself: this reciprocity (between himself and) others (one should mind).[142] 'Love your neighbour as yourself: 'As it would be unto thee.... so it is with him whom thou intendest to kill.' In the same way (it is with him) whom there intendest to punish, and to drive away.'[143] 'Life is dear to all' is the foundational principle. If hiṁsa is injurious and painful to one, the same will be painful to another because all beings hate pain; therefore, one should not kill them.[144] Sūtrakṛtāṅga holds this principle of reciprocity (with regard to non-injury) as the quintessence of wisdom.[145]
6. Comprehension of the truth about life, namely pain and sorrow, naturally leads one to renunciation: the pain of mundane existence is observed so keenly and it is considered to be the true knowledge.[146] The course of the world (regarding evil) is observed carefully and a truth is born out of experience namely, 'misery brings forth evil consequences'[147] and one has to cease from violent acts. But knowing that it is almost impossible to shun birth and the subsequent pain and the misery, renunciation and religious life is offered as the alternative: 'perceive the truth: from a desire of a pious end (they) chose a religious life.[148] Knowing pain and pleasure in all their variety and seeing his life not yet decline, a wise man should know *that* to be the proper moment (for entering a religious life).'[149]
7. Knowing the process of Karma, its root cause and its effects, is the true path of knowledge. Whether one is a religious or not one should follow this path of knowledge and it is this knowledge of the truth about the process of karman[150]

that leads one to the highest good namely liberation. 'The conditions of living beings arise from Karma'[151] and for him who is without Karma, there is no appellation (that which *condition* life as man, god, hell being, young, old etc.) Not only that Karma as its root is a conditioning factor but Karma as actions brings pain[152] the duly knowing upright men (are) aware that pain results from actions,[153] and every activity is caused by pleasure: First pleasures, then troubles; thus they are the cause of quarrels.[154] The continuity of action takes root in man in the first place, because of pleasure: 'desirous of pleasures they keep up Karma; influenced by it they are bom again.'[155] Thus pleasure, activity and birth seem to be a continuous vicious cycle one has to go through until the time of awakening and liberation.

8. Freedom from Karma has two aspects: one is the extreme path of ceasing from activities and the other from passion. The Discovering one is awakened and ceases to act...seeing that acts will bear fruit the knower of the sacred lore parts from (karma).[156] 'Shaking of greed, pride, deceit and wrath one becomes free from Karma.'[157] Those who engage in works and are held in worldly bondage do not know the law which leads to liberation.[158] The sinners cannot annihilate their works by new works; the pious annihilate the works by abstention from works.[159] Complete abandonment of act seems to be the only way to get rid of karma and it is an extreme from. of asceticism: He who does not undertake new acts does not acquire Karma; sinful acts are got rid of by him who does not undertake any new acts.'[160] But there are instances where pious acts are exalted and form the means of attaining liberation: Turning from worldly life they reach the goal by pious acts; by their pious acts they are directed towards (liberation) and they show the way to others.[161] But generally the Jaina Āgamas uphold that complete freedom is beyond good and bad acts.
9. Jainism is said to be the *Religion of Self-help:* 'Man, thou are thy own friend, why wishest thou for a friend beyond

thyself[162] and each one has to exert oneself in the rule of truth in order to overcome the evil one. 'Misery is produced by one's own works, not by those of somebody else (viz. fate, creator, etc.).'[163] Also 'mother, father, daughter-in-law, brother, wife and sons will not be able to help me, when I suffer from my own deeds'[164] because the door of the acts must suffer for them.[165] Hence it becomes a challenge for the aspirant to overcome the power of karma by his insight and pure conduct and no one can escape the effects of their own actions[166] because the karma follows the doer.[167] Jainism and the early Buddhism affirmed an innate power within oneself to realize here and now perfection and omniscience independent of a deity; they sought through the examples given by Mahāvīra and Buddha and their message that human beings are able to break the beginningless bond of Saṁsāra by themselves.[168]

10. The Concept of Nirvāṇa is both immediate and eschatological. It is immediate in the sense that complete annihilation of Karma is possible here and now and it is eschatological in the sense that the effort to annihilate Karma is continued also in the future course of lives and events. In both ways Nirvāṇa is final and complete. The Concept of Bodhisattva[169] can be compared to the one who is looking forward to the eschatological event of final Buddhahood. Even in Jaina tradition one who has crossed the 12th spiritual stage of formation is not touched by karma any more.[170] He can thereafter only look towards the final siddhahood. This is one reason why the Jaina path of purification is symbolised in an ascending order and once the formation is complete the soul reaches the top of the lokākāsa.[171] The self-effort nature of the Jaina ethics shows that the path the Nirvāṇa is gradual, long and tedious and hence several earlier births of Tīrthaṅkara are mentioned to give us the idea that the realization of the object and purpose of life (complete knowledge, etc.) is not restricted to one life or event.

3.3.3. Karma as the central theme of Jaina Dharma

The idea of Karma may have possibly originated in the context of agrarian experience: A well planted field yields good crop and the land will give birth repeatedly. Healthy seeds find in it a place to take hold and grow. As the seed dies the new life of a plant emerges. This process of death and resurrection to new life (rebirth) is a system of behaviour that keeps the world running smoothly. This agrarian experience is extended to the realm of human beings in which one's current situation in the world is regarded as the fruit of seeds planted by one's own behaviour and dispositions in the past. And it is also the view that in all of one's present actions the similar seeds will have continuity and determinative effect on one's life as they bear fruit in the future. This impersonal, trans-ethical law of cause and effect subsequently pervaded the ideology of Vedic ritualism, yoga, the Vedānta, āyurvedic medicine, sectarian theism, and it stands as a central theme in the scriptures of Jainism and Buddhism.

3.3.3.1. Karma in Ritualistic Tradition

In the early ritualistic tradition sacrifices to the gods in order to please them and to the advantage of the performer and the patron were regarded as Karma. These performances were believed to fulfil the desired end (iṣṭapūrta)[172] in the present also in the future (the Brāhmaṇas described the sacrifice as *apūrva Karma* - action the results of which have not yet been seen). The pūrvamīmāṁsā philosophers have a magical twist of this idea saying that the correct performance of the sacrifices would control the will of gods. It would automatically bring a response. This develops the view that a person is born into a world he has made for himself.

3.3.3.2. Karma in Upaniṣadic Tradition

In the Upaniṣadic time two ways were described for those who were diseased and dying: The lower path was the path of the fathers *(pitṛyāna)* for those who perform the rituals for material gain; the second and the highest path was the path of the gods *(devayāna)* or those who renounced worldly ends and practised tapas in the forest. There was a belief that a person's body became newer and newer and became a god by his actions;[173] and one becomes good through good action and bad by bad actions.[174] Thus the series of desire, will to act, and the result continued till the Upaniṣadic seers realized that there would not be a stop to this cycle of birth and rebirth, leading to unhappiness. Yama tells Naciketas that 'deluded by the glimmer of wealth' men seek the world thinking that 'there is no other world' beyond this.[175]

Thus the Upaniṣads lead the way to the notion that one has to free oneself from this bond of Karma, the cause of repeated births. Hence Patañjali proposed a system of activities (yoga) that would counteract those acts that trap the person in the wheel of life and death. Though ascetic renunciation of physical pleasures prevents all new *klelśas* (afflictions) from rising, and thereby no longer produces *karmaśaya* (receptacle of Karma) the person attains *kaivalya* or autonomy at the time of death.

3.3.3.3. Materialistic conception of Karma

The Upaniṣadic and Patañjali's description of Karma suggest that some *thing* is left behind by one's actions as a *substance*. Āyurvedic medical tradition too considers that Karma resides *in* substance and is one of the causes of physical health and illness and fertility techniques were undertaken for the embryo to acquire auspicious Karma.

This material nature of Karma was fully developed by the Jaina thinkers from ancient times according to which the spatial world is permeated[176] with a kind of subtle dust[177] that existed from time immemorial[178] which is sticky.[179] These sticky particles soil the Jīva infecting its original nature with a colour *leśya*[180] whenever Jīva is passionate[181] while performing an action. This determines the conditions and circumstances of its next birth. Jaina Cosmography[182] is structured in such a way that those who are infected with the heavy burden of sinful Karma sink downwards to the hellish world and those with less weight of puṇya karma enjoy the stay in the heavenly upper world indicating the physical nature of karma as a weighty substance. The soul will find eternal rest *absorbed in itself* (svasamaya) only when it stops accumulating new Karma and removes old Karma.

3.3.3.4. Niṣkāma Karma and Svadharma of the Gītā

Since all actions bring their consequences, either good or bad, one might think of *renouncing* act itself and embrace willful death. Aware of this problem the Bhagavad Gītā proposed the value of *disciplined action.*[183] Since complete inaction was impossible and as even the maintenance of the physical body required activity,[184] the philosophers of the Gītā proposed *Niṣkāma Karma*[185] (action without attachment or desire for its fruits). It advocated *Svadharma*[186] (action that pertains to one's own position in the society) and rebuked those who performed someone else's responsibilities.[187] By this the seers acknowledge that it was *desire* and not *action* itself that was the cause of repeated births. Hence the renunciation of the fruit of action suggested surrender to God's will and dedication[188] and God saved those who see their actions as God's actions and the results as God's will from the trap of karman.[189]

3.3.3.5. Intention-act-after effect of the Buddhist Tradition

According to the Buddhists, the fate of an individual is brought about by one's own behaviour and intentions (dravya and bhāva Karma). Karma depends upon volition (Cetanā), actual behaviour (samudācāra), impressions and dispositions (vāsana and saṁskāra) acquired from acts performed previously. It is the last one called the bija (seed) in Hīnayāna school that shapes one's character, constitution general personality. But as Prof. Kogen Mizuno says, it is the Buddhist doctrines of the causal efficacy of action (karmavāda), behaviour (kriyāvāda) and of effort (vīriyavāda) imply the freedom of human beings' intentions and his diligence and effort in reaching the Buddhist ideal.[190]

3.3.4. Factors responsible for the Cause of the Universe, Misery, etc.

In history there have been different schools of thought[191] giving prominence to either one or the other of the following factors which are responsible for the cause of the universe, cause of misery, etc.:

1. *Time* (Kāla) is described as the superior power to none in kālasūkta of Atharva Veda.[192] Gomaṭasāra says that time creates all, time destroys all.. time can be deceived by none.[193]
2. *Svabhāvavādins* established that everything behaves according to its own nature.[194] It denies any freedom of action.
3. *Niyativādins* or the determinists or the fatalists believed that nothing can be altered and everything has been fixed. And hence hope and fear are to be condemned; both depend upon viewing the future as uncertain and therefore spring from lack of wisdom.[195] Makkhali Gośāla, one of the contemporaries of Buddha and Mahāvīra, was a staunch fatalist. Pūraṇakāśyapa, another contemporary of Mahāvīra, says that to one who kills a living creature who takes what is not given, who breaks into house who commits dacoity or robbery to him thus acted, there is no guilt.... in generosity, in self mastery in control of the senses, in speaking the truth there is neither merit nor increase of merit.[196]

   This is an outright denial of moral responsibility for action to which the Jains and the Buddhists reacted sharply. Buddha refutes such philosophers saying that there exist a *heroic effort* (vīriya) in man, there exists a possibility of a successful exertion (utsāha) aimed at the disengagement of man from the vortex of rebirths provided he strives whole heartedly for this end.[197] Sūtrakṛtāṅga calls such philosophers *fools* and *ignorant* to understand that things depend partly on fate and partly on human exertion.[198] Jains favour a relative determinism but not at the cost of human efforts, which the Jaina dharma holds as the *supreme value* for all moral progress.
4. The *Yadṛcchāvādins* or the accidentalists believe that every event is merely a matter of chance and ultimate cause of

an event cannot be shown. The Jains uphold this theory to show the relative importance of instrumental cause (nimittakāraṇa) as against the substantial cause, which holds the prime position.

5. The *Bhūtavādins* or the materialists hold that matter is the only cause for everything and deny everything that is unseen. There is neither virtue nor vice, there is no world beyond. On the dissolution of the body the individual ceases to be.[199] The Jains hold matter *as real* but do not subscribe to the idea that matter is the only reality.
6. The *Puruṣavādins* hold that human beings. Brahman and God or Īśvara are responsible for the cause of misery etc. The first holds the *indeterminate* theory that everything is possible within the limits of human efforts even apart from the environments etc. The *Vedāntins* believe that consciousness is the only reality, which is the substantial as well as the instrumental cause of the universe. Such monistic view refutes the dualism of the universe as doer and action, good and bad, knowledge and ignorance, bondage and liberation, etc.[200] And finally God is made responsible for whatever takes place in the universe (*īśvaravāda*).

   Such theistic view is refuted by both the Jains as well as the Buddhists.[201] The physical world is ruled by physical laws and not by any divine law. God can only be the highest, noblest and fullest manifestation of the powers, which lie latent in the human soul.[202] According to the Jains the human soul is capable of realizing its own self or Siddhahood by shedding away all impurities. The purpose of the whole structure of mantras, worship, temple visits, prayer, meditation etc. is to awaken in oneself the latent potentialities of Godhead.[203]

3.3.5. Jaina view of Karma

1. It is the Jains who have treated the theory of Karma more extensively than others. The entire mundane existence of Jīva is based upon the theory of Karma. The cause of the

soul's embodiment is the presence of Karma matter in it. The inborn nature or qualities of the soul such as Jñāna (knowledge), Darśana (intuition, faith), etc.[204] are weakened or obscured by the presence of Karma. It is this Karma that has provided each soul a kārmanaśarīra.

2. The limited condition and circumstances of life like knowledge, faith, emotion, family, age, body, etc. are because of Karma.[205] This does not suggest a deterministic or fatalistic view of Karma. Jaina Karma theory concentrates on the nature of human efforts. Depending upon the passionate condition of the soul the person is motivated to act either in a conducive or a harmful way. In fact the path to liberation is a moral path and the auspicious karma aids it and it depends on the individual's efforts.[206] It is the moral effort of the individual that is ascertained and required.

3. When karma is made responsible for man's conditions and circumstances, Jaina theory gives relative importance to the theories that suggest other factors as solely responsible. Thus Jainism has given a relatively specific role to factors like accident (yadṛcchā), nature (svabhāva), human efforts (puruṣa), etc. It has also given correctives to fatalistic and theistic views giving fresh definitions of God, etc.
4. The Jaina theory of Karma gives due importance to the motives and intentions of the doer. When there is no motive or intention a person cannot be held morally responsible for his actions. The story of *Tandulamatsya*[207] is quoted in this connection. Merely by entertaining a violent idea the small fish had to go to lower hells than the big fish which actually committed the sin of violence.[208]
5. The idea *of grace of god* is a contradiction to the Jaina doctrine of Karma.[209] There is no necessity of bringing in the merciful God into human affairs; there is neither the acceptance nor the transferability of merits in Jaina morality as it is in the case of Buddhism or Christianity. It is only the doer who has to bear the consequence. The Jaina Ācāryas say that from the absolute point of view *(Niścaya*

naya) nobody can inherit the acts of others and everyone suffers the results of his actions all alone. From the practical point of view *(Vyavahāra naya)* helping fellow beings, as a meritorious action, is very much upheld.

6. The doctrine of the 6 *leśyas* (soul-colouring)[210] is closely linked to the Jaina Karma theory. This doctrine has been elaborately treated in Uttarādhyayana Sūtra.[211] Depending upon the type of action of the body, mind and speech, the soul acquires certain colours like black, blue, grey, red, yellow and white. Kṛṣṇa leśya is said to be the worst and the śukla leśya is the best. The sūtra depicts the type of man with the one or the other characters of the colour. The black, blue and grey leśyas are the lowest leśyas and through them the soul is brought into miserable courses of life. The red, yellow and white leśyas are the good leśyas and through them the soul is brought into happy course of life. The Jaina religious efforts are directed towards the acquisition of pure (white) leśya.[212]
7. Karma theory in general gives the justification for the sufferings of humanity: there are practical moral questions like the sufferings of a morally upright man and the happiness of the immoral evil person. Belief in the will of god or fate, or nature will not convince reason. But according to Jaina Karma theory, the reason is traced to the fruition or non-fruition of past Karma from the niscaya point of view and according to vyavahāra point of view it may be traced to circumstances, environment, etc. Jaina Karma theory takes into account its social significance (than man's activity is influenced by or influences his environment, etc.) and opens a fresh areas of investigation into the sociological, political, bio, psychological and ecological contexts.
8. Jaina theory of Karma upholds the theory of both *determinism and free will* of the human person. The former is not in the mechanistic or fatalistic sense that one cannot alter the courses of events in life and history as though everything is pre planned and pre determined. But still Jainism also accepts that even actions are to some extent determined by

the motives or the intentions or desire of the person. These causes belong to the agent. In this way the Jains are more accommodative and they believe that even free will must involve causality. Free will does not mean indeterminism. Both strict determinism and complete indeterminism have moral problems regarding responsibility etc. Freedom of will is seen in the Jaina glorification of human efforts. Although Jīva in the real sense is beyond *sūbha* and *aśubha* Karma (transcendental and beyond activities) which in a way suggests a deterministic view Jīva in its practical and embodied form is an agent full of activities. In Jaina moral theory, if an individual is to realize the highest good he needs to engage in śubha (auspicious) and śubha karma only. This again might sound deterministic and the agent is not free otherwise. But choosing a moral and good action is a practical utility in the realization of the goal. In the last two spiritual stages in the ladder of moral progress[213] the agent is not touched by karma at all although yoga or activity of the person remains in the 13th stage. It is in the last stage that even activities vanish.

9. Sūtrakṛtāṅga summarizes the creed of four different schools:[214] kriyāvādins, akriyāvādins, vinayavādins and ajñānavādins.) Kriyāvādins believe that misery is produced by one's own works, not by those of somebody else, namely, fate, creator etc.[215] They contend, according to Śīlāṅka, that works alone by themselves, without knowledge, lead to Mokśa[216]) Akriyāvādins ascertain that the whole world is unreal.[217] Śūnyavādins, who are considered to belong to the Akriyāvādins, deny all actions[218] even such as are perceived by everybody.[219] Mahāvīra refutes the doctrine of the Akriyāvādins[220] and describes them as those with *pervert intellect* and who can't believe what they see. He also gives corrective to the kriyāvādins: not works alone but right knowledge and conduct lead to liberation.[221]
10. Lastly, Jaina doctrine of Karma has a *reconciliatory* perspective: it takes into account the different views (for instance factors like fate, nature, accident, matter etc.) in the

cause of misery and of the universe and gives due role and place to them. Its approach towards different schools of thought (for instance, kriyāvādins, akriyāvādins, etc.) is constructive and complimentary. It is also balanced in its view regarding the causes, for instance, the significance of upādāna (efficient cause) and nimitta (instrumental cause) and seeks to accommodate both in their position.

Though finally Jaina dharma upholds the individual's efforts in conquering passions and activities, it also understands and accepts the relevance of social duties and responsibilities like helping others, etc. It is true that Jaina ethics lays more emphasis on individual efforts and on ascetic virtues than on social and positive virtues. It is so because it believes that ultimately it is renunciation of the worldly life alone that can reach the target, namely, the final liberation.

Notes

1. Monier-Williams, p. 519
2. ER, Vol. 4, p.328
3. Manu 2.6
4. Ibid 2.12 and 1.108
5. Satya Ranjan Banerjee has descirbed the vedic conception of Dharma as 'Laws and Orders' of this Universe actuating a relationship between the Universe and human person. See 'Janism through the Ages' in Jain Journal, Vol XXIX, N o, 4 April 1995, p. 133
6. Ṛg Veda i.105.12
7. Ṛg Veda x. 114, 189; 121
8. Śat Br, SBE, Vol.XII, P.309.
9. Majumdar, R.C.(Ed.), p.225.
10. Myths like the story 'Śunāhsepa', Ait Br Book VIII, Ch.3; the story of Naciketa, Tait Br Book II, 11; the geographical data of the Śatapata Brāhmaṇa point to the land of the Kuru-Pañcālas being still the centre of Brāhmaṇical culture. The Brāhmaṇical system had by this time spread to the countries to the east of the Madhyadeśa, to Kosala, with its capital Ayodhya and to Videha, with its capital, Mithila; Yāñavalkhya is referred to as a spiritual authority; the words; Arhat, Brāhmaṇa and Pratibuhddha occur here for the first time, announcing the firm footing of Brāhmaṇa culture in the eastern region; certain allusions are also suggestive of the beginning of the Sāṁkhya doctrine.

11. Ātman is described as the Eternal in the Br Up III, VIII.8, 11. The nature of Ātman is given in Kathā Up iv. 9, vi.912. Ātman or the Brahman as the universe in the begining; the evolutiion of man & woman from the Ātman. Chānd Up vi.8-16, Br Up IIV 6. It was already recognized in the Śat Br X. VI 3. Ātman as the inner guide (antaryāmin) Br Up III. vii
12. True knowledge and faith leads to Devayāna and practice of sacrifice and good works take me through the world of the Father. Br. Up VI. ii 15-16; The story of Naciketas. Kathā Up.I
13. The Yājñavalkya episode on renunication Br Up. II the Sannyāsa dharma enunciated in Muṇḍaka III. ii.8 Explanations on Brahman as manifest and unmanifest residing on oneself. Br. Up. iii 4,5 Final return by means of yoga. See Kathā Up first & last sections of Ch.I
14. Manu: I.31, 87; X 45
15. Ibid., IX. 317
16. Ibid., II. 135
17. Ibid., II. 40
18. Characteristics of an ascetic: Ap Ds II 9.21 Manu VI.33, 42-45; Yājñ DS III. 58 f.
19. Manu III. 78 vi. 37, 87, 97; Gaut DS III. 3.
20. Manu; VI
21. Of the Kṣatryas; Manu VII; of the Brāhmaṇas Manu VII & VIII etc; of the Householder. Manu VI; of the hermit: Manu VI and Ap DS II.
22. Macdonell, A p. 263
23. Dowson, p. 326
24. Manu 8.318
25. Ibid., 9.240
26. Peter Della Santina's article ' Conceptions of Dharma in the Śramanical and Brāhmaṇical Traditions' highlights the salient features in the dilemma of Arjuna in the Bhagaved Gītā. Finally 'Svadharma 'emerges as the supreme value in Kṛṣṇa's declaration. The demonstration of transcendality of the supreme self by means of the adoption of the transcendental technique (wise man do not mourn for the living or for the dead (Gītā 2.11); doctrine of non-origination (ajātivāda); agent and the object (2:19); the transcendentailty of the supreme self (2:17); serves only to vindicate in a somewhat moral way the paramount position of Svadharma. Moral Epic grealty emphasizes the caste duties for the true progress of man. Even a man of lower grade will be able to raise himself morally and spiritually by discharging his own duties with denotion). See Sharma, B: P.25
27. Ayodh Kāṇ, 13/1 44/4, 60/6, 105/34-37, 106/44, etc.
28. Yud kāṇ, 83/31-40
29. Ayodh Kāṇ, 21 /57-58
30. Āran Kāṇ, 9/30-33

31. Ayodh Kāṇ, 14/3 57-8
32. Goodness should be realized: Yud Kān, 9/16
33. Ayodh Kāṇ, 21/49
34. Ayodh Kāṇ, 21/36
35. Ayodh Kāṇ, 106/2294
36. Āran Kāṇ, 9/27
37. Āran Kāṇ, 12/26-27
38. Bāla Kaṇ, 1/12; Ayodh Kān, 12/33., 35/32; 58/32, Yud K94n, 119/28
39. Gītā, 18. 54-58
40. Ibid., 3.19;3.25
41. Ibid., 4.7-8
42. Ibid., Ch, 6, 9,12 and 3
43. ER, Vol 12, p. 89
44. Manu 2.9
45. Gītā 3.45; 18.47
46. In the first Council held at Rājagriha in C 483 B.C. the classification of the whole mass discourses (Sutta) was done into five groups (Nikāya), as also greater part of the disciplinary rules (Vinaya) in a separate collection.
47. There was an attempt to list and classify the main topics (mātika or matṛka), such as 'aggregates' (khandha), 'elements' (dhātu) and 'gateways' (of sense perception (Ātataba), on which the Buddha had discoursed. These became the nucleus of the third collection of Canonical texts, the Abhidhamma Piṭaka, dealing mostly with philosophical analysis and synthesis.
48 Sixty-two metaphysical views (ditthi) are discussed in Brahmajāla Suttānta (Dīg N, 1.12 ff). Many of these can be subsumed under one or the other of the ten undeclared (avyākrta) problems. The Culla-Māluṅkyaputta-sutta points out that the solutions to these questions do not lead to well-being and do not contribute to the higher religious lift, to renunciatin to dispassion, cesation.
49. Saṁ N 5.421 ff (as quoted in De Bary, p. 101 f)
50. ibid, Saṁ N. 5.421 ff.
51. Dīg N 3.180 f(De Bary, p,122f)
52. Budhacarita 7.20 ff (as quoted in De Bary, p. 169) also in SBE, XLIX, p. 72 f
53. Sikṣā, sanuccaya pp. 278 -83 and Āṣṭāsahasrikā Prajñāparamita 22. 402-3 (De Bary, pp. 161-2)
54. The great change has been clearly portrayed by Frof. Clarence, H. Hamilton pp. 22-23
55. Smith, V.A., P 248
56. P.S. Jaini has made a comprehensive analysis of the development of Abhidhamma scholasticism. See the introduction to his edition of Abhidhammadīpa.

57. Atthaśālini, Dhammasaṅgaṇi-aṭṭhakathā, p.21
58. Farquhar, J.N. P. 122.
59. Poussin, ERE, VIII, pp. 235-37.
60. Dasgupta, Vol I, p 145.
61. Suzuki, D.T. PP. 21f, 62 f
62. Suzuki Trans for 'Awakening of Faith ' Ibid, p. 55
63. Suzuki Trans for 'Awakening of Faith ' p 146
64. The cosmic order is seen in this doctrine. All physical and psychical phenomena are conditioned by antecedent physical or psychical factors and that whole of existence can be shown to be an uninterrupted flux of phenomena. 12 terms are used to set forth the doctrine. Old age and death (jarāmaraṇa) are due to antecedent rebirth (jāti); rebith is due to antecedent process of becoming (bhāva); becoming is due to clinging to life (upādāna); cliging is due to craving (tanhā); craving is due to feeling (vedana); feeling is due to sense impression (phassā); sense impression is due to the 6 bases of sense (āyatana); the 6 bases due to corporeality (nāma-rūpa); corporeality is due to consciousness (vinnāna); consciousness is due to karma formations (sankhāra); and karma formation is due to ignorance (avijjā). See Sam N. II. 7; Visuddhimagga of Buddhaghosa Ch. 17 trans. pp. 592 f. See Trevor Ling p. 158
65. Literally it means 'Thusness' or 'Suchness; It is a term used by the Mahāyanist for the ultimate and unconditioned nature of all things. In one sense, it is Śūnya expressed positively. It is that which is expressd in all things. Nothing can be denied or affirmed concerning it. it can only be understood by realising that one can neither find it by searching nor lose it by trying to separate oneself from it. Yet it has to be found. See Christmas Humphreys, pp. 195-196
66. As applied to man, anatta states that there is no permanent ego or self (essence of individuality). Man is made of 5 skandhas or groups of constituent factors. The Buddha, however, nowhere denied the existence of an ego or soul, but taught that no permanent entity, not subject to Anicca and Dukkha, can be found in any of the human faculties. Buddhism teaches that everything is subject to the Law of cause and effect and everything is the creation of preceding caused and is in turn a cause of after effects. There is in existence, therefore, no unchanging condition of being, but only an ever becoming flux. Dukkha is largely the effect of man's reaction of Anicca and Anatta. It follows then, that existence cannot be wholly separated from Dukkha, and that complete escape from it is possible only by liberation from the cycle of births and deaths. See also Trevor Ling p. 17, 18, 90 and 157-158
67. A schematic description of the Buddhist life is described in the holy or noble (Ārya) Eight-fold path. In earlier texts it is found as a three fold scheme: (i) initial faith (saddha) which ultimately becomes wisdom (panna); (ii) morality (sīla); (iii) concentration or meditation (samādhi

). Each of these aspects is subdivided: faith into right thought; morality into right speech, right bodily action and right livelihood, meditatiion into (spiritual) effort, right mindfulness and right concentration. The outcome of practice of this eight-fold way is held to be the attainment of state of wisdom. See Trevor Ling p.90

68. Regarded as Budha's First Sermon, viz. 'the setting in motion (pavattana) of the wheel (cakka) of the Dhamma or the sermon on the Foundation of Righteousness: This discourse is regarded as one of the 4 great events in the life of Buddha, the other 3 being the birth, enlightenmnet and passing into Parinibbāna. Saṁ N Verse 420; Vinayapiṭaka 1.10 f see Trevor ling, pp. 82-83

69. Nirvāṇa or Nibbāna (pali) is the supreme goal of Buddhist endeavour. It is the release from the limitations of existence. The work is derived from a root meaning 'extinguished through lack of fuel', and since rebirth is the result of desire (tanhā), freedom from rebirth is attained by the extinguishing of all such desire. The Theravāda school tends to view Nirvāṇa as escape from life by overcoming its attraction. The Mahāyāna views it as the fruition of life, the unfolding of the infinite posibilities of the innate nature than the saint (Arhat) who relinquishes all connections with it. See also Trevor ling, pp-149-150

70. In Mahāyāna tradition, Bodhisattva is the ideal of the path as contrasted with the Arhat of the Theravāda tradition. Having practised the six pārāmita (the 6 stages of spiritual perfection towards Buddhahood namely, the highest possible development of dāna (charity), sīlā (morality) ṣānti (patience), vīrya (vigour), dhyāṇa (meditation) and prajñā (wisdom) and attained enlightenment, he renounces nirvāṇa in order to help humanity on its pilgrimage. The Bodhisatvas are often called 'Buddhas of compassion. 'Trevor Ling points out that the concept of Bodhisattva implies possibility of existence within the world of many Bodhisattvas. Those who were regarded as having reached penultimate state of existence in the Tuśīta heaven were thought of as heavenly beings, upon whom ordinary mortals could call for help, and the compassionate Bodhisattva would not fail them. In such terms were regarded the major Bodhisattvas, such as Avalokiteśvara, Mañjūsrī, Maitreya, Samantabhadra and Kṣitigarbha. In this way the Mahāyāna Philosophy was able to provide a 'respectable rationale' for a popular cult. See Trevor ling, p.34; also see Conze, pp 234f

71. Trikāya of Buddha is a novel idea in the Buddhist thought in order to express the relationship of one aspect of Buddha nature to the other. See T.R. V. Murti, pp.284-287; The Dharmakāya or Truth body is self existent (Sva-bhāva-kāya) and it is in this sense the absolute aspect of the Buddha nature. See D.T. Suzuki, p.308; The Sambhogakaya or Bliss body is the celestial manifestation of the Buddha nature as it is perceived by celestial or non- moral beings because of their spiritual disclipline. The Nirmānakaya

or the 'assumed body' is necessitated because 'the Dharmakāya is too exalted a body for ordinary mortals to come into any conscious contact with. As it transcends all forms of limitations, it cannot become an object of sense or intellect....... The essence of Buddhahood is the Dharmakāya, but as long as the Buddha remains such, there is no hope for the salvation of a world of particulars. The Buddha has to abandon his original abode, and put upon himself such forms as are conceivable and acceptable to the inhabitants of this earth', See D.T. Suzuki, p. 310; Also see Trevor Ling, pp.42-43

72. The Yogācāra School developed the doctrine of Ālayavijñāna or store consciousness, by which meant a central or universal consciousness or pure consciousness, before it particularises itself as substratum of human mind or consciousness. This is a concept somewhat similar to that of Hindu idea of the universal Brahman. This 'store consciousness' performs the role of a permanent 'Self', although the Yogācārins., in accordance with the Buddhist tenets, denied the existence of a self. In this respect they have been accused of attempting to reconcile the irrconcilable. See Conze, p. 133 f; The ālaya is also called the Thathāgatagarbha or the womb of Tathāgata, pregnant with all posibilities and throbbing with seeds of all vijñānas.
73. Maj N 19, 26; Saṁ N 38
74. Aṅg N3. 134; Saṁ N 12.20
75. Rhys Davids, SBB, i, 26.
76. Maj N 13 Dukkhakāṇḍa
77. Saṁ N 36, Vedana Saṁ N esp. 3,5, etc. Aṅg N 3.33.69; SBE X i...61; Rhys Davids, SBB, ii 129; Saṁ N 64.4
78. Two fold system of morality - one that of monks and nuns and the other, that laity Maj N 117; A detailed description of the wordly norality is given in the sermon to Siṅgālaka Dig N 31
79. Vinaya, Chulavagga 10.14 and Aṅg N 8.51
80. Women discliples of Buddha; People of mean origin occupied important places in Buddhist Order: Punna and Punnika (slave girls); Sumangala mata (daughter and wife to mat weavers); Subhā (daughter of a smith), etc. (examples cited by Rhys Davids).
81. Illustrated by the whole book of Sankrityayan, R.
82. Trevor Ling writes: 'An important reform movement which began in the 14 th century under the leadership of a teacher named Tsong Kapa (1357-1417) resulted in the formation of the Gelug-pa, sect popularly known as the yellow hats. This sect revived the tradition of strict monastic discipline. It also maintained a high level of morality. It was believed that one of its abbots, who died in 1475 was reincarnated in a yound monk and that he in turn was at his death reincarnated in another. It was to this reincarnated and highly revered lāma that the name Talāi (ocean) was given and hence began the line of the Talai or Dalai Lamas. Dalai

Lama is considered as the spiritual and temporal Head of Tibet. He is regarded as the earthly manifestatioin of Chenresi, the 'precious protectors' the Tibetan terms for Avalokiteśvara', Trever line, p.186-187

83. It refers to the Varṇa and Āśrama structures of the Brāhmaṇic scheme of life. The growth of asceticism is considered to be a revolt against the caste structure of the Brāhmaṇic society. An ascetic is beyond caste and he is respected even by kings. (The conversation between Gautama and King Ajātaśatru). Again it refers, in contrast to the Brāhmaṇic social order, to the attitude of tribal societies, its grouping and functioning which Buddha admired very much (the conversation between Gautama and his disciple Ānanda).
84. Dig N 27. Agganna: this is the appellation of the Tathāgata, his body is of truth (dhammakāya) he is made up of Truth (dhammabhūta), etc.
85. Dīg N 4; Aṅg N3, p.81-90.
86. Saṁ N33.3.4, p.47.13.
87. Tat Sūtra 5.17
88. Ibid., 5.18
89. Bhargava, p.12, Footnotes
90. Ibid., footnote 2
91. Sikdar describes the three aspects of reality, namely, Utpāda (origination), Vyaya (decay) and Dhrauvya (permanence) and also explains in brief that reality is 'permanence-in-change' See Dr. J. C. Sikdar, pp. 80-82. Filita Bharucha mentions that the Jaina view of reality resembles modern thought of space and time. See Filita Bharucha, pp 7-8
92. Das Sūtra, 4.12
93. Tat Sūtra, 1.4. A lucid description is given by Glasenapp, See pp. 178 f.
94. Dr. Lalitha describes how every living being gets the character or name through the effect of the Karman relating to that particular being. See Jain Journal, Vol. XXX, No. 1, 1995
95. Samayasāra. 2
96. Dravyasaṁgraha, 3
97. Tat Sūtra, 2.13
98. Ibid., 5.19
99. Ibid., 5.20
100. Ibid., 5.29
101. Ibid., 5.37
102. Ibid., 5.30
103. Pañcādhyāyī, 2.35-36 Bhargava p.53 no.
104. Ibid 2.57 Bhargava p.53, n 2
105. Tat Sūtra, 6. 1-2
106. Ibid 8.5; Muni Shivkumar describes the 8-types of Karma in all its details. See Muni Shivkumar, pp. 64-69; Dr. N.L. Jain descibes the scriptural as well as the scientific concepts of Karma theory in the four

table he has shown in his book 'Jaina Karmology' a translation of Ch. VII of Tattvārtharājavārtika of Akalanka. See N.L. Jain, pp. 75-80

107. Ibid., 6.11
108. Ibid., 7. 14-15
109. Ibid., 8.14
110. Ibid., 6.12-13
111. Ibid., 6.24-25
112. Ibid., 6.16-18.20
113 Ibid., 6.61-22
114. Ibid., 6.26
115. Ibid., 6.5-8.2
116. Pūjyapāda on Tat Sūtra 6.5
117. Tat Sūtra, 8.2-3
118. Pūjyapāda on Tat Sūtra, 8.1
119. Ibid.8.1
120. Akalaṅka on Tat Sūtra 8.1
121. Pūjyapāda on Tat Sūtra, 8.1
122. Tat Sūtra, IX. 1-2
123. Ibid., 9.4
124. Ibid., 9.5
125. Ibid., 9.6
126. Ibid., 9.7
127. Ibid., 9.8-9
128. Ibid., 9.18
129. Ibid., 9.19-20
130. Ibid., 10-2.3
131. Ibid., 10.5
132. Ibid., 10.5
133. Ibid, 10.8
134. Animism, a theroy set forth by the English Scholar E.B. Taylor, one of the founding fathers of Anthropology.
135. Ācār Sātra, 1.1.2.3
136. Ibid., 1..1.6,7
137. Ibid., 1.6.1.4
138. Ibid., 1.2.3.4
139. Ibid., 1.2.3.3.5
140 Ibid., 1.2.3.5
141. Ibid., 1.2.3.5
142. Ibid., 1.1.7.1
143. Ibid., 1.5.5.4
144. Sūt.Kr. I.11.9
145. Ibid., I.11.10
146. Ācār Sūtra, 1.2.6.2
147. Ibid., 1.3.3.2.1

148. Ibid., 1.3.2.1
149. Ibid., 1.2.1.5
150. Sūt Kr II. 3.37
151. Ācār Sūtra, 1.3 1.4; Sūt Kr. 1.2.3. 18
152. Sūt Kr 1.2.1.4
153. Ācār Sūtra, 1.4.3.1
154. Ibid., 1.5.4.5
155. Ibid., 1.3.2.4
156. Ibid., 1.4.4.3
157. Sūt Kr I. 1.2.12
158. Ibid., 1.1016
159 Ibid., 1.12.15
160. Ibid., 1.15.6-8
161. Ibid., 1.15.10
162. Ācār Sūtra 1.8.3.4
163. Sūt Kr. 1.12.11
164. Ibid., 1.95; Utt Sutra, 6.31
165. Ibid., 1.9.4
166. Utt Sātra, 4.3
167. Ibid; 13.23
168. Ahimsa Voice, July '90, p.8
169. Bodhisattva in Mahāyāna Buddhism is prefinal stage towards Buddhahood: Aṣṭasāhasrikā Prajñāparamita, 22.402-3., Sikṣāsamuccaya, pp 278-83, Tatā gataguhya Sūtra Sikṣāsamuccaya, p.274
170. Kalghatgi. T.G. p.78
171. Ibid., p.79
172. Ṛg Veda x.14.8
173. Tait Up 2.8; Up. 4.3.33
174. Br Up. 3.2.13
175. Kathā Up 1.2.6
176. Kalghatgi. T.G. p.67
177. Just as water flows into the pond from different streamlets, so also karma flows into the soul from different directions due to various types of activity (Sūt Kr. 2.5.17)
178. Kalāghatgi, T.G. p. 53
179. Pravacanasāra, Book II, 237-741; Tat Sūtra, 2.6
180. Sūt Kr 1.6.13; The classification of living beings in terms of six colours may be traced in Pārśvaś doctrine of six jīva nikayas (Ācār Sūtra, II.15.16)
181. Samayasāra, 23; Tat Sūtra, 6.5
182. The Cosmological details have been worked out in the Uttrādhyayana Sūtra and the Bhagavatī Sūtra. See Utt Sūtra, 36.50;36.54
183. Gītā, 3.7
184. Ibid., 3.8

185. Ibid., 4.19.23
186. Ibid., 18.41-44
187. Ibid., 3.35; 18.45-48
188. Ibid., 12.6-7
189. Ibid., 3.31
190. ER, Vol.8 p. 266
191. Śvet Up gives the summary of all these Schools (Śvet Up. 1.12)
192. Atharva Veda, Aundha, 19.53.4
193. Gommatasāra, Karmakāṇḍa, 879, Bhargava, p.16, n.1
194. Ibid., 883, Bhargava, p.16, n-2
195. Russel, p.597, Bhargava, p.17, n-1
196. Dīg N 1.2 Bhargava, p.18, n-1
197. Zimmer, p.226, Bhargava, p.18, n-2
198. Sūt kr. 1.1.2.4; also Gom Sāra, p. 882, Bhargava, p.18 n.4
199. Ibid., 1.1.1.12, Bharagava, p. 19, n.3
200. Āptamīmāmsā, 24-27, Bhargava, p.22, n.1
201. Mahāpurāṇa, 4.16-31, 38-40. Syādvādamañjarī; and Ṣaḍdarśanasamuccaya bring out a refutation of the existence of an eternal, ommiscient God, See Syādvādamāñjarī, p. 29 f; Ṣaḍdarsanasamuccaya, p.54f. The Jaina devotion to the ideal arises essentially from the belief in the autonomy and centrality of the doctrine of Karma. Neverthless, the Jains and the Buddhists admit innumerable heavenly beings in various degrees of perfection, but non-eternal. But the devotion to these people is nothing but a genuine, transcendental attachment, praise and admiration, veneration and adoration of the Ideal one for the ideals he represents. See Sekhar, Vincent, 'Jaina Religious Consciouness- A Paradigm for a Religio-secular involvement' in Jinamañjarī, Vol. V, No. 11, October 1992, P 53, 55; The human being in an absolute and 'real ' sense is God (to put it theistically), but looks and behaves as though a 'God' who tries to climb the ladder of perfection. See Sekhar, Vincent, ' Early Śramaṇa Concept of Soul Jand the nature of personhood' in Jinamañjarī, VOL.XIV, No. 2, Oct. 1997. p, 59; The doctirne of a 'personal' God who created the universe 'ex nihilo' is not found in Buddhism. Such a being is neither explicityly affirmed nor denied. "Inconceivable, Oh, Monks, said Buddha, is this samsara; not to be discovered is any first beginnings of beings".
202. Radhakrishan, S. Vol. I. P.331
203. Bhargava, p.26
204. Prav Sāra Book II 90, 100, 108 Samayasāra, 2; See also Yuvraj Krishan, Karma as the causative force of the cycle of existence, pp.42-44
205. Tat Sūra. 8.5
206. Ācār Sūtra, 1.3.3.4; also Sūt kr 1.13.18
207. Upāsakadhyāna, pp. 141-142; Intention plays an important role in any act. Among kṛta, kārita and anumita, the last refers to mere intention

even without any act. Further, a Śrāvaka is prohibited to saṅkalpa hiṁsā. Bhagava, p.30, n.1

208. 'Pramattayogat prāṇavyavaropanam hiṁsā' Tat Sūtra VIII.8; The doer is to face the consequence fo his acts and no transfer of merit. Also see Prav Sāra II.288-307
209. Karma is understood as the Law of Retributive Justice and Personal Responsibility, See Yuvraj Krishan, pp.44-46
210. Sūt Kr. 1.6.13; also see Ācār Sūtra, II. 15.16.
211. Utt Sūtra, 34
212. Sūt Kr. 1.10.15
213. Tat Sūtra, 6.5. Com by Suklalji, pp. 232-33
214. Sūt Kr. 1.121; Ib d., 1.12.11
215. Ibid., I.12.11
216. SBE, Vol. XLV, P.317, footnote 4
217. Sūt Kr 1.12.7
218. Ibid., 1.12.4
219. SBE, Vol XLV, p, 317. footnote 1
220. Sūt Kr. 1.12.8-10
221. Ibid., 1.12.11

CHAPTER IV

AN ENQUIRY INTO JAINA ETHICS

4.1. Ethical and moral significance of Jaina Dharma

Every religion is a motivating and guiding force to people, who profess that religion. Even to an atheist, general and common good or general moral principles are guidelines to his or her life. Every religion professes a value system that has an impact on the wider society. What are common in all religions help human persons to have a meaningful relationship with each other. Every religion through its human institutions and social traditions, rules and regulations, injunctions and prohibitions, channelizes the growth and the moral progress of those belonging to that religion.

Every system of ethics seeks to answer questions like what is intrinsically desirable or good or worthwhile in life, what intrinsic values are to be pursued, what is morally right in a certain situation, what is the criteria for rightness action, what is obligatory in a certain situation, how duty is to be determined, what is the nature of ethical judgements, what is their justification, etc. The present chapter deals with answering such questions from the Jaina point of view.

4.1.1. **Self-realization** *as the End of Moral Life*

In the first place we ask a question: what is that which motivates a Jain to act? Motive is that which moves or causes one to act in a particular way. It is said to be the spring of action. Feeling of pleasure and pain can be motives of actions but man is not merely a sentient being but rational too. His actions are not merely impulsive but essentially *purposive* in nature. A Jain's moral life is characterised by purpose or end.[1] It is the thought of a desirable end. Moral activity or conduct is purposeful action... it is moved by the thought of some end to be attained.[2]

The end or the purpose of life in Jaina tradition is *self-realization* i.e. to realize the true nature of one-self.[3] It is, in other words. Karma nirjarā[4] or getting rid of the accumulated karma that defiles the soul and the subsequent realization of anantacatuṣtaya,[5] or the fore-fold perfection, namely, perfect knowledge, perfect vision, perfect strength and perfect bliss. The highest good of a human person consists in the fullest self-consciousness or fullest realization of one's spiritual nature. The end of ethics is the realization of spiritual capacities and this is the highest aim of moral life.

Self-realization in ethics means the perfection of the self as a whole, namely, both the sentient and rational self, also individual and social self. *Hedonists* seek to realize their sentient self and the *Rationalists* seek to realize their self in their self-sacrifice or control of impulses and feelings. *Eudeamonists* transcend the limitations of Rationalism and Hedonism. They seek to realize the total self, sentient as well as rational. The *Utilitarianists* consider the rational self as the social self. Apart from the social group there can be no such thing as self-realization or perfection of the self. Hence the highest good of the self is the highest social good.

Jaina doctrine of self-realization sounds individualistic from a particular point of view. The extreme ascetic tendency of the Jains, the meticulous following of the ascetic rules (Mahāvrata)[6] of the munis different from *anuvrata,*[7] a less intense level for the laity, the niścaya or the absolute point of view[8] in following the rules of conduct for the sake of karma nirjarā, etc. suggest that it is individualistic in its approach and does not concern society as a whole. But on the contrary, the Tīrthaṅkaras, who are said to have attained self-realization and the *Pañcaparameṣtin*[9] or the *Holy Pentad* in Jaina soteriology are the visionaries or the prophets of the Jaina community. Hence the doctrine of self-realization suggests that the highest good of the self is for the sake of the highest social good. Since each individual is organically related to the Jaina community (saṅgha), one can realize one's self only in and through it. The Tīrthaṅkaras suggest the common moral or spiritual principle for the community to emulate. It is self-realization for the sake of the whole.

From the absolute or the niścaya point of view, self-realization is individualistic because the path of self-realization depends substantially upon the individual (no god, nor any Siddha comes to the help of the individual). From the practical or the vyavahāra point of view, self-realization accommodates the instrumental causes in the effort, such as helping others, sharing others sufferings, etc. Prof. Bhargava[10] says that our obligations vary as we ascend the ladder of spirituality. The Jaina goal of life suggests that spiritual realization and not social service is the ultimate aim of life. But social service can and often does prove a stepping stone to spiritual realization.

The same problem can be looked at in a different way. A man may be moved to act by pleasure or by reason or purpose. Here we can raise a question: what is the motivating factor for a Jain towards self-realization? Is it pleasure or reason? One is spell-bound when he studies the Jaina doctrine of karma and the process of the stoppage of Karma (saṁvara) and clearing of the accumulated Karma (Nirjarā) and the code of conduct[11] in these areas. The hardships involved in these do not suggest that it is a path of pleasure. Instead, one marvels at the rationale behind the system of Jaina ethics. Psychological hedonists like Bentham and Mill construe that we owe all our ideas to pleasure and pain and we refer our judgement and determination of life to them. Man's nature is to seek pleasure and shun pain.

The Jaina Ācāryas have taken into consideration these motives, so natural to all living beings and have enunciated the ethical principle of Ahiṁsā. Life is dear to everybody[12] is the foundational creed for restraining one from violence to any living being. Ultimately it is the feeling that gives one the will to do. Although the act is guided by a feeling, it seeks a good, reflecting the rationality of the system. Thus, reason and passion go hand in hand and not that Reason is and ought to be the slave of passions.[13]

This suggests that what one intends decides the morality of an action. The rightness or wrongness of an act depends very much upon the motive from which it is done, although consequences of actions are no less important than the motives themselves. Samantabhadra argues that truth is not to be spoken when, by so doing, the other is entangled in miseries[14] and Swami Kumāra in the Kārtikeyānuprekṣā disallows the purchase of things at a low price in order to maintain the vow of non-stealing,[15] whereas the general rule is *speak the truth* (satya), *do not be extravagant* (aparigraha). This incidentally refers to the *situational* ethics, where moral implications of an action are evaluated in its context. This only shows that Jaina ethics does not allow a blind worship of rules.

One can realize one's true self or the complete good only by realizing the social end. In order to do this one must negate the merely individual self, which is not the true self. One must realize oneself by sacrificing oneself.[16] It is by the sacrifice of one's own good one realizes the importance of others as members of the one great universe.

Again no one can realize oneself in isolation because the human mind expresses itself in terms of social institutions, like the family, civic communities and the state. The individual can find his good by identifying himself with the life and institutions of his time because they are all vehicles of the expression of the Absolute mind. The Jaina tīrtha or the Four Holy Orders[17] becomes the vehicle for achieving the purpose or the end of life for a Jain. The Jaina church (muni and śrāvaka) is the visible manifestation of the eschatological fulfillment. The monk and the laity and their mutual relationship in terms of respect, support, discipleship, etc. and the social relations among individuals and families provide ample facilities for the perfection of the whole person and for expanding one's spiritual life.

The muni, although an individual, is linked to society. While he is maintained by the community, he in turn preaches the Dharma to the community. We can give one concrete instance in this context: the mahavrata and the anuvrata of the Jains. Apart from the specific rules for the monks and the laity, the five vows[18] are observed by all in the Jaina community. The difference lies in the intensity of observance. Another common element between the muni and the śrāvaka is the worship of the Pañcaparameṣtins or the Five-fold obeisance to the Siddha, Arhat, Ācārya, Upādhyāya and the Sādhu. This pañcanamaskāra mantra, when recited, relieves them from the bondage of Karma.

4.1.2. Choice of Moral Act

4.1.2.1. Conduct backed by Knowledge

Conduct generally consists of voluntary and habitual actions. It involves deliberation, choice and purpose. An action, which is not chosen by the moral agent after deliberation and does not reflect his purpose therein, cannot be regarded as a constant of conduct. In Jaina terminology a *right conduct* is one which takes into consideration right knowledge and right intuition[19] The common Jaina example is the act of taking medicine. The act of taking medicine is preceded by knowledge of the medicine and faith in the one who prescribed the medicine. Jaina ethics gives preferential importance to conduct (ācāra), because it is by building up the character that one can build up one's moral life.

4.1.2.2. Self-determination of the Moral Agent

It is true that the influence of environment is great on the formation of character, such as social, and physical environment, climatic and geographic condition, economic conditions, education etc. But much depends upon how an individual adapts himself to a particular type of environment. We have the power to mould our environment by our endeavour. Jaina path of purification amply testifies this truth. For instance, Jainism does not believe in a personal god, who is a creator or redeemer, etc. nor in his/her grace.[20] And it esteems the efforts of human beings. No one can save another unless he saves himself.[21] Jaina doctrine of Karma prescribes self-imposed obligations and responsibilities. And Jainism as a profound system is a *Religion of Action* and

Self-determination. Any moral judgement is never simply passed on something done (action) but always on a person doing it (self).[22]

Self-determination in Jainism expresses elements of freedom and responsible behaviour in an agent. Cunningham says that freedom is not to be sought in an uncaused, spontaneous act of choice among alternatives, but in the capacity inherent in each moral agent to determine the bent of his own character. Freedom, in short, means not indeterminism but self-determinism, self-expression and self-development.[23] Where there is self-determination there arises accountability and moral responsibility.

4.2. Moral Judgements and Jaina Justifications

4.2.1. Subject and Object of Moral Judgement

Any moral judgement has a subject and an object. The subject of moral judgement is the conscience or the self within. It has two functions, (a) The reflective function which considers the intentions, motives, actions, consequences and the character of the person with a view to judging their goodness or badness, rightness or wrongness, (b) an authoritative function, which deals with the taking of decision on a particular line of action judged to be good. The conscience becomes an impartial spectator when it judges our actions. It is the conscience that can be the authoritative and critical judge of moral actions just like an art piece being reviewed by an artist. While judging an action there is an appcal from the universal consciousness. Hence the conscience adapts a universal and rational point of view. This brings about objectivity in moral judgements. It is ultimately the Ideal self that guides us.

4.2.2. Moral Worth of an Act

But how to judge the moral worth of an action? In Jaina terminology how does an action become Puṇya or Pāpa or virtuous or vicious, praiseworthy or blameworthy, morally good or bad? Prof. K.C. Sogani[24] discusses this matter in his article on Jaina Ethical Theory. We have four possibilities in our actions:

1. Right action and a bad motive;
2. Wrong action and a good motive;
3. Right action and a good motive, and
4. Wrong action and a bad motive

The third and fourth possibilities are termed as śubha and aśubha karma in Jainism. They are not complicated. The first possibility (right action and a bad motive) does not have any moral worth because of its bed motive. The second possibility (wrong action and a good motive) is rather complex and it has to be evaluated in that particular context. Although motive is given due importance in Jaina Ethics yet the act and its consequences are taken into consideration. Jaina Ācāryas do not 'exclusively' choose to emphasize one point (ekānta) either internal motive or external action alone but views it comprehensively (anekānta)[25] in order to evaluate its moral worth.

4.2.3. Nature of Moral Judgements

They do not merely state the nature of some action but compare them with an objective standard and by means of this standard determine its value. In other words, moral judgements are not judgements of facts but are essentially judgements of value. It is a judgement of *what ought to be* and not merely *what is.* Its characteristics can be described in two ways:

1. Moral judgements are not merely statements but are often, accompanied by expressions, feelings.
2. Moral judgements are guidance to action. They come to the help when we seek advice from them. They are prescriptive by nature. When the Jaina Ācāryas prescribe a vow 'Thou shall not injure living beings', the act of injuring is not like saying 'This table is made of wood' or 'water is colourless'. There is neither emotional content nor prescriptive nature hidden in these affirmations. In other words the value of the statement is zero. Whereas in the vow 'Thou shall not injure

living beings' contains feeling of abhorrence at the thought or at the sight of injury of an animal, feeling of sympathy at the thought or at the sight of that animal, feeling of anger at the thought or at the sight of the person injuring, etc. These feelings subsequently evoke in us a decision that we should not injure any animal. It becomes a law unto us.

4.2.4. Jaina Value System

When we talk about the value of non-injury to living beings there is a moral standard implied. The value is concerned with what is good and what is bad. In other words it means how we can justify our moral statements like 'Thou shall not injure living beings'. The justification comes when we evaluate the rightness or wrongness of the action on the basis of a moral standard. When we are asked to justify action we have recourse to intrinsic values like truth, beauty and goodness. Based on truth, beauty and goodness we say an action is right or wrong.

The Jaina value system is based on intuition and thus they are self-justifying. The conscience immediately perceives the moral worth of the action and evaluates it without any reference to some ends extrinsic to it. Actions are judged intuitively and immediately. Prof. Sidgwick[26] classifies forms of intuition as follows:

1. *Perceptional:* We perceive something to be right or wrong intuitively and immediately.
2. *Dogmatic:* We immediately apprehend the rightness or wrongness of a certain class of actions.
3. *Philosophical:* We immediately and intuitively apprehend some moral principle whereby we can evaluate actions to be right or wring. In the case of intuition no reasoning is done, no evidence is presented and no investigations are carried out.

But the Jaina Ācāryas know the limitations of this theory. Say, if the conscience itself is misguided? We know that a bad character has a bad conscience. Sometimes our impulses and passions are so strong that the voice of conscience is purposed.

4.2.5. The Doctrine of Triratna

Having such practical difficulties in mind, the Jaina Ācāryas have propounded the Doctrine of Triratna or three jewels. Tattvārthasūtra[27] pronounces that the path of goodness can be traversed only by right knowledge, right faith or belief or vision and right conduct altogether. False beliefs and evil conduct corrupt the *moral sense* of an individual. Also if morality is to be absolute and unconditional it must originate in the rational nature of man.[28] Western schools of ethical philosophy have stressed different perspectives like the perspective of the cognitivists, the emotivists and the intuitionists. But the Jaina anekānta attitude does not rest content with any one of these absolutist view. Their comprehensive knowledge of the problem of moral judgements and their justification have made them profound Ideals of right knowledge, right faith and right conduct.

The Tīrthaṅkaras stand a testimony to this comprehensive vision of the three ideals. Hence they are called the perfect ones. They have shown in their lifetime the path of deep rootedness in spiritual realization.

Through right faith and conduct they acquired the highest knowledge and were known as the *Omniscient* (Sarvajña).[29] They could intuitively know the universe, sentient and non-sentient beings, and the dynamics of their mutual relationship, the rise and fall in spiritual progress of ātman, etc., and thus show the path to liberation and purification. All these knowledge is handed down from generation to generation in the form of the Āgamas and the teaching the gurus.

4.3. Practical Application of Jaina Ethics

4.3.1. The basis and the end of Morality in Jainism

Morality is not an end in itself. It is only a means to achieve the total happiness of oneself, known in terms like Nirvāṇa or Mokṣa. The basis of conduct in Jaina Ethics is the individual i.e. each individual has to prepare himself for his own salvation. The theory of karma says that one is fully responsible for one's own deeds and their results. The personal element in the quest for salvation is very much emphasized in all Śramaṇic culture. Yet the altruistic motive is also seen in the principles like Samatā or equality, Ahiṁsā or Non-violence, Sāmāyika etc. It is said in Uttarādhyayana Sūtra that a Śramaṇa becomes a real Śramaṇa only through samatā.[30]

4.3.2. The two levels of Jaina Morality

In Jaina ethics, morality, whether it is individualistic or altruistic, is only a practical way of speaking (Vyavahārika). Wordily happiness achieved for oneself or for the other is not the ultimate end of morality. The ultimate aim of morality is to uproot even the subtlest form of passions. Therefore the *relative life of virtue and vice is to be abandoned*[31] in favour of life of pure consciousness (śuddhopayoga). In śuddhopayoga the self is absorbed in itself.[32] In the case of both śubhopayoga and aśubhopayoga, the self is not absorbed in itself whereas it involves with extraneous objects. Any activity, whether good or bad, is extraneous to oneself.[33] From the transcendental point of view the ultimate distinction between good and evil cannot be held.[34] And hence emancipation from mundane existence, which is the ultimate end of life, cannot be attained by mere observance of virtue.[35] So a person has to transcend the duality of good and bad actions. Paramātmaprakāśa suggests ironically that even meritorious actions can lead one to sin: the meritorious actions leads to wealth, wealth to pride; pride to infatuation; and infatuation to sin; and hence let, therefore, be no good actions for us.[36] Then what about practical conduct in wordily life, like speaking the truth, obeying the master, etc.? They are practical morality, which are again followed with the ultimate aim of transcendental morality.

4.3.3. Virtue and Vice: Its Preference

Though the Jaina ethical literature proposes a way beyond good and evil (i. e. transcendental morality) they also encourage one to prefer good to evil deeds.[37] Vice and virtue are chain of iron and gold respectively and as such are equally bad.[38] But it is better to wait in the shade rather than in the hot sun.[39] Once the soul is engaged in the mundane world it has to act in order to keep itself going and hence from the practical point of view 'good actions' are approved by Pravacanasāra.[40]

We might ask why good actions alone are preferred or even approved by Jaina Ācāryas. The answer is that virtuous acts are indirectly helpful in the achievement of liberation[41] if and only if the ultimate aim is kept in mind. One reason is that for a man engaged in worldly affairs it is not possible to remain absorbed in pure consciousness.[42] So when he turns to activities under compulsion it is better to indulge in virtuous acts (śubhopayoga) which leads to happiness rather than in vicious acts (aśubhopayoga) which leads to misery.[43] Secondly, good actions generally demand self denial and sacrifice on the part of the doer. If one is to be liberal he has to do away with greed and hence a virtue like liberality is a sort of penance[44] and, thirdly, a good act does good to the neighbour and the society at large. So for the sake of the society's well being one is not to engage in evil deeds. Thus a person in the temporary shed of this world will try his best to engage in it fruitfully and avoid evil deeds for the sake of one's own good and the good of others.

4.3.4. The Muni and the Śrāvaka dharma

4.3.4.1. Ascetic and Lay person: representations of two Levels of Morality

What we have so far dealt with is the two levels of morality as transcendental and practical, which only suggests the real nature of the soul as self-absorbed and the practical aspect of it as embodiment in the mundane world due to Karma. A Jain is supposed to aim always at the higher degree of perfection.[45] At a saṁsāric level (also vyavahāric level), he will not be able to attain this perfection. He can only get for a higher place in the next birth and his śubha karma will bring him that. On the contrary, a monk is *homeless*[46] and has nothing to do with the worldly desires and ambitions. His life style can easily aim at the higher degree of perfection and attain the ultimate end of life, which is the complete shedding of Karma. For him activities are of no avail. Even religious discourse, a good and pious act, can bring him only reward, which would commit him once again to higher birth. But he knows that activities whether good or bad will ever keep him in bondage. Hence he wants to purify himself religiously by choosing religious purification or *sallekhanā*.[47]

4.3.4.2. The close link between the Ascetic and the Lay Person[48]

Munidharma and Śrāvakācāra (ascetic and lay ethics) are the representatives of the two levels of morality. The former seeks to attain the ultimate end of ethics, namely, the complete shedding of karma. In other words it is to realize the *true* and *real* nature of the self as absorbed in itself and nothing to do with the outside world of activity, enjoyment, etc. The lay ethics[49] occupies the lower ladder in the path of perfection, although with the same ultimate motive in mind. Given their conditions in the world they cannot but be engaged in activities. They have to act in such a way that their next birth will secure them a higher status in perfection.

The ideal of a muni or monk has inspired the lay followers of the Jaina Community and this is manifested in their deep respect for the religious (monks and nuns) in their genuine wish to take to religious ordination (Dīkṣā), spend at least sometime in the monastery along with the religious. We can even say that the state of a laymen is only preliminary to the state of a monk. In fact most of the regulations or the rules of conduct for lay person (anuvrata, guṇavrata, sikṣāvrata,) are intended apparently to make them participate in the merits and benefits of monastic life without obliging them to renounce the world altogether. For example, the rules for Sallekhanā have a similar end in view. It cannot be doubted that this close union between lay persons and ascetics brought about by the similarity of their religious duties, differing not in kind but in degree, has enabled Jainism to avoid fundamental changes within, and to resist dangers from without for more than two thousand years.[50]

Muni dharma is sometimes understood as individual ethics and that of the laity is called social ethics. The morality of the laity is called *social ethics* because of their choice of life and its demands, their responsibility over the society and the duty they are committed to, etc.

4.3.5. The Common practice of the Five Vows

What is prominent in the moral way of life of both the ascetics and the lay persons is the practice of Pañcavratas or the Five Vows.[51] The great vows, which are called the place of peace, the great teachers and the producers of disinterestedness have, in all quarters of the earth, been proclaimed by the infinite Jina, the knowing one, as light illumining the three worlds, (repels) darkness.[52] These five vows are a must for both the monk as well as the lay followers of Jainism. For the monks it is absolute. The five small vows known as anuvrata are meant for the laity keeping in view of their social obligations in the society.

Besides these Five Vows, the laity is supposed to follow three guṇa vratas and four śikśā vratas. The spiritual welfare of the society increases by the faithful observance of these twelve austerities on the whole. Each vow has aticaras or violations or errors of commission and omission. For the performance of the austerities these violations have to be given up. A lay person who would like to go in higher stages of spiritual development practices the Eleven Pratimas or the stages of moral development towards the ideal personality. They include right attitude, practice of vow, equanimity, fasting, restriction in food habit, right profession, clothing, family affairs, etc.

4.3.5.1. The Vow of Non-violence

The vow of non-violence is so absolute for a monk that he has to be careful in his movements, speech, thinking, handling of things and food, etc. not to injure living beings.[53] Violence to any of the living beings will amount to deviation from the path of self-realization.[54] Such intense practice is not possible for the householder because he needs to engage himself in several activities, household duties, business activities, etc.

But a lay person chooses a profession that involves least violence. As a doctor or a soldier in the army, he is compelled to cause injury to his neighbour who cannot be avoided. Under such circumstances his violence is tolerated (Udyogami hiṁsā). During household duties like cooking, etc. a person cannot be free from violence. Such unintentional violence (Āraṁbha hiṁsā)[55] is tolerated.

Though violence to vegetative life is a lesser evil to violence done to animals in order to obtain meat etc., a householder cannot avoid this. The preference of vegetarian diet among the Jaina community is closely linked to this vow of non-injury to life. Similarly whatever food stupefies the mind and provokes evil practices like wine, etc. is condemand throughout.[56] A solider needs to defend himself and his country during war (Virodhi hiṁsā). Such necessary evils are tolerated. But no intertional violence for the sake of fun, etc.[57] For example the typing of the living beings tightly, beating them, mutilating them, overloading them and withholding their food and drink are condonable if done under the pressure of passions.[58] Generally as the aspirant ascends the steps of spiritual progress minimizes all types of violence in his conduct. Meanwhile he has a constant feeling of guilt and self-condemnation (nindanā garhaṇa) for the violence he has been committing all along.[59]

4.3.5.2. The Vow of Truth

To a monk truth is not only a negation of lie but a negation of all that is injurious, such as injurious speech, teasing speech, harsh speech, exciting speech, etc.[60] It means avoidance of all words under the influence of attachment, aversion, jest, fear, anger and greed.[61] All truth necessarily involves violence, for it is cussed by negligence, which is the backbone of violence.[62]

While truth is an absolute guide to a monk, for a householder it takes a relative position.

There are four types of truth: *Satyāsatya* (wholly true), *asatyāsatya* (intermixture of truth and falsehood where asatya is predominant), *sayasatya* (where satya is predominant) and *asatyāsatya* (wholly false).[63] Circumstances will decide the relative position of truth. For instance, truth has to be avoided if it is harmful to others.[64] In this case truth is subservient to Non-violence. Even professional lie is allowed[65] under the second and third types of Truth, namely, asatyāsatya, satyāsatya. Yet there are several transgressions a householder has to be aware of, like false preaching, divulging one's secret, forgery, breach of trust, disclosing one's secret purpose, etc.[66]

4.3.5.3. The Vow of Non-stealing

As regards the third vow, (Non-stealing), the monk should refrain from taking anything without being offered not only in the village or a town but also in the forest[67] (adattādāna: to take what is not being given).

In the ordinary plane of life where there is so much of business transactions and relations, the householder is warned against buying valuable articles for cheap price because it might be stolen articles,[68] taking things whose ownership is doubtful;[69] and appropriating something that is not offered or placed, dropped or forgotten by others.[70] The use of false weight and measures, all illicit business and adulteration which are transgressions or aticara. The third vow (non-stealing) is very significant even today and have been severally mentioned in Jaina ethical literature.[71]

4.3.5.4. The Vow of Celibacy or Purity

For a monk, Brahmacarya or Celibacy is deeper and wider in sense. It strictly forbids dealings with the outside world. The rules of conduct prescribed for munis show that he cannot have talks with the householders while wandering[72] and he has to avoid visiting relatives' house.[73] He is supposed to make use of couches that are unused by the householders.[74] He is not supposed to go to places of censure and listen to the sounds of instruments,[75] renounce sexual pleasures.[76] A monk should abstract from women, then friendship and company[77] and he must avoid talks about women.[78] Mūlācara describes a celibate monk in these terms: he abstains from sexual intercourse, bodily decoration, sense indulgence, exciting food, excessive food, songs and dance, association with woman, exciting surroundings, passionate thinking, recalling past sexual enjoyment and planning for future sexual enjoyment.[79] Uttarādhyayanasūtra gives ten conditions for a monk to observe celibacy. Most of them deal with women and their company, excessive eating and drinking, ornamental dressing, etc.[80]

For a householder, the vow of celibacy would mean fidelity to one's wife[81] (svadāra santuṣṭi and paradāra nivṛtti) add to keep off from a harlot or a kept-woman[82] or any woman leading a disorderly life.[83] Excessive desire for sex pleasure and use of artificial means for excessive sex enjoyments are to be avoided.[84] In practice, it is one way of aspiring for a monastic way of life.

4.3.5.5. The Vow of Non-attachment

Non-stealing goes along with the fifth vow, namely, non-possession. Stealing and possessing goods show the attitude of attachment, which is the cause of bondage.[85] Aparigraha has been defined as renunciation of sentient and insentient paraphernalia.[86] There are evidences where the Jaina monks were granted gifts of land by their royal patrons[87] especially to the Yāpanīya sect of Jainism, evidenced by inscriptions in Karnataka and Tamilnadu and hoarding of things in case of emergency by the monks. Mūlācāra warns against the attitude of attachment towards possessions.[88] Non-stealing and non-possession in a monk's life is manifested in their activity of 'begging' and the attitude of detachment. Ācārāṅgasūtra abounds in references to show the significance of the virtue of begging.[89] The only possession that a monk can have (differs from tradition to tradition) include śāstra, peacock feather, kamaṇḍala,[90] clothe, alms bowl, blanket and broom.[91] There are means of attaining knowledge, observance of vows and of purity.

Puruṣārthasiddhyupāya gives a list of ideas and activities that may alienate the nature of the self, and calls it 'inner possessions', such as false belief, seeking passions, likes and dislikes, sorrow and fear, etc.[92] A householder should constantly try to limit his activities for possession. The vows of limiting one's directions, regions, etc. *(Dig vrata or Deśa vrata)*[93] are facilities offered to a devout Jaina to be content with what he has.

Apart from these five vows, which are the cardinal virtues for both the monks and the lay person, penance or tapas, both external land internal, is made very special in Jaina morality. It embraces repentance of sin,[94] confession of the same to the teacher, penance done for it, the study and the teaching of the only faith, pious meditations,[95] the renunciation of all worldly possessions, temperance, begging, different kinds of self mortification, especially by fasts which my be continued to starvation known as religious purification (sallekhanā).

The motives for moral behaviour differ from one another depending on the understanding of their objectives of life. Jaina understanding of Mokṣa is the realisation of the self in its true nature devoid of the slightest tinge of Karma, which keeps the Jīva in bondage. Buddhism does not admit any permanent substance like Ātman but believes in the phenomenality of existence itself. While the realisation of the true nature of self guides the ethical sphere in the life of a Jaina, Right Belief[96] and Right Knowledge[97] about the phenomenal nature of reality and existence form the basis for the rest of the principles of conduct[98] mentioned in the 8-fold path. Buddhism holds that the objective of life in the knowledge of the Ātman, etc is itself a hindrance rather than a help in the achievement of the end. For in Buddhism the self is an abiding ego and the self in bondage is just the negation of the liberated self. It is rather the knowledge of the human situation that is relevant and of practical significance instead of the knowledge of anything purely theoretical. It is for this the 4 Noble Truths have been suggested and it is the knowledge of the 4 Noble Truths that constitutes the cognitive background for any moral life in Buddhism.

Incidentally, we could see another distinction within these two

Śramaṇa traditions: Jainism becomes too individualistic in its ascetic practices and general moral behaviour whereas Buddhism stresses the social dimension of ethical life. Although Jainism considers social work, helping others, etc. as instrumental and practical in the realisation of the end, it does not totally acknowledge them as constitutive of human liberation. Only from practical point of view that social institutions and duty to society etc. are acknowledged. One another reason for such an understanding is that Jainism believes in the self-determination of human effort. Jainism is known as the *Religion of Self-help.* Both Buddhism and Jainism deny the existence of god as creator, protector, sustainer etc. as well as the grace of such an Almighty. It upholds the dignity of human personality and human effort. Jainism has given much emphasis to this in relation to self-realisation: each one is responsible for his own liberation. But Buddhism has concentrated the whole human effort through 'right conduct' the last six of the 8-fold Path as part of the way of the elimination of suffering which is the consequent attainment of liberation. Therefore Buddhism would say: act that your action is in no way determined either directly or even indirectly by the desire for personal immortality which, according to it, is the counter part of the dread of death.

In Jaina theory of action there is no allowance for vicarious suffering nor any acceptance of transfer of merit. From niscaya point of view one has to eliminate one's own karma and he cannot either remove the karma of another or transfer his merit on to somebody else. For practical reasons one can undertake actions for social cause, etc. But in Buddhism, as in Christianity, the Bodhisattva is ready to sacrifice himself (like the *Suffering Servant of Yahweh* in Christianity) for the sake of the liberation of others. For this, the Bodhisattva undertakes special vows (the pārāmitas). Buddhism attaches much importance to the virtues of maitrī, karuṇā, muditā and upekṣā. The ideal of supreme self-sacrifice as the highest of human conduct is acknowledged more in Mahāyāṇa Buddhism than in Jainism.

The Anekāntavāda of Jainism comes to the aid of its belief and practice whenever internal contradictions need to be solved.

For instance, the niścaya and vyavahāra points of view makes distinction between the two level of understanding and experiencing. The point of focus is the realisation of Self in its true and original nature. Thus Jaina ethics suggests the way of the ascetics as the *absolute way* but it also accepts the moral conduct of the lay persons as the *practical way* because to them societal life is part of their daily phenomenon. Thus right action is viewed from two different angles.

The same theory holds good when the Jains are to judge the moral justification of any action. The Anekānta attitude takes into account the intention of the doer, the act proper the effects of the act and all the circumstances that enabled the person to act besides the formation of character etc. of the doer although it gives more stress to the act proper. For instance, Jainism holds that living beings with one-sense etc. accumulate karma through their acts of injury in spite of their limited perception and knowledge. On the other hand it also proclaims that knowledge and perception must accompany conduct.

This theory of pluralism or implied wholeness has penetrated deep into their epistemological system based on which several important concepts like Jīva, Karma, etc. are understood and morality prescribed and practised. Buddhism too subscribed to a theory like this but there is no distinct two-tier ethical system, as seen in Jainism but the code of conduct is meant for the monks in la special way, although social duties are prescribed for the laity in the isolated passages like the Siṅgālovādasutta.

Both Buddhism and Jainism with their indigenous character and systematization of their belief and practice more or less in a similar way in the same socio-political and religious milieu, have made a tremendous impact on Indian life and society. The special features of these living Śramaṇa traditions such as the phenomenality of life, the urge to eliminate misery and suffering, the meticulous practice of moral and religious codes like that of Ahiṁsā, the ascetic renunciation and the spirit of detachment, etc. have gone deep into the nerve of the Indian system. The next and the last chapter expound this special feature of impact by analyzing its relevance to the contemporary society.

Notes

1. A commentary of the Sūtrakrtāṅga Sūtra indicates how the novices on Jain path should not fall a prey to the misconduct of heretics, etc, and how they should keep in mind their 'nirvānic' goal and adhere to the discipline. As quoted by Dr. Lalitha in Jain Journal, XXX, No. 1, July 1995, pp. 2-3
2. Mackenzie, pp, 51-52
3. Samayasāra, 2.
4. 'Ekādeśa karma sankṣaya laksaṇa Nirvāṇa,' Sar Sid X.1-3
5. Sar Sid X.4.
6. Ibid., VII, 2.
7. Kalghatgi, T.G. p.81.
8. The introductory discourse in Samayasāra, 2-14.
9. Obeisance to the Five-fold deities is described in Pannavānasuttam, Part I; Text p.3 and footnote 2 and tr. by P.S. Jaini, pp.162-63.
10. Bhargava, p.30
11. Tat Sūtra, 9.2-3, 18-20
12. Ācār Sūtra, 1.2.3.4
13. Hume, D. Book II, Part III, Ch. 3
14. RKSA 5 also Amit SA, 6.47
15. Kar AP 335
16. Mackenzie, pp. 273-74
17. Four holy Tīrthas are the Ascetic Order of the monks and the nuns and the Lay Order of men and women.
18. Sar Sid VII, Kalghatgi, T.G. pp. 81-84
19. Without knowledge there is no virtuous conduct (Utt. 28.30). Right faith preceedes right conduct (Pūjyapāda on Tat Sūtra, 2-3).
20. Complete rejection of grace of god, etc. because the doer of the acts must suffer for them (Sūt Kr 1.9. 4-5).The belief in an eternally free person capable of dispensing salvation by grace is a feature conspicuously absent in the heterodox systems. The Jains and the early Buddhists rejected this special category of and eternally free soul as purely arbitrary and obseved that the activities of a teacher were inconsistent with one deprived of the means of communicatin, namely, mind, body and speech.
21. Spirituality of self-help: A man must come and go (according to his karma) alone (i.e. without deriving any help form others) Sūt Kr 1.13-18
22. Mackenzie, p 111
23. Cunningham, p 391
24. Dwivedi, pp. 175-76
25. An important contribution by the Jainas in the field of Pramāṇas is the theory of Anekānta. A comprehensive pictue of reality is sought to be presented by the Jaina theory of Anekānta. Ekānta or dogmatism or one-

sided approach is not inherent in the reality (Vastugata dharma), but it is due to the working of the intellect. It is the product of intellectual discrimination.

26. Sidgwick, Book I, Ch. 8
27. Tat Sūtra 1.1
28. According to Kant, an action is right if it is done on a principle which is 'categorical imperative.' Categorical imperative is a command of our rational self.
29. Mati, Śruta, Avadhi, Manahparyāya and Kevala: these five are the types of congnition (Tat Sūtra, 1.9); of these, the Kevala jñāna is the highest (Tat Sūtra, 1.30)
30. Utt Sūtra, 25.32
31. From the pure, absolute point of view, the self is immaterial and has nothing to do with good or bad, virtue or vice. Both are to be transcended. The self is 'unattached' to either of them. See Sekhar, Vincent, in his paper 'Jaina Concept of Person—A textual Study of Samayasāra of Ācārya Kundakunda' in Jain Journal, Vol XXV, No. 3, January 1991 1991., pp 110-118
32. Complete self-absorption is described in Samayasāra, 36-7; 205-6
33. Samayasāra clearly distinguishes self from non-self (Samayasāra: 2,7, 16-17, 24-32, 43 etc.
34. Amṛtacandra on Prav Sāra 1.72, 77 also Samayasāra, 145
35. Prav Sāra 3.56
36. Paramātmaprākaśa 260 Comm. by Brahmadeva
37. Sūtrakṛtāṅga points out thirteen kinds of sinful activities; Sūt Kr II 2.4
38. Samayasāra 146
39. Iṣṭopadeśa, 3
40. Prav Sāra 3.51
41. Bhāvasaṅgraha, 610-18
42. Ibid., 607
43. Ibid., 611-12
44. Ibid., 616-17
45. Dr Madhusudana Mishra discources the rules of conduct of Jaina laypersons in the study of Amṛtacandra's Puruṣārthasiddhyupāya. To the question 'who is a real Śrāvaka', he says that only a 'samyagdṛṣṭi' can be a real śravāka. See, House Holder 's Discipline in Jainism, See Ch. 1 on Right Belief; Ch. 2 on Right Knowledge, and Ch, 3 Right Conduct.
46. N. Shanta has done an extensive study on the Jain women ascetics and she describes their consecration, work, itinerary trip, final purificatin, etc. See N. Shanta, pp. 420-560
47. Ācārāṅga 1.4 ff: also in the Aurapachakkhana and Saṁthāra, the 2nd and 4th Painnas.
48. Surendra Bothara indicates in his paper ' Sādhu and Society ' that a Sādhu is an integral part of the society. especially of the Jain society, and he

or she is duty-bound to repay the obligations of the society that maintain them See Jain Journal, Vol XXIX, No. 2 Oct 1994.

49. The 11- Pratimas describe the stages of spirtual growth of a House Holder, See Muni Shivkumar pp. 108-109
50. SBE, Vol.VII, p. 470
51. Pūjyapāda on Tat Sūtra, 7.1-2
52. Ācār Sūtra II.16.6
53. Tat Sūtra, 9.5; Mūlācāra 5.140, Barghava p.152, n.2
54. Amṛtacnadra on Prav Sāra 3.16 Barghava, p.152, n.3
55. Amīt SA 6.6-7
56. Pur Sid 62, 64, 71
57. RKSA, 53
58. Upāsakadaśāṅga, 1.45, Siddhasena on Tat. Sūtra 7.20
59. Amit SA, 6.8
60. Sthān Sūtra, 6.3.527
61. Mūlācāra 5.141; Bhag Ar 1207
62. Pur Sid 99
63. Handiqui, K.K. p.265
64. Amit SA, 6.47
65. Pur Sid 101
66. Amit SA, 7.4; Pur Sid 184
67. Mūlācāra. 5.290
68. Kār AP.335
69. Sāgār Dhar 4.49
70. RKSA. 57; Vas SA, 211 Sāgār Dhar. 4.48
71. Tat Sūtra, 7.22;RKSA, 58, Pur Sid 185; Amit SA, 7.5
72. Ācār Sūtra, II.3.8
73. Ibid., II.1.4
74. Ibid., II.2.8-12
75. Ibid., II 11.1.14-19
76. Ibid., II 15.4
77. Sūt Kr 1.4.2. 19-20
78. Niyamasāra, 67
79. Mūlācāra, 10.105-106; also see Utt Sūtra, 16.1-10
80. Utt Sūtra, 16
81. RKSA, 59
82. Siddhasena on Tat Sūtra, 16.1-10
83. Sāgar Dhar 4.58
84. Sidhasena on Tat Sūtra, 7.23
85. Every attachment is a cause of sin. Sūt Kr I.3.2.13
86. Mūlācāra, 1.9
87. Epigraphica Indica, PP 232-40
88. Vasunandin on Mūlācāra, 5.142

89. Begging of food (Ācār Sūtra, II.1); Begging of Couch (Ibid., II.5); Begging of Bowl (ibid., II.6); Regulations of Possessions (ibid., II.7)
90. According to Digambara tradition, mūlācāra, 1.14
91. According to Śvetāmbara tradition, Ācār Sūtra, 1.2.5.3
92. Pur Sid 116
93. Bhargava, p.126
94. Sūt Kr II.2.4
95. The 12-fold reflections or meditations are given in Bhag Ār 1715
96. Utt Sūtra, 28.15
97. Right Knowledge about the nature of the soul: Das Sūtra, 4.12; The saving Knowledge: Utt Sūtra, 29.60
98. Right Belief, Right Knowledge and Right Conduct are intertwined: Utt Sūtra, 28.30

CHAPTER V

TECHNICAL DISCUSSION OF THE TERM *DHARMA*

PART-I IN BUDDHIST ABHIDHARMA TRADITION

5.1.1. *Abhidharma* and its Purpose:

Mrs. Rhys Davids[1] clearly mentions that the burden of Abhidharma (one of the Tri-pitakas of Buddhist canon) is but analytical and logical and methodological elaboration (of the knowledge ... revealed in the Buddhist Pāli canon), the chief methods of which were: first, the definition and determination of all names or terms entering into the Buddhist scheme of culture; secondly, the enunciation of all doctrines, theoretical and practical, as formulas, with coordination of all such as were logically interrelated, and finally, practice in reducing all possible heterodox positions to an absurdity ...

The Abhidharma is said to be the instruction in the ultimate nature of things and the ultimate way of explanation.[2] Abhidharma brings about pure Prajñā, which deals with the discernment of harms.[3] Apart from the discernment of the dharmas there is no means to extinguish the defilements; and it is by reason of the defilements that the living being wander in the ocean of existence. Hence with a view to discern the dharmas the Abhidharma has been spoken by the Blessed One. Abhidharma is called abhi-dharma because it envisions (abhimukha) the dharma which is the object of supreme knowledge or the supreme Dharma, Nirvāṇa,[4] and it was the supremely enlightened one who first knew the Abhidharma while sitting under the Bodhi-tree. He penetrated the Abhidharma and became the Buddha.[5]

Hence the aid of Abhidharma is nothing less than to open men's eyes to that ... which can be immediately apprehended and is applicable to us.[6] But the only criticism is that the Abhidharma centred its attention to the numerical definition and became oblivious to the spirit, which laid down the analysis of mind and its functions, etc.[7] as a guide conducive to Final Liberation

5.1.2. Purpose of Dharma Vicara:

The shortest statement of the essence and spirit of Buddhism is declared in the Mahāvagga.[8] Buddha discovered the elements (dhamma) of existence,[9] their causal connection, and a method to suppress their efficiency forever (nirodha). Vasubandhu[10] makes a similar statement about the essence of the doctrine. It is a method of converting the elements of existence into a condition of rest, out of which they will never emerge again. It is for this reason that the discernment of the dharmas, their distinct nature and characteristics has been explained in the Abhidharma. The novices in the Buddhist church before obtaining admittance into the order went through a course of instruction in what may be called the Buddhist catechism, i.e. an exposition of the elements (dharma) of existence and their different classifications into skandhas, āyatanas, dhātus.[11]

5.1.3. Meaning and the nature of dharma:

The Abhidharmakoṣa Bhāṣya of Vasubandhu describes the meaning and nature of dharma:

1. Dharma is that which bears (dharma) self-characteristics[12] which is unique.
2. A dharma is included in its own nature for it is distinct from the nature of others.[13]
3. There are four criteria for distinction between dharmas: its nature or characteristic, its function, its manifestation as how it appears to the mediator and its immediate or proximate cause.[14]
4. A dharma does not change its characteristics in the course of time and all dharma are impersonal.[15]

5. Dharmas are numerous, sensations, ideas etc. The best of them is considered Nirvāṇa.[16]
6. Dharma arises, lasts, gnaws old and perishes at one and the same time.[17]
7. All dharmas are kāraṇa hetu (reason for existence) with regard to all with the exception of itself and no dharma constitutes an obstacle to the arising of the dharmas susceptible of arising.[18]
8. No dharma arises from a single cause[19] that indicates that the world is not produced from a single cause that is called God, or Puruṣa or Pradhāna or any of the names.[20]
9. A dharma is the result of the virile activity of the dharma through the force by which it arises and a dharma grasps a result when it becomes its seed. A dharma produces a result at the moment when it gives this result the power of arising, that is, this dharma gives it the power that causes it to enter into the present.[21]
10. The material dharmas arise by reason of two conditions, causes as condition and predominating influences as conditions[22] whereas mind and mental states are causes through association.[23]
11. The world and the dharmas submit to the mind. The world is led by the mind, conducted by the mind: all dharmas obey this one dharma, the mind.[24] Rightly said so because it is the faculty of Prajñā (wisdom) that discerns the dharmas.[25] Buddha declares that if there is a single dharma that is not known and penetrated, one cannot put an end to suffering.[26]

The general characteristics of dhamma can be summarized in the following manner:

1. Every dhamma is a separate (Pṛthak) entity or force.
2. There is no inherence of one element (dharma) in another which implies that there is no substantiality[27] in dharmas. What we mean by substance is only name and form; there is no chariot except that it is made of parts - no substance apart from its qualities, no matter beyond sense data, and

no soul beyond the separate mental dāta (dharma = anātman = nirjīva).

3. Dharma is momentary and has no duration.[28] Each dharma represents a flash of moment. Dharma has no movement; the whole world and the phenomena of life and existence are only consecutive appearances, flashes of dharmas.
4. Dharmas cooperate with one another (saṁskṛta) and this activity is controlled by laws of causation called pratītyasamutpāda[29] Hence the whole dynamism in the world is a process of cooperation between 72 dharmas, each subtle and evanescent, coming into existence because of some cause (hetu-prabhāva) and steer towards extinction (nirodha), in serial succession.[30]
5. Dharmas experience unrest[31] due to Avidyā and they tend towards rest due to Prajñā. An ordinary man and a saint are two representatives of two distinct combination of dharmas, the former of Avidyā and the later, of Prajñā.
6. The Final liberation is the suppression of all dharmas, an Absolute Calm. These characteristics are fundamental, and the knowledge and discernment of dharmas in their nature and characteristics lead the worldlings to Final Perfection.

To put it in simple term, Dhamma[32] refers to the 'ultimate unit of existence'. Whatever we can think of, animate and inanimate beings, the dynamism of life and relationship, problems and solutions to life and existence, etc. are all constituted by dhammas. There is no mind, body, matter, spirit, world, planetary motions without dhammas. All these are composed of dhammas.

5.1.4. **Dhamma,** ***the Essence of Buddhism:***

The essential doctrines of Buddhism, namely, the anātman theory[33] (no substantiality), anitya theory (kṣanikavāda or momentariness) and Duhkha (Pain or suffering) and their corollaries are built on the fundamental and foundational concept of dhamma.

1. In the Anātman theory whatsoever be designated by ātman as personality, an ego, a self, an individual, a living being, a conscious agent etc. is not a real and ultimate fact. What

is real in them is a multitude of inter connected facts, which Buddhist philosophy is attempting to analyze by reducing them to real elements, namely, dhammas. Hence Soullessness or Anātman is a negative expression for the existence of ultimate realities[34] called dhammas. Therefore an element (dharma) technically means *non-self*[35]

2. Similarly since the elements of existence (dharma) are of momentary nature, a moment becomes a synonym of an element (dhamma). Two moments are two different elements. The elements do not change but disappear. In Prof. Stcherbatsky's words[36] what does not disappear does not exist. This implies that there are some universal forces working within each dharma. These are the characteristic feature or the manifesting forces (saṁskāras) of phenomenal existence: the force of origination (utpāda), decay (jarā), maintenance (sthiti) and destruction (anityatā). These forces affect every element at every moment of existence. But the characteristic of kṣanikatva of dharmas seems to deny motion. This problem is carefully resolved in the series of separate apparitions, or flashings, arising one after another. The conception of a plurality of separate elements includes the idea of causality, controlling their operation in the worldly process. The theory of elements means that if something appears, such and such result will follow.[37] Extending this reflection further, *time*, in general, is not different from the dharmas taken collectively. In fact 'the times' is one of the synonyms used to designate collectively the elements appearing in ordinary life.[38]
3. What follows then is the meaning of Duhkha. The understanding that the ultimate constituent of existence (dharma) has no substance, that it is evanescent, that it is in a beginningless state of commotion and unrest, that it can be brought to rest only in its complete suppression etc. gives the real meaning of Duhkha.[39] The total unrest of elements is duhkha. The unrest is caused by existence or saṁsāra the deliverance from which is possible only by the total suppression of it.

The whole of existence and the whole phenomena of life namely mind and mental states, body, the senses, thought processes and other activities, attitude, volition etc. are the outcome of the various dharmas combining in different ways caused by different factors, forming a stream of unrest. Hence as long as existence continues so long the flashings of the dharmas would be. One can only contemplate to reverse this course of events (suppression of the dharmas) caused by the voluntary action of volition or the will (cetanā) through knowledge and ecstasy (Prajñā and Bhāvana): these are mental faculties always present in every conscious moment. Their presence gives the whole stream (santāna) of dharmas a special power to purify the feelings, ideas and volition.[40] For, complete suppression of the elements of unrest, which is duhkha, are needed to enter into new worlds of existence, gradually from the world of purified matter (rūpa dhātu) to higher worlds where sense experience is gradually replaced by the purely spiritual (arūpa dhātu).

The important conclusions are:

1. Existence is reduced to dharmas.
2. Plurality of dharmas implies a causal connection.
3. Though momentary, they are held together in a dynamic manner.
4. All movements and stability are only apparent and the very nature of dharma makes this possible.
5. In this dynamism all dharmas serve as the connecting link.
6. The world of inanimate and the animate existence are because of such causally connected dharmas.
7. The entire body and mind function because of their specific dharmas.
8. Dharmas explain the nature of very existence as non-substantial and momentary.
9. Their unrest causes the phenomenon, called duhkha.
10. Dharmas cause unrest and deliverance from it is possible. This feature converts the dharma theory into a doctrine of salvation. This implies the whole practice of morality, etc.
11. Each individual possesses distinct types of dharmas[41] and

each dharma has special characteristics. They cannot inter change. Such understanding of dharma does not warrant an outside *force* or *saviour* who would deliver the individual from the total unrest.

12. Dharmas, through their causal link, provide dynamism and movement to the whole and the parts of all states and stages of existence. The whole of Buddhist understanding of the world and its functions is based on the fundamental belief in the Doctrine of Dharma. The aim of life and the goal of existence again fall back on this central doctrine. Ethics has no place without its understanding. Buddhist theory of karma and Nirvāṇa rest upon the basic faith in the doctrine of Dharma.

5.1.5. Classification of Dharmas

In order to understand the working of the dharmas in the phenomenon of existence it is important to present their general classification. The very classification will indicate to us their specific nature, functions and the rationale behind them.

5.1.5.1. General Classification of Dharmas

There are a number of ways in which the dharmas are categorized according to groups and functions:

1. The general division of all dharmas is into matter (rūpa), mind (citta) and forces (saṁskāra).[42]
2. The simplest classification of all dharmas of existence is represented by a discussion into Five groups (skandhas)[43]: Matter, Feelings, Ideas, Volitions and other Faculties and Pure sensation or general consciousness. Matter represents the physical elements of a personality including external objects. The mental ones are distributed among the four others.
3. Another classification of elements is made with a view to a division into cognitive faculties and their objects. There are six cognitive faculties and six categories of corresponding objects (e.g. Sense of vision corresponds to colour and

shape, sense of audition corresponds to sound, etc.). Thus they make 12 *Āyatanas*[44] or bases of cognition and all dharmas are distributed in the 12 Āyatanas.

4. The division of the elements of existence into Eighteen Dhātus[45] is made from quite a different view point. Just as different metals (dhātus) might be extracted out of a mine, so does the stream of an individual life reveal elements of eighteen different kinds (dhātu = gotra).
5. Another category of division is made corresponding to the denizens of various worlds. All the varieties of consciousness exist only in the ordinary plane of existence (kāma dhātu). In higher worlds (rūpa dhātu) sense-consciousness gradually disappears and in the immaterial worlds (arūpa dhātu) only non-sensuous consciousness is left.[46]
6. From the point of view of Final Deliverance all the dharmas of life may assume two different characters: they are either characterized by a tendency towards life, commotion and turmoil, and thus they are called Sāsrava, i.e., 'influenced' by passion, or they are uninfluenced (anāsrava), i.e., they exhibit the opposite tendency towards reduction of life, appeasement of commotion and even annihilation.[47] The first set of dharmas correspond to the ordinary man and the second make up the saint (ārya).
7. Factors of being, i.e. the twelve terms of Dependent Origination,[48] is another classification of the entire dharmas: concealed by ignorance, mutually dependent, continuity due to karma, etc.

5.1.5.2. Abhidharmakoṣabhāsya of Vasubandu gives yet another classification

Skandhas, Āyatanas and dhatus are the triple designation of the dharmas.[49] Dharmas classified in the eighteen dhatus are Visible and Invisible dharmas. Resistant and Non-resistant dharmas and good, bad and morally Neutral dharmas.[50]

Dharmas are divided into conditioned and unconditioned dharmas:[51] conditioned dharmas are called paths (so called because they have the nature of having gone, of going, of shall be going); they are devoured by impermanence and are dependent on causes; they are also 'endowed with leaving'.[52]

All conditioned dharmas are necessarily generated with their saṁskṛta laksanas: arising, duration, old age, and impermanence.[53] Only conditioned dharmas have causes and result and belong to time period.[54] All the conditioned dharmas are included within the totality of the skandhas.[55] The conditioned dharmas are of different natures: physical matter, sensation, ideas, etc.[56] Conditioned dharmas could be pure as well as inpure. Impure conditioned dharmas are the five skandhas and they constitute the five defilements; they proceed from defilements, are governed by the defilements, give rise to the defilements. Hence they are called the 'Battle'. They are also suffering, arising, the worlds the locus of false opinions, existence - all from defilements.[57] The unconditioned dharmas have neither cause nor result and they are outside of time.[58] All the dharmas, conditioned as well as unconditioned, are 'objects of consciousness' of the mind and its mental states in a discriminate way.[59]

Dharmas are generally divided into four categories: Defiled dharmas. Retributive dharmas, the first Pure dharmas and the other dharmas.[60] Dharmas of defilement are lack of discipline, moral transgression, the cutting of the root of good. Dharmas of purification are discipline, acquisition of the fruits, and detachment.[61]

Universals are the only cause of defiled dharmas. It is through their power that there arise defilements belonging to categories different from them. These universals are abandoned by seeing the Truths.[62] Bad dharmas and impure good dharmas are retributive causes (vipāka hetu). Pure dharmas are not retributive causes because they are not moistened through desire. Pure dharmas are not bound to any sphere of existence.[63]

There are certain dharmas which can be 'acquired through effort' such as qualities (guṇa) proceeding from hearing (śruta), that is from the word of the Buddha, from reflection (cintā) and from meditation (bhāvana).[64] There are dharmas which are called the companions of the mind[65] and dharmas not associated with the mind,[66] dharmas existing at every moment of the mind,[67] and those that are found in all good minds,[68] dharmas that are causes[69] and dharmas belonging to a certain category and to a certain stage (Bhūmi), etc.[70]

Analysing this classification one comes across the function of dharmas in the growth process, particularly of living beings, towards the Buddhist ideal of Nirvāṇa. In actual life-situation one sees the working of the innate dharmas and the dharmas though acquisition towards this purpose. What conditions all animate beings in this growth process is the arising of the new dharmas with their causal relations in the lifetime. But since they are endowed with the characteristic of 'leaving', it is possible for the animate beings to experience the different stages of annihilation of dharmas through Discipline and Wisdom. Thus the actual life turns into an Ideal Path of spiritual realization. All the conditioned dharmas are to be purified in the process. Freed completely from the defiled state the person is no more conditioned by causal relationship; he is detached and no more bears the burden of retribution. This movement of 'growth towards Extinction' (Nirvāṇa) can only be realized if proper discernment is made on the nature and functions of dharmas in the whole phenomena of life and existence.

5.1.5.3. Dr. W. F. Jayasuriya's Classification

Dr. W. F. Jayasuriya puts the subject of all higher teachings into Four categories of elements: Cognition, Mental Factors, Matter and Nibbāna. These four groups of elements are the Reals[71] in phenomena, because they exist and perform particular functions. He also presents a complete list.[72] of all the elements into the category of units of Matter and units of Mind. He points out a relation of the two without mixing.[73]

Interaction between elements do take place and various kinds of activity or functions may be carried out within the unit, whether physical or mental with their specific structure in different degrees of intensity. For instance in the 'act of thieving' the mind operates and performs its various functions without any overriding door or self. Any unit of matter arises on account of one or the other of four categories of causes or condition, namely, past Action or Kamma, Thought, Energy and Nutriment.[74] Similarly any thought unit arises out of twenty-four causal relations.[75]

Every thought unit has a cognitive element and a number of mental Factors. There are three main principles of classification of thoughts: a) According to the plane of Existence: the Sense plane, the Form plane, the Formless plane and the Supramundane plane b) The second relates to the Ethical Nature of thoughts: moral thoughts, Immoral thoughts and Ineffective thoughts. These Ethical thoughts bring about respectively agreeable effects, disagreeable effects and no effect at all. Actions done in the past with moral and immoral thoughts yield effects (material and mental). The material effects are property, power etc. and the mental effects of past actions are known as the Resultant thoughts over which we have no control. The Inoperative thoughts do not lead to further effects because they are not conscious effects, (c) In respect of underlying sources of motivation - Attachment, Ill-will, Delusion and their opposites.

Ultimately, thoughts are classified into eighty-nine classes. Out of them, one finds fifty-two mental factors or non-cognitive psychic elements. Some are found in each and every thought unit (called the universal Mental Factors); some others arise irrespective of whether the thought is moral or immoral; a third group refers to those psychic elements found in the wholesome thoughts and the fourth group is that found in the immoral thoughts.[76]

In the category of Matter we find twenty-eight kinds of elements of which four are primary and twenty-four are secondary i.e., they are dependent on the primary one. The Directly caused elements include Four primary elements and fourteen secondary elements. The Indirectly caused elements are ten, and they refer to certain properties of the atoms (physical unit) themselves. This division has its rationale in the recovering of all elements as functions and yet admitting the necessity of regarding matter substantially as particles.[77]

There is no unit of matter without qualities of hardness, cohesion, energy, motion, colour, taste, smell and nutriment.

Matter is deeply involved in a continuous process of being with reproduction of atoms of the same kind or changing into atoms of a different kind.[78]

The interaction between the atoms (units of matter) leads to differences in their total quantities of the primary elements. Thereby we get certain qualitative or property changes as of state and also other changes such as in colour, smell and sound. Changes in properties can be produced by the Energy element being supplied from outside. Accordingly new atoms resulting from changed conditions may have a greater or lesser quantity of any one of these four primary Elements and so cause changes in the states or mode of being in things as solid, liquid, flame and gas.[79] Similarly occurrence of youth and old age is explained due to a maturation process from the continuing action of Energy as atoms generated at various times. Because the Motion element is a part of the structure atoms, which have only a life of very brief duration, are ever springing anew in different places.[80]

Of the twenty-four secondary elements, fourteen of them are directly caused and the rest, indirectly caused:

The first category includes a) the sensitive elements on which the impact of the object takes place b) the stimulating elements which refer to the external stimuli such as colour, sound, odour taste and touch c) the sex elements as male and female d) the Heart or Mind-base Element referring to the thoughts of awareness and reception of the sense object e) the Life element which has a protective function and by the loss of which death occurs and f) the Nutriment element energising the cells and dispelling the fatigue of the body.

The second category, namely the Indirectly caused secondary elements include a) the Space element that prevents the fusion of atom b) the Intimating elements which are responsible for bodily action and speech c) the Alterable elements such as Buoyancy, Pliancy and Efficiency and d) the Phasic elements which refer to the qualitatively in distinct periods in the life duration of an atom.

The fourth Real, namely the Nibbāna element belongs to the supramundane reality. It is a release from cravings of every kind.[81] It has an independent existence with radically different characteristic when compared to that of the mundane elements. It is uncaused, its nature is stillness, free from all defilements but full of purity; it is not bound by time (eternal) and it is permanent and deathless. It is a state of peace. Supramundane thoughts can take only the Nibbāna element as object. It can be the object for certain other wholesome thoughts of the sense plane too. The individuals, purified from all defilements can evolve into the order of saints.

5.1.6. Dynamic Conception of dharmas

The nature and characteristic of each dharma and particularly the grouping of all dharmas into Skandhas, Āyatanas and Dhātus and their specific functions suggest their dynamic character. As the whole phenomena of life and existence are reduced to their ultimate constituents (dhammas) they imbibe in themselves in a unique manner, the essence of existence, of arising, staying, decay and extinction. In all these stages the dharmas experience a dynamism through complex system of inter-relations,[82] through changes in properties qualitatively and quantitatively, something very significant of existence itself.

The motivating or the generating 'forces' that operate in each dharma whether material or mental, primarily account for the 'movement' in the potential as well as in the actual stage, although the dharmas themselves do not move nor mix with one another. The appearance of every dharma in a constant flow bears the resultant characteristics of all the preceding dharmas. Their effect becomes the seed for future dharmas. In every thought process there are several causes at work, which relates all the dharmas in the process.

It is through these causal relations that certain mental elements are associated with one another as a tree depending upon its root: that an object causes the genesis of thought; that one psychic element, out of many, assumes more powerful position; that one depends on something because it is of great value because it influences him (passions, pleasures, etc.); that one is consequent on the other like when information of an approaching doom influences one's conduct; that one is respectively engaged in certain action (habit); that one is actively conditioned, like volition (cetanā) brings out effects (Karma relation); that something brings about a natural effect, like flowering forth on plants; that one experiences superior or trance thoughts; that one is led to the fortunate or unfortunate path; that one experiences association or dissociation; that one witnesses certain events in the presence or absence of certain things, etc.

Similarly, the 'moving forces' of material dharmas, namely, the Kamma or Past action. Though, Energy and Nutriment are responsible for the arising of any unit of matter into existence. The force of striving or the volitions in past actions creates in the present life certain kinds of matter such as the life element, the sex elements and the sensitive elements of the body. Thoughts too generate a number of different kinds of atoms that can cause the health of the body, maintain posture, cause respiration and also cause muscular movements. Energy or heat, which is an integral property of every kind of matter, internal as well as external, is responsible for most of the different kinds and states of matter. Similarly Nutriment too causes birth of several atoms giving growth and vitality to living bodies. It is Energy, which generates new atoms in the physical world, outside living bodies, whereas all the four generative forces operate in animate beings.

5.1.7. **The Movement Dynamics *of Human Personality***

*5.1.7.1. **Formation of Healthy and Unhealthy attitudes***

The following reflections are to show how dharmas function in a specific way in human psyche bringing about distinct personality especially in the formation of healthy and unhealthy Attitudes. Attitude (citta) plays a vital role in human personality because it discriminates.[83] Without this we cannot account for the differences in individuals: An attitude in which passion is predominant is different from an attitude in which aversion prevails and it is different from an attitude which bewilderment holds its sway. And an attitude concerned with the world of sensuous object (kāmāvacara) is different from an attitude concerned with the world ofgestalten (rūpāvacara).[84] Attitude is the determining element in our life because activity and affectivity build it up (citta).[85] This attitude is not a single entity but a definite organization and the resultant of many factors (function-events) and the following 5 function-events are always present in an attitude: Sparśa, Vedana, Saṁjñā, Cetanā and Citta.[86]

These events take place when there is a sensuous relation between Object and Emotion - the object (the three realms of existence) is passionately desired and the emotion passionately desires[87] in the human personality: Sparśa acts as a pillar that supports all other psychic events[88] by 'touching' (relating) the object and bringing it into the focus of consciousness.[89] Thus Sparśa is said to produce feeling, to give rise to it.[90] Feeling imparts a definite value in the sense of acceptance (like) or rejection (dislike) or indifference.[91] Saṁjñā (sensation) in the meanwhile recognizes the object, helps in transmitting to consciousness the perceived image (as a whole or as a part).[92] Cetanā or volition arouses and sustains the activity and functions as a motive and a drive. Its function of arranging and effecting comes to pass in healthy or unhealthy effects.[93] In this way cetana and karman are synonymous. By cetanā, an individual is bound and fettered to saṁsāra until he has reached Nirvāṇa and moved out of the range of Karma.

Again Emotions are the principal condition for Karma. It is by the dominating influence of Emotions that karman is able to present a new life. Emotions are the root of the fact of continued existence. Where Emotions are exhausted the worlds cease to exist.

Healthy attitudes are rooted in detached love and knowledge whereas unhealthy attitudes are tied to the worlds of sensuous relatedness (kāmāvacara)... They do not admit any spiritual levels (bhūmi) which can be realized by detachment and not by attachment, by love and not by cupidity, by knowledge and not by ignorance.[94] An absence of confidence, inspection, analytical appreciative understanding, and the ease, straight forwardness, and adaptability of all psychic functions mark all unhealthy attitudes.[95] Unhealthy attitudes are infected by various effective instabilities such as cupidity (lobha), antipathy (dveṣa or doṣa), delusion, bewilderment (moha), preestablished ideas (diṭṭhigata) and conceitedness (māna).

5.1.7.2. Formation of Concentrated and Distracted personalities

The need for Deliverance and the Path of Deliverance do not possess any value until one is aware of what is meant by Bondage and what leads one to Bondage. The Noble truths and the 8-fold Path do not serve a person in his spiritual pursuit if his mind and attitude are misguided, if his faith is in false-views and his morality deviates the path of Perfection. Hence the discerning of the dharmas that constitute one's mental life is an extreme necessity; also because it is the seed for continued existence.

Though concentration is one of the 8-fold path suggested by the Buddha in attaining Liberation, it is the summum bonum of the path of morality, because the stages of spiritual perfection rest on this. Concentration suggests 'freedom from' distraction. What distracts mental life is the 'unrest' caused by the continuous interaction between the various categories of dharmas, arising, staying and leaving due to the several causal relationships between the subject and the object.

The agitatedness in human being is because of the perceptual situations with colour, sound, etc.[96] and the sensitivities of the sense organs which are manifested to a person himself by a mass of bodily feeling and to others through certain visual and factual sense.[97] The technical term *Rūpa* is said to possess lightness (lahutā), pliability (mudutā), workability (kammaññata),[98] and a life of its own (jīvita)[99] and in Buddhism qualities are dynamic. Hence when we encounter the external, objective situation we deal not merely with 'bodies' or 'things' as such, but with concepts having a dynamic flux. When the external world exhibits such a flux, manas or mind receives the sense perception and discriminates from other objects 'developing toward a certain effect'.

It is again an energetic process that bridges the gulf between itself (mind) and the external object, the effect developing into unhealthy process, as accompanied by a joyous feeling... developing in and toward a healthy atmosphere and as accompanied by an indifferent feeling.[100] Such an inter related activity between the mind and the matter takes place due to karman, an energy inherent in every activity in the process. Hence suppressing this karman process is synonymous with suppressing the stream of constant flow of dharmas. This suppression (Absolute calm) is the reverse of agitatedness suggested by concentration.

Aṭṭhasālinī[101] defines concentration as 'absence of distraction' (avisāharā), 'non-confusedness' (avikkhepa) and 'non-dividedness' (avisāhatamānasatā) because concentration scatters and reverses the agitative and uncertainty processes and leads the whole attitude towards pointedness. The different stages in the process of concentration are vitarka,[102] a process of positing, implying examination leading upto judgement and decision; Vicāra,[103] a process by which all details are taken in and that all coexistent events and processes of the psyche are activated and involved; Prīti,[104] which makes both the function patterns (kāya) and the mental outlook (feeling) satisfied and quivering with exultation; Śukha,[105] a feeling (judgement) of pleasure imparted to both the function patterns (kāya) and the whole attitude of the individual (cetasika); and samadhi or Cittaikagrata,[106] 'one-objectness', directing one's whole being and whole mental operation (citta) towards one object (ekagga).

In such a process of concentration one acquires values like *śraddhā* (confidence and certitude), vīrya (energy), smṛti (recollection and inspection), samādhi (absorption) and prajña (analytical understanding). All these values becoming dominant, they subdue their opponents. In the constant flux and change, which characterize every living process these values acquire an intense energy or power (bala). The moral path propounded by the Buddha increases and intensifies this energy in the attainment of the goal, namely, Nirvāṇa.

PART- II TECHNICAL UNDERSTANDING OF DHARMA AND ADHARMA IN JAINA TRADITION

5.2.1. Meaning and Genesis of the concepts Dharma and Adharma

Dharma and Adharma are peculiar concepts in Jain Metaphysics. Unlike in Hindu thought where dharma and adharma refer to virtue and vice respectively, these terms carry special meaning concerning *movement* and *rest.* They suggest certain natural laws of the universe to work as a system in order. Prof. Chakravarti[107] says that the very system of the universe calls for the existence of dharma and adharma in establishing the Order of the universe. Certain scholars[108] have made the reasonable suggestion that these principles are traceable to an ancient notion of fluids flowing through the universe. Prof. Jacobi[109] contends that these terms originally had their natural meaning denoting subtle fluids, which caused merit and demerit.

Abhayadeva,[110] the famous commentator on the canonical literature of the Jains, explains both the terms dharma and adharma taking them to mean merit and demerit, as well as the medium of motion and rest respectively. Siddhasena Divākara[111] did not feel any necessity of including dharma and adharma into the sphere of Jain metaphysics. He thinks that it is due to prayoga (motion imparted by another object) and visrasa (motion imparted by itself) that an object moves or is at rest. But Pūjyapāda and Akalaṅka tried their best to establish the doctrine saying finally that it must be accepted, as it is the speech of the Omniscient One (Sarvajña).[112]

In the discussion whether dharma and adharma meant ethical or metaphysical categories there is also a suggestion that what these terms originally meant from a metaphysical standpoint later on developed into ethical categories. Dr. Harisatya Bhattacharya[113] says that there is a tendency to think that the metaphysical sense of dharma is its old and original significance, which has determined its ethical sense later on. He points out an example: Jīva as has a natural tendency to rise upward and *uddha-goi* dharma is the

Principle of motion, which helps the soul in this motion towards the blissful upper regions. But a soul is enacted to go upwards only doing good or pious deeds. Thus the word dharma which originally meant the principle that helps the soul in its motion came to signify a good or meritorious act. In the same way with Adharma, which is the principle helping the stoppage of a soul in this universe came to be identified with Pāpa or sinful acts which cause the continuance of the soul in saṁsāra.

5.2.2. The Nature and Significance of Dharma and Adharma:

1. Dharma and adharma are, first and foremost, substances (dravya): A substance is that which maintains its identity while manifesting its various qualities and modifications and which is not different from satta and it is called dravya.[114] This definition presents three distinct characteristics of a substance, namely, existence, modifications and qualities. On being asked by Indrabhūti, the foremost disciple of Mahāvīra, 'what is the nature of reality?' (Kimtattvam), Mahāvīra is reported to have at first answered origination and then after the same question was successively repeated, destruction and persistence.[115] Umasvāmi[116] defines it as possessing origination, decay and permanence. While *dhruvatva* signifies the static aspect of reality, called by various terms like being, identity, unity, oneness, continuance, statism etc.[117] *Utpāda* and *vyaya* refer to the dynamic aspects of reality. Thus nothing that is real can be thought of without the triple constituents of Utpāda, Vyaya and dhruva.[118] Hence Dharma and Adharma as substances possess these three characteristics.
2. Dharma and adharma belong to the Ajīva dravyas. This means that these substances do not possess conscious animation. They do not, in any way, animate themselves or other substances. This implies that their function is only to facilitate.
3. Dharma and adharma are Arūpi Ajīva. These two dravyas do not possess form like matter. Only matter or pudgala

among the Ajīvas is tangible. And they have none of the five sense qualities possessed by pudgala. Arūpi Ajīva are further subdivided in terms of dravya (substance), kṣetra (place) kāla (Time) and guṇa (Qualities): For instance, dharmāstikāya and adhamiāstikāya are substances; their place is the entire universe; with regard to time both are without beginning and without end as distinguished from pudgala; their nature is without colour, without smell, without taste, imperceptible to touch and without form; only their quality is distinct: dharma helps motion and adharma arrests motion.

4. Dharma is called the principle of motion and Adharma, the principle of rest. Puruṣārtha siddhyupāya[119] says that the whole universe would be at a standstill but for this substance (dharma) and without adharma the whole universe would be constantly moving.
5. The principle of movement (dharma-dravya) does not itself set the souls and material atoms in motion. Rather it provides the medium, the external efficient cause (Nimitta kāraṇa), through which movement can occur:[120] 'As water assists the movement of moving fish so adharma (assists the movement of moving) pudgala and jīva. But it does not move (pudgala and jīva which are) not moving.'[121] Jīva and pudgala have the capacity to move (the chief cause or the metrical cause: Upādāna kāraṇa), and yet they cannot realize this potential unless dharma dravya is present.
6. Similarly Adharma is the Principle of rest and it becomes an auxiliary cause of rest to the soul and matter.[122] Dravyasaṁgraha[123] gives an illustration: 'As shadow (assists the staying of) the traveler (so) adharma assists the staying of the pudgalas and Jīvas which are stationary. But that (i.e. adharma) does not hold back moving (Pudgalas and Jīvas).'
7. Both dharma-dravya and adharma-dravya are unitary substances which like Jīva, pudgala and Ākāsa, extend (*Astikāya*)[124] in space: in terms of uncountable (asaṁkhyāta) infinite number of space points[125] (*Pradeśa*)'. Dharma and adharma are known to be Astikāyas which means that they

are existent, real and are related to space by being in it. Another aspect of the Astikāyas is that they are all manifested in their changing modes and differing qualities. The most significant characteristic of astikāya is that it has existence and is also extensive.[126]

Since dharma and adharma are extensive in the space they occupy the 'space points' within Lokākāśa. It is only in Lokākāśa that movement or rest is possible and Alokākāśa refers to space in which these two dravyas along with Jīva and Pudgala are absent. Hence when a Jīva makes an attempt to move upwards, in its gradual stages of spiritual development (14 Guṇasthānas), it is able to do so through the assistance of Dharma. By gradually moving higher and higher the Jīva reaches the limits of Lokākāśa beyond which there is no dharma. Dravyasaṁgraha[127] says that the liberated Jīvas stay at of the top of Lokākāśa and, though possessing the characteristics of having an upward motion, they do not proceed further. It is only Lokākāśa that allows the substances dharma and adharma to penetrate itself.[128]

Dharma and adharma are coextensive with Lokākāśa because all these have innumerable 'spacepoints' The predeśa or the spacepoints of dharma and adharma are beyond calculation because they can pervade all parts of the universe (Lokākāśa) as oil pervades the whole portion of mustard seed.[129]

5.2.3. Implications of dharma and adharma

Although dharma and adharma have distinct meaning and characteristics from other substances in Jain metaphysics these when they are related to other metaphysical categories, yield ample reflections. Dharma and adharma are thrown, as it were, in the space (Lokākāśa) so extensively as to hold in them the innumerable Jīvas and material substances (pudgala) like fishes in water-pond.

The relationship between Jīva and Pudgala results in karma formation within the universe (Lokākāśa) in the course of time (kāla) assisted by movement and rest (dharma and adharma). Karma is a kind of matter (karma pudgala), a subtle fine matter imperceptible to the senses which enters into the soul and causes great change in it. It produces in the soul certain conditions.[130] This fine matter which can become Karman fills the whole cosmos. The soul has *Vīrya* or infinite capacity for activity and this characteristic causes the movement of the particles or attracts the matter which is necessary for the body, the organ of speech and manas, change into specific essence of these organs, and finally, emits it again because it continually conveys matter to the soul. It is the chief cause (Upādāna kāraṇa) of the assimilation of new Karma. Salvation is therefore only possible, if every activity of body, mind and speech (yoga) has disappeared.[131] Dharma and adharma in their movement and rest are supplying the auxiliary cause (nimitta kāraṇa).[132]

Thus the relation between Jīva and Karmapudgada is made actual in the very presence and help of Dharma and adharma. If Karma is understood as the dynamic element in the path of purification by which bondage occurs, mokṣa is another similar dynamic process of the gradual resting of Karma flow into the soul. The implication is that the process of bondage and release described in the process of Āsrava (inflow of Karman), Saṁvara (stoppage of karman) and Nirjarā (purifying the accumulated karman) is fundamentally due to the process of movement and rest. In other words, Āsrava and Nirjarā, which happen because of the inflow and out-flow of karma particles, represent the two dynamic categories, movement. This means that the life of the embodied beings (Saṁsāri Jīva) from one sense to five senses with their limited knowledge (they are yet to attain Sarvajña or Omniscience) are conditioned in every way and move about in the worlds of existence (the four gatis).

The doctrine of Karma involves the idea of an eternal metaphysics.[133] Actions performed anew must be expiated in future life and hence the migration of the souls continues without end. The matter that has penetrated into the jiva in the form of certain karman-species (Bandha) exist in potential (Satta) from the moment of its annihilation to the moment of realization (Udaya),[134] The unrealized, latent karmas are the causes of the future existence. Thus the Saṁsāri jīva (worldly soul) migrates from existence to existence until through spiritual development it exhausts all Karman.[135] Dharma and adharma again, facilitate the migration of the souls from existence to existence and their rest. Since dharma and adharma are spread in all the three worlds (the ūrdhvaloka, and madhyaloka and the adhamaloka), the jīvas existing in all these three realms experience the support of movement and rest.

Pertinent in this context is the concept of fourteen guṇasthānas, the stages of spiritual development. The guṇasthānas refer not to the chronological order but to the qualitative state of a soul in its spiritual development. The soul gets purified in the gradual and intensive manner that it sheds karma as it climbs the stairs of spiritual hierarchy. This is also being described as the soul becoming lighter and lighter because of the shedding of the material karma burden and finally rises to the top of the universe to enjoy the free state. Thus the movement upwards of the soul takes place as it climbs the stairs of spiritual perfection. Relating Jain cosmography (the shape of the universe conceived as flat and in a straight line) to the guṇathānas, the bottom of the world (the pātāla loka) weighs down with the burden of inauspicious Karma and as one goes upwards to the top of the world the soul gradually sheds such a burden. Although dharma and adharma do not directly cause the movement or rest of souls and material substances they do play important roles in the jīva's life towards perfection.

The moral discipline is closely linked with the shedding of karma. The two categories of Jain metaphysics, namely. Pāpa and Puṇya (virtue and vice) are symbolic of Karma accumulation. Activities, even if they are spiritual, bind the soul with karman. This is fundamental in Jain philosophy. Karma, both good as well as bad bind the soul. Accumulation of good karma may help the soul in achieving a better status, which means a higher stage in the spiritual development, but mokṣa is possible only when complete shedding of Karma takes place. The whole process of moral and spiritual discipline is possible only when assisted by dharma and adharma. In short, the whole dynamics of conversion from the state of bondage to the state of release (with necessary moral and spiritual attitudes and activities) is being facilitated by the dynamic presence of dharma and adharma. As the wheel, the stick, etc. are the necessary auxiliary cause in the making of the pot though mud is its material cause, dharma and adharma are necessary for jiva and the material substances. Dharma and adharma provide dynamism to the whole process.

PART-III COMPARATIVE ANALYSIS OF BAUDDHA *DHAMMA* AND JAINA *DHARMA AND ADHARMA*

Studying the above-mentioned things concerning dharma or dhamma from the Buddhist and dharma and adharma from the Jaina perspective, the following differences and similarities are seen.

5.3.1. Differences

1. Dharma or dhamma in Buddhist terminology refers to the ultimate constituent of existence or an element with distinct nature and function. Jain dharma refers to the medium of motion and, adharma, to the medium of rest.
2. Buddhist dharma is divided into different categories from different standpoints; for instance, into 5 Skandhas, 12 Āyatanas and 18 Dhātus, all referring in some way to the reality of existence. But there is no such classification with regard to Jain Dharma or Adharma. But the latter could be described in terms of dravya (substance), kṣetra (place), kāla (time) and guṇa (quality). They are substances, spread out everywhere with regard to place and eternal with respect to time. But they have distinct functions of motion and of rest with respect of qualities.
3. Every dharma in Buddhist tradition arises out of Karma (past action), thoughts, energy and Nutrition and each category of dharma (according to Skandha, Āyatana and Dhātu) has distinct nature and they do not mix with one another. Thus *Nāma* and *Rūpa* have distinct characteristics and one does not become the other. The material elements

and the mental elements remain separate but dependent on one another by causal connections in a series of flow constituting existence. In other words, dharmas are active in their characteristics. Jain dharma and adharma do not possess such characteristics. They are merely 'passive' substances facilitating movement and rest. They do not possess 'active energy' to move other substances like Jiva or Pudgala. It is only Jīva and not harma or adharma in Jain metaphysics, which has vīrya or energy. It is due to the characteristic mark of activity of Jīva that fine matter particles have a flow into Jiva in order to form the karmaprakṛtis.

4. The whole of existence is reduced to dharmas in the Buddhist tradition. Dhammas constitute the physical and the non- material worlds whether it be karma dhātu (the sensory plane), or rūpa dhātu (the form plane) or arūpa dhātu (the formless plane). The Jain dharma and adharma themselves are different substances and they do not constitute the whole phenomenal existence. They are spread out in all the three worlds of Jain cosmology (the ūrdhva loka, the madhya loka, and the adhama loka) holding, as it were, in their laps, other substances like souls and material substances.
5. Buddhist dharma consists of material and non-material dharmas. They are all included in the five skandhas (dhammas of matter, dhammas of sensation, dhammas of feelings, dhammas of volition and dhammas of consciousness). Since none of these dhammas have a subsisting substratum (they are all devoid of any substance), the distinction between material and mental dhammas disappears. In Jain metaphysics dharma and adharma are Ajīva dravyas i.e. inanimate substances and hence there is no conscious element in dharma and adharma as in the case of manodhatu or immaterial element of Buddhist reals. The only animate being in Jain metaphysics in the Jīva or the Soul. There is no such thing as animate dharma or adharma in Jain reality.
6. The fundamental difference between Buddhist dhamma and Jain dharma and adharma is that Buddhist dhamma is not

a substance, though real. The dhammas are said to be momentary evanescent and changing states. There is no substantial presence of a stranger, called god or the self. All phenomenon of existence is a stream of flow of dhammas, causally connected, which presents an apparent static, permanent state. In Jain metaphysics what is permanent and substantial is the six dravyas or substances including Dharma and Adharma. The animate or the inanimate substances do not fundamentally change. But changes occur in their modifications (Paryāya) and qualities (guṇa). But in both Buddhism as well in Jainism the changes are real. In Jain metaphysics dharma and adharma are called Astikāya with the characteristic marks of existence and extension.

7. Subsequently, there is no transmigration of dhammas in the Buddhist tradition. There is no substantial thing in the dhammas that transmigrates but the residue or the vāsana of the whole series precedent to the present dharma is being borne by the latter. This residue or vāsana has a binding effect but the person has no control over it. The fresh activity (body, speech, and mind) generates new atoms, which would carry not only the fresh kamma but also the resultant of all that preceded. Buddhism accepts karma and rebirth without transmigration of any substance. This is not the case in Jainism. It is the saṁsāri Jīva (the worldly soul) which carries the karma from birth to birth until the final liberation. The saṁsāri jīva is the only animate substance, which undergoes transmigration.

   Although Pudgala, Dharma, Adharma, Ākāśa and Kāla are also substances they are inanimate and they do not transmigrate yet changes are found in all dravyas. But nobody can deny that transmigration takes place due to karma-formation and karma-formation cannot take place unless the soul is related to pudgala, Dharma, Adharma, Ākāśa and Kāla. It is due to the interrelations and inter-dependence between jīva, the animate substance, and ajīva, the inanimate substance (which comprises of pudgala, etc.) that karma-formation takes place. For instance, the presence of material substances (pudgala) produces passions (kaṣāyas) in the soul due to which the fine-matter particles flow into the soul and form themselves as karma particles. Dharma and adharma facilitate movement and rest of such particles. It takes place in lokakasa and in time. Hence transmigration of Jīva in Jain tradition directly as well as indirectly depend on other dravyas like dharma, adharma, etc.

8. Dharmas in Buddhist tradition are affected by moral, immoral and non-moral (indifferent, inoperative) activities. Conversely, you can not think of any activity without dhammas. Hence activity is synonymous with the flow of dhammas. The Buddhist goal of Nirvāṇa aims at the complete cessation of all dhammas. Hence the Eight-fold path of the Buddha, all moral and spiritual discipline, are aimed at the total rest of chaotic elements. Freedom from unrest or chaos of dhammas is synonymous with Nirvāṇa.

In Jain tradition dharma and adharma neither move themselves nor move Jīvas and pudgalas. Their presence is everywhere in the lokākāśa and eternally. There is nothing that could reverse their laws or systems. The unrest is said to take place in Jīva in contact with pudgala. Hence we can say that Buddhist dhamma is, to that extent, synonymous with Jain Jīva (In Buddhist tradition existence, including Jīva, is constituted by 72 dhammas). All moral and spiritual disciplines undertaken by the Jains are towards the only aim of Mokṣa, complete liberation from Karma. But moral, immoral and indifferent activities do not depend on dharma or adharma in a direct manner. The higher development of spirituality and the subsequent movement of the soul in the upward direction (ūrdhva gati) is facilitated by Dharma. Total rest is possible only at the higher spiritual stage called Siddhahood! But the liberated soul (Mukta jīva) is still active. The fullness of energy virya or activity can be achieved only in the highest state of development. It is a paradox to call it a state of complete rest (as in Buddhist understanding of Nirvāṇa), but rest in the sense of freedom caused by the shedding of the Karma.

5.3.2. Similarities

1. Dhammas in Buddhist tradition is real but non-substantial scene, and they are not perceptible to the senses. Dharma and Adharma in Jain tradition are unitary substances, which have existence with extension and not perceptible to the senses.
2. Dhammas constitute three realms of the universe (kāma, rūpa and arūpa dhātus). Dharma and adharma in Jain metaphysics pervade the whole universe (in the three lokas). While dhammas are constitutive of the three realms, dharma and adharma are two of the six substances, which have separate existences.
3. Dhammas are dependent on one another in the constant stream but they do not mix with one another. They retain their identity. 24 causal relations link them. Dharma and adharma, though independent substances in Jain metaphysics, are linked to other substances like jīva and pudgala in their activities. Jīva and pudgala depend on dharma and adharma as nimitta kāraṇa or auxiliary causes for their movement and rest.
4. Buddhist dhamma and the Jain dharma and adharma are related to the doctrine of Kamma or Karma and the doctrine of Nirvāṇa or Mokṣa. New dhamma as a momentary element appearing in the series bears the burden of the vasanas of past dhammas. It bears the resultant forces of all that preceded. Any activity with passion produces new dhammas with moral and immoral results. The resultant Karma could be latent or apparent as the case may be. Until all karmas are exhausted the series of flow of dhammas continue. In this case birth and death are not new beginning and end. They form part of the series.

Buddhist tradition treats dhamma as equivalent to duhkha and kamma. The unrest created by the flow of dhammas - i.e. kamma at work - has to be stopped by some means. Thus dhamma is not merely linked to kamma but also to Nirvāṇa. The moral path propounded by Buddha, particularly

Prajñā or wisdom, helps in the stoppage of the flow of dhammas. Morality and ethical courses will be futile and irrelevant without fulfilling this aim, namely, the stoppage of the flow of dhammas.

In Jain tradition the karma formation takes place due to the entry of fine matter particles (karma pudgala) into the soul due to various causes like activity. The dynamic forces Dharma and Adharma facilitate in their movement and rest. In this way the two media of motion and of rest are associated with Jīva and Pudgala in the karma-formation. In Jain metaphysics Āsrava brings about bondage and saṁvarā and nirjara lead the soul towards its release. The moral discipline and the spiritual steps prescribed for release are ultimately to stop the flow of karma particles and to clear the already accumulated karmas. As dharma and adharma are associated with the inflow of karmas they are also be associated with the complete shedding of karmas, namely, Release or Mokṣa. Any process involving movement and rest is not possible without dharma and adharma. Thus dharma and adharma are related to the salvation history of the soul.

Notes

1. Aṭṭhasālinī III, 488 as qrpted in Guenther, p.2. No.1
2. Ibid 1.3; III, 304, 484, 486, 488
3. Pruden Vol. 1, p.56, Pruden gives a long list of defintion of Abhidharma as formed in the Buddhist Pali Canon, pp. xxxii -xxxiv
4. Ibid., p.57; Chaudhuri, p.70
5. Aṭṭasālinī I.44 as quoted in Guenther, p.3, No.1
6. Guenther, p.3
7. Guenther, p.86
8. Mahāvagga, i.23.as quoted by Stcherbatsky, p.3
9. Warren, H.C. Buddhism in Translations, p.84 'When to the strenuous, meditative Brahman, There came to light the elements of being, Then Vanish all his double and eager questions, what time he knows The Elements have causes... what time he knows How causes Have an Ending'.
10. Abhidarmakoṣa, ii. Tib. text; p.3, 11.12-13; Stcherbatsky, p.3

11. Theragāthā, 1255, Stcherbatsky, p.3
12. Pruden, Vol I, P.57
13. Ibid., p.76
14. Jayasuria, p.17
15. Pruden, op.cit., p.108-109
16. Ibid., p.86
17. Ibid., p.245
18. Ibid., p.255
19. Ibid., p.308
20. Ibid., p.306f
21. Ibid., p.291
22. Ibid., p.308
23. Ibid., p.272-273
24. Ibid., p.155
25. Ibid., p.130
26. Ibid., p.73
27. Waren, H.C. p.251, 'In considering the factors of being in the light of their lack of an Ego....'
28. Ibid., p.251. In considering the factor of being in the light of their transitoriness, what is the knowledge of truth thus achieved? Wherein consists correct insight ? How does it become plain that all the constituents of being are transitory ? Where is doubt abandoned?
29. Ibid., p.166 this is known as the middle doctrine between 'that things being' the 'that things have no being'
30. Ibid., p.149, the illustration of the 'light burning through the night' how element of being join one and there in serial succession.
31. Ibid., p.266-7, This unrest or agitaion is beautifully protrayed in the verse: 'while eagerly man culls life's flowers, with all his faculties intent, of pleasure still insatiate – Death comes and overpowereth him.' The Tathāgata exclaims 'when will ever get free from misery.'
32. Full connotation of the term Dharma has been treated by Rhys Davids, pp.97-104; Warren, pp.116, 209; Aung, S.Z. p.179n and pp.254-9; S. Levi, Sūtrālaṅkāra , 17, 21
33. Refutation of the theory of the soul, Chaudhuri, pp.132-133
34. Stcherbatsky, Soul theory of the Buddhists, p.836
35. Ibid., op.cit., p.27
36. Ibid., p.38.
37. 'Asmin sati idam bhavati'-Abhidharmakoṣa. iii.18 and 28. cf. also in ii.47, 50.; Stcherbatsky, p.28
38. Upādāna Skandha, cf. Abhidharmakoṣa 1.7, p.42
39. Warren, pp.84 166 Through the Doctrine of Dependent Origination the Blesed One enunciates the entire aggregation of misery and causes. The dependency or the conditioning in the total unrest of elements is misery. pp.368-369. The Blesed One instructs about the noble truth of misery:

Birth, old age, disease, death, sorrow, lamentaion, misery , grief and despair are misery... Bodily misery, mental misery ... all the five attachment group are misery. All these indicate the unrest of elements.

40. Abhidharmakoṣa, 1.2. Stcherbatsky, p.50. On 'Bhavana' see Chaudhuri, p.176f
41. Pruden, op.cit., p.207. No one possesses the dharmas of another. No one possesses the dharmas which are not of a living being.
42. Stcherbatsky, op.cit.p.7
43. Ibid., p.6-7. The Skandhas carry on the functions of the world, Chaudhuri, p.80
44. Stcherbatsky, op.cit. pp.7-8; Chaudhuri, p.81 Āyatana signifies 'gate of entry' 'gate of arising' of the mind and of the mental states. See Pruden, p.77-78
45. Stcherbatsky, p.9; Chaudhuri, p.81; 'Dhātu' signifies gotra, race, lineage. See Pruden, p.77-78
46. Stcherbatsky, p.10
47. Ibid., p.49. 'Sāsrava' and 'Anāsrava'- Abhidharmakorṣa i.3; Chaudhuri, p.70
48. Warren, H.C. op.cit. p.245.
49. Abhidharmakoṣabhāsyam, tr. Pruden, op.cit.vol.I, p.70
50. Ibid., p.90
51. Chaudhuri, p.71; Complete list in pp.98a-b
52. Ibid., p.62
53. Ibid., p.188, 238
54. Ibid., p.278
55. Ibid., p.76
56. Ibid., p.184
57. Ibid., p.62-64
58. Ibid., p.278
59. Ibid., p.302
60. Ibid., p.295
61. Ibid., p.154
62. Ibid., p.273
63. Ibid., p.274
64. Ibid., p.269, 210
65. Ibid., p.257
66. Ibid., p.206
67. Ibid., p.189
68. Ibid., p.191
69. Ibid., p.257
70. Ibid., p.263
71. Paramo uttamo aviparito attho paramattho: The term Parmattha means the highest, essence, ultimate, non changing nature. Jayasuria, op.cit. p.3

72. Table of classification of primary elements, Jayasuria op.cit.p.80, note.3; Table of clasification of Secondary Elements, Ibid., p.82, Table of classification of thoughts, Ibid., p.32
73. Jayasuriya, p.14, Note.1. The relations are called the Dependence and the Disociation Relations.
74. Ibid., p.19
75. Ibid., p.22, more details on pp.128-131
76. Ibid., p.68
77. Ibid., p.80
78. Ibid., p.88
79. Ibid., p.81
80. Ibid., p.81-82
81. 'Vanato nikkantam nibbānaṁ': Nibbāna is the nature of being freed from the cravings or Vāna. Again 'Sāntilakkhanaṁ nibbānaṁ': Nibbāna is that which has tranquility as its characteristic. Ibid., p.94, Note. 2
82. ibid., p.131. Dr. Jayasuriya presents a number of causal relations between Mind to mind, Mind to mind and matter, Mind to matter, Matter to Mind, concepts, mind and matter to Mind, Mind and Matter to mind and matter.
83. Aṭṭhaśālini, iii. 3., Guenther, op.cit., p.12.
84. Ibid., iii.43, Guenther, p.13.
85. Poussin's trans. of the Abhidharmakoṣabhāṣyam Ch.II, verse 34.
86. Guenther, pp.12, 30-31.
87. Aṭṭhaśālini, iii.26, Guenther, p.6.
88. Ibid., iii. 177, Guenther, p.32.
89. Ibid., iii. 179, Guenther, p.33.
90. Ibid., iii. 183, Guenther, p.36.
91. Ibid., iii. 184, Guenther, p.37.
92. Ibid., iii. 188, Guenther, p.39.
93. Ibid., iii. 190, Guenther, p.42.
94. Ibid., iii. 540.
95. Ibid., iii. 546, Guenther, p.94.
96. Ibid., iv. 2, 3, Guenther, p.145-146.
97. Ibid., iv. 26, Guenther, p.152.
98. Ibid., iv. 77-78, Guenther, p. 163.
99. Ibid., iv. 67, Guenther, p.163.
100. Viśuddhimagga xiv, 119, Guenther, p.24.
101. Aṭṭhaśālini, iii. 282, Guenther, p.60.
102. Ibid., iii. 198, Guenther, p.50.
103. Ibid., iii. 199-200, Guenther, p.50.
104. Ibid., iii. 202, Guenther, p.52.
105. Ibid., iii. 208, Guenther, p.53.
106. Ibid., iii. 211, Guenther, p.57.
107. IHQ, Vol. ix, no. 3, p. 292.

108. Dr. B.N. Seal makes dharma somewhat like the preestablished Harmony of Leibnitz, ("Positive Sciences of the Ancient Hidus", See Dharma Saṁgraha, SBJ, Vol. 4, pp.1,9). Adhrama is compared with the law of Newton's gravitation. See Chakravarti, p.96. Dharma is said as an all pervading, non-atomic medium, circulating internally as a perfect fluid and possessing a tremendous velocity comparable to that of light. IHQ, Vol. ix, No.3, p.793
109. SBE, Vol. XLV, p.xxxiv, see also note Dharma and Adharma are treated in crisp manner in Utt Sūtra, SBE, Vol. XLV, pp.153-154 and 207-208
110. IHQ vol. ix no.3, p.793
111. IHQ vol. ix no.3, p.793
112. IHQ vol. ix no.3, p.794
113. Jaina Gazette, Vol. xxii, p.290
114. Pañcāstikāya, 8
115. Padmarajiah, p.127
116. Tat Sūtra, v.29
117. Padmarajiah, p.127
118. Gopalan, p.123
119. Pur Sid, 22; Comm. by Amrtachandrasuṛi, SBJ. Vol. 4, p.18
120. Jaini, P.S., p. 99
121. Dravyasaṁgraha, 17. In all works of Jaina Literature, we have nearly the same illustration given of Dharma. The illustration is as follows: As fish moves in the water, without being impelled in their movement by water, but only receiving assistance of the water in their movement, so pudgala and jīva move, assisted by dharma, but not impelled by it. Dharma has no form, i.e. eternal and void of activity. See Vardamāna Purāṇa by Sakala Kirti, Canto xvi, verse 29; Pañcāstikāya Samayasāra, verse 85; Tattvārthasāra by Amṛtacandra Sūri, 3.33.34; Dharmasarmābhydayam, 21-83 and Candraprabhācaritam 18-69-70 See Ghoshal. pp.52-54).
122. Niyamasāra, 30 SBJ. Vol 9
123. Dravyasaṁgraha, 18. The following examples are invariably found in all Jaina works illustrating Adharma. First, Adharma is likened to earth which does not stop creatures form moving but becomes a support of them when they are at rest. Secondly, Adharma is said to be like shaddow which does not forcibly stop the travellers scorched by the rays of the sun from moving, but assists in their rest while they on their own accord come to sit in the shade. Dharmasarmābhyudayam, xxi.84; Tattvārthasāra, iii, 35-36; Candraprabhācaritam, Canto xviii, Verse 71.As quoyed in Ghoshal, p. 55.
124. 'As these exist. They are called 'Asti' and because (they have) many pradeśas, like bodies, therfore (they are called) kāyas (Hence they are called) Astikāyas.' Dravyasaṁgraha, 24

125. 'Paradisyanta iti pradesah' paramanuh! Yavatiksetre Vya as pradeśa iti Vyavahriyate- Sarvārthasiddhi, 541, as quoted in Stevenson, p.98
126. Dravyasaṁgraha, 24
127. Ibid., p.14
128. Ibid., 20, also see Ghoshal, p.57
129. Tattvārthasāra, 3.14.23, See Ghoshal, p.67
130. Glasenapp, H.S., p3
131. Ibid., p.45
132. Niyamasāra, 30, SBJ, Vol IX
133. Glasenapp, H.V., p.xi
134. Bandha, Udaya and Satta as explained in the Karmagranthas, ibid., p.28
135. Ibid., pp.65-66 The spiritual development is attained by 6 means: gupti (control), samiti (carefulness), dharma (the 10 duties), bhāvanā or anuprekṣā (12 reflections), parīṣahā (endurance of 22 trobles), cāritra (5 degreses of conduct). The last included 'tapas', both internal and external austerity. From the point of view of Darśana, it is the gradual process from mithyatva to sarvajña, ibid., pp. 49-50

CHAPTER VI

CONTEMPORARY RELEVANCE OF ŚRAMAṆA DHARMA

PART-1 THE PHENOMENON OF VIOLENCE: EVIL AND ITS REMEDIES

6.1.1. Introduction

Religion gives meaning to society. It operates from ultimate perspectives, in terms of end or goal of life. It does not provide merely an abstract creed as a set of beliefs, but offers at the level of behaviour certain ethical principles through which the believing community seeks to reach the proposed goals. It is the task of religion to orient the whole of life, the common good of humanity, etc.

Religion and society shape each other in history. Society, its cultural and other changes might affect the external structure of any Religion. There might be adaptations, even renewals. For instance, religions like Buddhism and Christianity had adapted local cultural and traditional elements. But this does not mean that the basic outlook of Buddhism or Christianity have changed due to changes in cultures and traditions. The central figures of these religions, their worship, adherence to their precepts, etc. have by and large remained the same in history. It is such 'changeless' elements that offer 'newness' to life everywhere.

There is a basic ethos in Śramaṇa culture and thought. Buddhism may not believe in a permanent substance called Ātman, but it believes in karma and rebirth, the ills of the world and of the human beings, their remedy, etc. In the same way, Jain Dharma upholds the sanctity of life and urges its promotion and protection. These Śramaṇa traditions are realistic about the existence of misery and its root cause, propound a path of purification and deliverance from all that is evil and all that is limiting.

These Śramaṇa religions have recourse to conduct as the major means of liberation. Of all moral principles, Ahiṁsā or non-injury to life is the focal point round which the whole gamut of religion and philosophy is built. Without this there is no life, no existence. In other words, it is this moral principle of Ahiṁsā that describes briefly these Śramaṇa religions - *Jainism is sometimes called 'the Religion of Ahiṁsa'*. It is Ahiṁsā that guides both at the level of conduct as well as ideas and reflection. Down the centuries, Ahiṁsā has acquired new meanings, particularly in the social and political planes. Persons like M. K. Gandhi have translated this concept into every sphere of life.

The Śramaṇa religions believe that it is hiṁsā or injury to life, which is the root cause of all ills in this world. Hence they offer Ahiṁsā as the method and means to revert this situation. The following pages roughly portray the ugly situation life is drawn into, and how the Śramaṇa religions offer a suitable remedy to such a situation.

6.1.2. The ugly face of the human situation:

The human predicament especially in India can be broadly characterized by inequality, poverty and religious and cultural (ethnic, lingual...) fundamentalism. The caste discrimination is a strong impediment to the development of the individual and society. The prevailing injustice in the agricultural sector in land ownership and illiteracy, the degrading economic scene, the problem of inflation, inequality in income distribution. Black money, the social injustices done to women and children, the dowry system, child labour, juvenile delinquency, gender discrimination in family and society and many others are basically the outcome of inequality both at the conceptual as well as at the actual levels.

6.1.2.1. Poverty and inequality:

What gives a low profile and an unstable condition to an individual is the thought that one is poor. Not only that poverty affects the development of personality it also leads, because of inadequate resources, to illness, mobility and mortality. The culture of poverty suffocates the breath of hope and confidence in living. The economically poor realize a sense of the improbability of achieving success in terms of values and goals of the larger society.

Inequality, caste discrimination and poverty give birth to categories like the untouchables and the evil called untouchability. In the words of M.K. Gandhi: Socially, they (the untouchables) are lepers, economically they are worse than slaves. Religiously they are denied entrance to places we miscall 'houses of God'. They are denied the use, on the same terms as the caste Hindus, of public roads, public schools, public hospitals, public wells, public taps, public parks and the like. In some cases their approach within the measured distance is a social crime, and in some other rare enough cases their very sight is an offence. They are relegated for their residence to the worst quarters of cities and villages where they practically get no social service. Caste Hindu lawyers and doctors will not serve them as they do other members of society. Brahmans will not officiate at their religious function.'[1]

To abolish this inhuman practice, the Government had given a number of provisions in the Constitutions and had undertaken necessary steps.[2] For instances, the abolition of untouchability (article 17, constitution of India); appointment of a minister in charge of the scheduled castes in some states (article 164); reservation of seats in the Loksabha (article 330) and in the Legislative Assembly in every state and union territory (article332); safeguards for the claims of the member of scheduled castes while making appointments to the Central and State Government jobs (article 335); appointment of a special officer to take care of the interests of the scheduled castes (article 338) and in pursuance of these provisions, the parliament and the State Legislatures have enacted numerous laws but India has suffered, to this day, blame from global community.

6.1.2.2. Environmental degradation:

Another area of concern is the environment and the people who are affected by it directly. Nature and humans are so close to each other for mutual existence and sustenance. Only by acting on nature can man develop his drives and abilities. Humans appropriate more and more of nature making it the object of their knowing, feeling and acting, by adapting objects of nature to satisfy their various needs. They transform it into material inorganic body that is to say, nature excluding the human body itself. To say that humans live from nature means that nature is their body with which they remain in a continuous interchange in order not to die.[3]

But the growing menace of pollution of nature is like stripping the mother goddess naked and insulting her. For instances, the spoiling of water resources like rivers, ponds, lakes and even oceans and the poisoning of the atmosphere with chemicals because of the high concentration of industries and factories, the throwing out of the garbage and solid wastes anywhere at people's convenience, the high level noise specially in urban areas that harms the human nervous system, the petrol and diesel fumes from vehicles which affect even some sensitive plants like tobacco, potato and some cereal crops and certain flowers, etc. are but some of the results of the pollution menace.[4] Such pollution harm life in general.

The problem that the environmental science faces today is the preservation of its forest assets. Deforestation is not merely an ecological problem but a problem of human beings. The human element gives meaning to ecology and the environmental question becomes relevant to society only when it is viewed in relation to the people who are affected by it.[5] The environmental destruction has led to the intensification of poverty and destitution of the forest dwellers by way of non-availability of food, fuel, fodder, fertilizer and construction material, non-availability of medical herbs, etc. An increase in the reserve forests that cater to the needs of industry has deprived the forest dwellers very much. And those who are displaced and uprooted from their homeland due to natural calamity and planned destruction of forests.

While the social cost in such a despicable condition is being ignored, the material side of the scene is still worse, namely, floods, droughts, sedimentation and other forms of ecological damage like soil erosion, wind and water erosion etc. Food and droughts follow as a natural consequence to soil erosion since water does not seep into the soil and the ground water level goes down. Increased salutation and rise in the level of rivers, reservoirs and dams results in the reduction both with capacity of the dam to hold back heavy flood waters and in its irrigation potential. A result of the salutation of the major dams is floods that ravage the country every year.[6]

6.1.2.3. Problem of fundamentalism:

One of the foremost problems that India faces today is religious fundamentalism. Basically fundamentalism is a defect in attitude. We often do not know the faiths of other believes and their practices. This type of ignorance sometimes leads us to petty quarrels, fights and other harmful relationships. At times it takes the form of a tolerance which almost negates the other or, at the most, have nothing to do with the other. Such an attitude does not lead one to a healthy encounter. It sabotages seriousness in mutual learning and relationship. To the extent one affirms one's own faith or ideology to be the only truth there is not much of an opening to healthy encounters. Fundamentalism is a form of closure. The eyes are turned inside and there is a refusal to see the world at large.

Dr. Michael Amaladoss[7] points out that fundamentalism can go to the extent of creating a state religion. It is seen widespread in the world today. While fundamentalism often refers to religious fundamentalism, it is also seen in other spheres of life like politics where political ideologies do not make easy way to encounter the rest. Today inter-religious or even inter-political dialogue is useful and necessary not merely to come to know the other better and to dispel prejudices, etc. but also for a healthy collaboration between religious communities and political parties in order to promote common humanity based on justice and freedom.

6.1.3. Evil and its root cause:

Indian philosophical and religious traditions have reflected on the causes of such a situation and have also offered suitable remedies. Nirvāṇa or Mokṣa is a stage of life where one experiences cessation from pain, from birth, from ignorance, from karma, etc. Religious scriptures affirm that liberation is a state of good after overcoming evil. Now one cannot find solution to evil unless one is aware of the root cause for it.

The root cause of all evil according to Jain and Buddhist traditions is violence to life (hiṁsa). According to the Jain tradition, ignorance (abodhi) and carelessness (pramāda) cause violence. Ignorance is with respect to right knowledge, right vision and right conduct and carelessness is by way of certain types of activities, like alcohol, sensual pleasures, the passions, sleep and unprofitable conversation.[8] Hence Mahāvīra preached discrimination (viveka) and renunciation (vairāgya).

Buddhism too acknowledges that it is the passionate heart, which is the primary cause of evil. Many Buddhist schools of thought like the Theravādins, Sarvāstivādins and the Yogācāra schools term these following six as the morally defiling passions (kilesa): greed (lobha), hatred (doṣa), delusion (moha), conceit (māna), speculative views or heresy (ditthi) and doubt or uncertainty (vicikkiccha). To these are usually added mental idleness (thina), boastfulness (iddhacca), shamelessness (ahirika) and hardness of heart (anottappa).[9] Milindapanha too confirms this.[10] All these amount to a foundational cause known in Buddhist term as desire (tṛṣṇa) and, in Jain traditions, passion (kaṣāya).

Indian philosophical and religious traditions assert that the root cause of all evil is the desire to be and the desire to have. Having weighed life experiences, the Śramaṇa sages have come to the conclusion that the outcome of all existence is pain and suffering. Hence Nirvāṇa or Mokṣa would primarily mean cessation from all suffering. Early Buddhist and Jain traditions therefore sought to practise good conduct and penance in order to achieve this goal. The personal effort in achieving this end is seen in the Hīnayāna ideal of the Arhat, which later got developed into a collective social meaning found in the Bodhisattva ideal in the Mahāyāna tradition. But it has often remained primarily a personal endeavour in both these traditions.

The root of desire is again traced to egotism or ahaṁbhāva or the I-ness. This attitude expresses itself in acts of violence in order to gratify oneself, such as act of grabbing, retaining, etc. In Jain tradition, the intrinsic nature or svabhāva of the Soul (Ātman or Jīva) is pure consciousness and it has nothing to do with all others like egotism, desire, passions, activities, relations, etc. and they are extraneous to it.[11] And hence realization of the true self is not possible without abstinence from all passions and, subsequently, from all forms of violence. We could see this type of extreme ascetic life in a Jain monk. In the Buddhist tradition, Buddha chose a middle path by avoiding both extremes of luxury and austerity. A Bodhisattva takes hardships upon himself (an act of self-suffering and infliction of violence to oneself) in order to remove the pain and ensure salvation to others.[12] Both the systems recognize hiṁsā or injury to life as the ultimate cause of all evils and hence lay stress on personal and collective morality to overcome it.

Suffering, pain, etc. are forms of violence. Inequality results in caste/class discrimination, unequal income distribution, environmental disasters and ecological imbalances. All these are but a few manifestations of violence to life (Jīva hiṁsā). Jain metaphysics believes in the pluralism and equality of Jīva.[13] Life may show itself in a variety of forms. But life-as-such is the same in each living being. The plurality of Jīva manifests itself in many spheres of life. But the individuality of a being, be it a plant, or an animal or a human being or a higher spirit has to be acknowledged and respected. The intrinsic capacity or value of life (Jīva) is beyond bounds. The Jain system proclaims that any form of violence done to any living organism is ultimately violence done to oneself.

6.1.4. The phenomenon called 'violence':

Ācārāṅgasūtra, one of the earliest Jain Canon expounds the phenomenon of violence in these terms: 'the (living) world is afflicted, miserable, difficult to instruct and without discrimination. In this world full of pain, suffering by their different acts, see the benighted ones cause great pain.'[14] The very first Sermon of Buddha in the Deer Park has all the elements of maitrī and karuṇā[15] and at the same time the 4 Noble Truths lay stress on pain and suffering as results of violence.

Prof. Das Gupta contends that both Jainism and Buddhism appear to have arisen out of a reaction against the sacrificial discipline of the Brāhmaṇas marked by a strong aversion to the taking of animal life and against the practice of animal sacrifice.[16] Whatever may be the context in which these traditions evolved, the phenomenon of violence and the consequent stress on Ahiṁsā have been the hallmark of their attitude, religiosity and moral life down the centuries.

6.1.4.1. Meaning of violence:

Violence is understood as malevolence, hatred vengeance, enmity, murder, injury, war, cruelty, barbarity, torture, deception, rape, exploitation and so on. Praśnavyākaraṇa[17] gives nearly thirty Prākrit equivalents or synonyms to the word hiṁsā. Of these the following are considered important: destruction of life forces (prāṇavadha), carelessness (asaṁjamo), wheel of birth and death (parabhāvasamkāmakaro) and that which makes one devoid of virtues (Guṇānam Virahaṇa). Hiṁsā is the destruction of life forces caused by carelessness actuated by passion like attachment and aversion.[18] It destroys goodness and purity of the soul. In Buddhist tradition, destroying life intentionally is termed as violence.[19] In other places,[20] it is understood as cruelty, harming (killing), hurting, etc.

6.1.4.2. Aspects of violence

Hiṁsā is both mental and physical in Jain tradition. Hiṁsā does not depend on acts alone. The law of love will be broken by the absence of compassion shown when a person is carried away by anger. Hence a distinction has to be made between the intention to hurt (bhāva hiṁsā) and the actual hurt (dravya hiṁsā).[21] Violence is committed when either the inner self of a being (bhāvaprāṇa) or the outer vehicle of it, namely, the body (dravyaprāṇa) is in anyway hurt.[22] If one acts carelessly moved by passion, hiṁsā is certainly present whether a living being is killed or not.[23]

In Sūtrakṛtānga,[24] there is long discussion between Sudharma and Jambusvamin as regards the judgement of an act, whether it is violent or not. It finally concludes that there is sin though the preceptor of an action does not posses sinful thoughts, speeches, etc. And those creatures such as the earthbodies etc. which have no development or mature reason nor consciousness nor intellect, nor mind, nor speech (those which lack judgement) are still full of hostility and wrong against all sorts of living beings. Thus even senseless beings are reckoned instrumental in bringing about slaughter of living beings.[25]

It may look irrational and unjust to think how these senseless beings are led to violent deeds. But the Jain spiritual masters say that Soul or Jīva is the same in all the six types of living beings, from earth-bodied (one sensed) to human beings (with the internal organ as the sixth sense). It is this self due to wrong belief (mithyādṛṣṭi) that commits sin of violence by doing cruelty to other creatures.[26]

Buddhist tradition pays greater attention to the intention of the doer. It posits five necessary conditions in the crime of killing: the knowledge that life exists, the assurance that a living being is present, the intention to take life, some actions must take place and some movements towards that action, and the life must actually be taken.[27]

6.1.5. Justification of violence to the self:

6.1.5.1. Self-suffering, Self-mortification, Self-purification, Self-restraint in religion:

There are debates whether one is allowed to take one's life in the process of saving oneself or others. In other words, how are self-mortification, self-persecution and the like are justified? Can a person harm himself/herself or others to safeguard one's own interests?

We see in the Brāhmaṇic tradition the sacrifice of animals, birds, etc. in order to obtain wealth and prosperity to the owner of the sacrifice or the yajamāna. Sacrifice of these birds and animals were justified by stating that the victims will enjoy a better status in the life to come.[28] L.C. Burman argues against this contention saying that the same soul works in all and it is sinful to kill any kind of animal at any time and at any place: Śruti does not set down injunctions to kill. Self-protection is the aim of every creature and Ātman has no narrow domains. It is all and everywhere.[29] It is this sacrificial attitude of the Brāhmaṇas that led Hemachandra to call the Law of Manu as 'hiṁsā śāstra' or the Law of Violence.[30] The Jain Ācaryas, particularly Amṛtacandra and Amitagati, maintain absolute Ahiṁsā and preach that it is wrong to kill even destructive animals.[31]

Self-mortification is usually understood as inflicting pain upon oneself. But in a religious and ethical sense it does not result in pain. It is rather the joy of offering oneself in sacrificial service. To an observer the act might evoke sympathy, etc. but the motivation offers tremendous satisfaction and joy to the one who is involved in such a practice.

In Buddhist tradition, there are examples of self-sacrificial attitude in a Bodhisattva. According to Prajñāpāramita sūtra, Sikṣāsamucchaya and certain other Mahāyāna texts, a Bodhisattva shows compassion or karuṇā by resolving to suffer the torments and agonies of the dreadful purgatories during innumerable aeons, if need be, in order to lead all beings to perfect enlightenment.[32] The story of Pūrṇa in Samyutta Nikāya explains to what extent forbe..rance of an individual can go.[33] A Bodhisattva is the greatest forgiver and embodiment of forbearance. Even if his body is destroyed and cut into hundred pieces with swords and spears he does not conceive any anger against his cruel persecutors.[34]

Jain moral tradition upholds a practice called Sallekhana. This vow is taken with the objective to fulfill what is known as samadhi marana or peaceful passing away, sannyaśa maraṇa or disease in asceticism, pāṇḍitya maraṇa or the wise man's demise. This practice has been frankly recognized as *religions self-purification*[35] and it is highly commended for both the laity and the monks. It is described at length in the first anga of Ācārāṅgasūtra[36] and its preliminaries are described in detail in the Aurapaccakkhana, the Saṁthāra, the Mahāpaccakkhana and the Caṇḍavejjhaya, the 3rd, 4th, 5th and 6th of the Painnas. Jain tradition also gives a list of those who took to Sallekhana: Tirthaṅkara Pārśva and Ariśṭanemi[37] monk Khandage[38] Layman Ambada[39] and all those celebrated in Uvāsagadasāo. From middle age till recent years this practice of extreme asceticism is seen: Hemachandra in 1172 AD, King Kumārapāla[40], a monk at Ahmedabad[41] and a nun at Rajkot and so on.

A Jain monk undertakes this extreme form of self-mortification when he suffers from a fatal disease or when he is unable to follow the rules of his Order[42] or when he is faced with obstacles to follow his religion. Puruṣārthasiddhyupāya claims that Sallekhana is not suicide because the passions are attenuated. But he who acts with full of passion is guilty of suicide. There are five desires that are fatal at the time of Sallekhana: desire to live, desire to die, attachment to friend-, recollection of pleasures and desire for future pleasures.[43] It is almost killing of activity in oneself besides the abnegation of desires.

Extremism is not accepted in Buddhism as it chooses the middle path for its goal. Hence suicide is condemned without qualification: A monk who preaches suicide, who tells man, 'Do away with this wretched life, full of suffering and sin; death is better' in fact preaches murder, is a murderer, is no longer a monk.[44] Buddhists object to thirst for non-existence (vibhāvatrṣṇa) as they object to thirst for existence (bhāvatṛṣṇā). A saint must abide in indifference without caring for life, without caring for death. He will not commit suicide in order to reach Nirvāṇa sooner. Is not suicide a desperate act of disgust and desire - disgust with existence and desire for rest? The pilgrim I-tsing says that Indian Buddhists abstain from suicide and, in general, from self-torture.[45]

But there are a number of stories[46] to show that suicide in certain cases may be the actual cause of or occasion for the attainment of Arhatship, one step lower than the ideal of Buddhahood, although in certain other cases it may be pre-mature and sinful. The Mahāyāna Buddhism praises suicide as self-surrender and worship. The Bodhisattva of the past practised in that way[47] any heroic deed (duḥkara), for instance, in the ancient Buddhist canon Chariyapiṭaka Jātaka.

Religious suicide is approved in India. But it is significant to note that it has been in the case of men who have lived a full life and acquired a high measure of power. Suicide in other cases has never been authorized; rather it has been strongly condemned. In Buddhism as well as in every Indian system (except Cārvāka) it is held that suicide results in another life still burdened with the consequences of the individual's previous karma.

6.1.5.2. Duty and promotion of social good:

Apart from religious suicide and self-mortification that are justified on religious grounds, both Buddhism and Jainism seek justification for violence in certain other cases. Although Jainism is absolute about non-injury to life and living beings, yet it prescribes a practical way of life to the laity who engage daily in unavoidable injuries to living beings because of duty and responsibility.

To ascertain the truth that absolute non-injury is the only requirement for Mokṣa, Jain tradition believes that as long as one engages oneself in worldly life one cannot attain salvation. Hence one has to become a monk for sometime in life or aspire to religious life in order to practise Ahiṁsā in a more perfect manner. History reveals that there had been Jain kings, generals and soldiers who, by duty, had to engage themselves in political wars. But the Jain Ācāryas do not call them heretics (mithyādṛṣṭi) because of blood they shed during wars.[48]

Such illustrations as these show that unavoidable circumstances and duty consciousness make allowance for violence. While the Jains profess that there is no hiṁsā, which has purely pleasant and agreeable consequences[49] they also concede to certain activities of the laity performed by way of duty (for instance, punishment), etc. Buddhism considers daṇḍa or punishment as unattached violence. The crime includes both punishment of criminals and waging a righteous war.

In Buddhism, a Bodhisattva can kill a person who intends to murder a monk or his own parents: 'it does not matter if I suffer in purgatory for this sin but I must save this misguided creature from such a fate.'[50] Harsh speech is sometimes permissible to a Bodhisattva: 'he may speak harshly in order to retain foolish persons from evil actions.'[51]

While Buddhism is more liberal in its understanding of hiṁsā, Jainism holds on to its ideal way. For instance, it condemns Euthanasia or mercy killing. Puruṣārthasiddhyupāya warns against wielding a weapon in the false belief that those living in great pain ought quickly to be released from their misery. Even those who are suffering should not be killed.[52]

Generally violence is not justified except as a necessary evil, an evil done out of love, piety, pity or duty, and this is the most controversial part of the doctrine of Ahiṁsā. Questions are asked as to when violence is justified and in what forms and to what extent.[53] There can be situations in which the use of violence alone can set the process of transformation in motion. What is important is not to know whether violence is required or not but to know whether violence is necessary at all and whether it is oriented towards positive, meaningful changes in the social order or whether its objectives tend toward its total destruction.

For instance, to fight against unjust authority, to participate in military or revolutionary violence in order to attain social just objectives, etc. is not condemned. To refuse to take relevant action while injustice does its work and subsequently the poor die of hunger is one way of promoting the unjust system. It is often violence of the oppressor that prompts counter violence of the oppressed. Although debatable, today in practical circumstances, it is violence that assures the defence of the poor and it is violence that stands in the face of exploitation, coercion and oppression by the rich and the powerful. Today people realize that poverty is not a result of fate but the result of forms of social and economic oppression. Anything that tends to perpetuate poverty or to divert forces that should be devoted to this collective struggle against oppression is treason to the poor. Jacques Ellul says that remaining silent or passive in the face of evil reinforces evil.[54]

Indian history, even until Gandhi,[55] has accepted violence as a means to promote social good. Mahābhārata says that there are two things: 'abstention from injury and injury done with righteous motives. Of these two, that which brings in righteousness is preferable. There is neither act that is entirely pure nor any that is entirely simple. In all acts, right or wrong, something of both prevails.'[56] Violence as such is ethically bad but in life one has to consider the whole situation before deciding whether the use of violence is justified as a mixed good. The whole situation may not be dominated by one, single ethical principle.[57]

6.1.6. Countering the many faces of violence: The Śramaṇa call to Life-saving

6.1.6.1. Social inequality and caste discrimination:

Śramaṇa culture is said to be a reaction to the Brāhmaṇical system of social stratification and to the authority of the Vedas. Dharmakīrti says that there are five sins or folly of those who have lost their intelligence: belief in the validity of the Vedas, belief in a creator, expecting ethical merit from ablutions, pride of caste and engaging in violence to be rid of sin.[58] All these five elements are linked to the Brāhmaṇical system of life and society.

The social system was such that the Brāhmaṇas as priestly

community occupied the prime place of honour, were propitiated and consulted not merely in religious matters but also on every aspect of social and political life. Their authority was the authority of the Vedas. Their sanctity was the sanctity of the various gods. Their honour was the propitiation of these gods by way of gifts and sacrifices. Until post-Vedic period, Sannyāsa was not considered as the last stage of life and everyone who wanted to renounce this world had to go through the other stages of life. Gṛhastha dharma or the householder's life was considered meritorious and significant. Only certain types of people were admitted to Holy Orders of priesthood and women could not have access to it. Similarly, recitation of the Vedic texts was restricted only to the Brāhmaṇas and no outcast was accepted to the learning and life of a Brahmacārin.

It is during the post-Vedic time (the time of the Upaniṣads and the great Epics) we see a drastic change in the thinking pattern. The Śramaṇas must have made a significant influence on the Brāhmaṇic society and its traditional ideals. For instance, there is a reversal in the traditional understanding of a Brāhmaṇa. In the new definition, there are five requisites for being regarded as a Brāhmaṇa: Varṇa (ubhato sujato hoti), Jāti (avikkitto anupakutto jātivadena). Mantra (ajjhayako hoti mantrādhāro),' śīlā'and pāṇḍitya. But what really makes a person Brāhmaṇa is conduct and learning.[59]

Vajrasuci Upaniṣad[60] traces the source of Brāhmanhood to the purity of heart. In Mahābhārata[61], king Yudhisthira is asked, 'who, O King, is a Brāhmana?' The answer is 'a Brāhmaṇa is one who evinces the truth, liberality, forbearance, virtue, mildness, austerity and pity. Anyone who possesses these qualities should be called a Brahmāṇa; anyone bereft of these should be called a Śūdra.' It is no more by birth that someone claims to be Brāhmaṇa but by austerities (tapas) and good conduct (cāritra). Viśvāmitra, a kṣatriya, claims the birth and rights of a Brahmana by austerities.[62] The Jain non asserts that it is by one's deed that one becomes a Brāhmaṇa: one does not become a Śramaṇa by tonsure, nor a Brāhmaṇa by the sacred syllable Oṁ, nor a muni by living in the woods, nor a tāpasa by wearing clothes of kuśa grass and a bark. One becomes a Śramaṇa by equanimity; Brāhmaṇa by chastity, a Muni by knowledge and a Tāpasa by penance.[63] Anti-caste attitude is noticed in the legend of Harikeśa Bāla in one of the early Jain canons, Uttarādhyayanasutra.[64]

There are instances of declaration that the status of Kṣatriya was higher than that of the Brāhmaṇa.[65] Thc Kṣatriyas placed themselves in a superior position decrying the caste hierarchy, in favour of spiritual learning and achievement: 'Among those who claim a lineage or gotra, the Kṣatriya has a superiority. However, the person who has learning and character is superior to men as well as gods'.

To a question relating to gotra, Buddha answered Sundarika, a Brāhmaṇa of the Bharatvāja gotra: 'I am not a Brāhman, or the son of a king or a vessa; having taken a gotra that of common people, I wander about in the world, without possessions, meditating. Clad in the Sanghati, I wander about houseless with my hair shaven, tranquil, and not consorting with men in this world. Inopportunely O Bṛāhman, does thou make enquiry of my gotra.'[66] Implicit in the words of Buddha is that ascetic life itself becomes a protest against the tyranny of caste. An ascetic surpasses caste and other such institution of mundane life. He is casteless not because he iṣ below caste but because he is above it. An ascetic is free from the bondage and artificial restrictions of society, which an ordinary man might not transgress.

The Śramaṇa movement was a threat to class/caste division and Brāhmaṇa supremacy. It was originally a monastic structure. The Saṅgha or the Holy Order admitted all types of people, even outcasts and women.[67] This was not possible in the Brāhmaṇic set up. Even the administration of the Saṅgha was similar to the tribal organization, democratic form of government was followed especially with regard to admission into the Order, regular meetings and consultations, authority and accountability among the residents, general governing of the Body, etc.[68] All these were prompted by the belief in social equality and understanding of hierarchy on the basis of conduct and experience.

6.1.6.2. Accumulation of wealth and private ownership:

The attitude towards wealth and riches among the Śramaṇas was highly contemptuous. They were well aware of the transient nature of things, of the harm these riches did to the moral progress of human persons: 'great wealth and women, a family and exquisite pleasures - for such things people practice austerities. All this you may have for your asking. What avail riches for the practice of religion, what a family, what pleasures? We shall become Śramaṇas possessed of many virtues and wander about collecting alms.[69] In Uttarādhyayanasūtra there is a dialogue between a father and his sons. The father tells his sons, 'the study of the Vedas will not save you; the feeding of the Brāhmaṇas will lead you from dreaminess to darkness and the birth of sons will not save you... pleasures bring only a moment's happiness but suffering for a very long time, intense suffering, but slight happiness; they are an obstacle to the liberation from existence and are a very mine of evils.'[70] Finally the father persuades his sons to embrace the life of renunciation: 'my sons, after you have studied the Vedas and fed the priests, after you have placed your own sons at the head of your house and after you have enjoyed life together with you wives, then you may depart to the woods as praise worthy sages.'[71]

One of the major ethical principles of the Jains is Aparigraha, literally meaning non-grabbing. The metaphor generally refers to non-accumulation of wealth and simplicity of life. Several instances in the Jain canon point out to the deadly nature of wealth persuading the believer to follow the course of religious mendicancy. Every attachment is a cause of sin,[72] an accumulation of karma for which one has to reap the consequences. They call for subduing desire by desirelessness,[73] giving up the world,[74] his possessions and relations and all undertakings and become a wanderer and homeless without worldly interests.[75] A Muni is said to be the one who knows the doctrine of sin, who knows the time, the occasion, the conduct, the religious precept and disowns all things as not required for religious purposes.[76] In him there is no worldly desires and attachment. Uttarādhyanyanasūtra describes a conversation between King Nami and the god of gods Śakra in the guise of a Brāhmaṇa. Śakra asks King Nami, 'Your place is on fire, why do you not look after your seraglio?' To this the king replies, 'Happy are we, happy we live, we who call nothing our own; when Mithila is on fire, nothing is burnt that belongs to me. To a monk who has left his sons and wives and who has ceased to act, nothing pleasant can occur, nor anything unpleasant. There is much happiness for the sage, for the houseless monk, who is free from all ties, and knows himself to be single and unconnected (with the rest of the world).'[77]

Ideas cherished by such mendicants give us a different perspective to the understanding of wealth and the rich blessings of the world. Such an attitude towards wealth keeps Religion as priority and religious living as the sure means to attain the goal of life. 'Making faith his fortress, penance and self-control the bolt (of its gate), patience its strong wall... making zeal his bar, its string carefulness in walking (īriyā) and its top (where the string is fastened content, he should bend (this bow) with Truth, piercing with the arrow, penance, (the foe's) mail, karma (in this way) a sage will be the victor in battle and get rid of the saṁsāra.'[78]

From the Śramaṇa perspective, wealth cannot give what is necessary to man: 'If there were numberless mountains of gold and silver, as big as Kailāsa, they would not satisfy a greedy person; for his activity is boundless like space.'[79] 'Wealth cannot really save me: It is only a fool who thinks that his wealth, cattle and relations will save him; they him or he them. But they are no help, no protection.'[80] Uttarādhyayana describes how two sons took refuge in the path of the Jina. As the father discourages and dissuades his sons from a life of austerities, the sons reply to him, 'if the whole world and all treasures were yours you would still not be satisfied, nor would all this be able to save you. Whenever you die, O king, and leave all pleasant things behind, the law alone and nothing else in this world, will save you a monarch.'[81]

It is easier for a monk to lead a life with frugal means. The life style of a mendicant provides austerity measures. An individual may be weak and slip back into his old ways[82] but by assisting one another the mendicants would strengthen one another's efforts. The mendicants' way of life has provided rules for begging food, clothes, couch, bowl and it also regulates the possession of a mendicant.[83] A householder, on the other hand, is in the midst of a world with vast differences in attitude and behaviour. When the worldly ways pose a challenge to a life of Dharma and Mokṣa, a householder is at a loss to balance between needs and wants, between extremes of life.

6.1.6.3. Attachment and dominance:

The word parigraha refers to possession and private ownership. Aparigraha is an attitude of detachment, and in the economic realm it may mean non-obsession with material things or, simply, non-possession. Aparigraha, besides being a vrata or vow, is an attitude toward life and specifically toward the material universe. Implicit in the vow is the great reverence to the autonomy of the material universe. What we call wealth, possessions and the pleasures, etc. are strictly outside one's self. They may be meant for oneself but does not really belong to the self. This basic understanding comes from the idea that Jīva or the self is identical only with consciousness and all others like pleasures, activity, etc. are extraneous to it. This is the quintessence of Jain philosophy. Hence, in order to attain the objective of life, namely the realization of the true self devoid of all that is extraneous to it, Aparigraha or the vow of detachment and non-possession is proposed. Aparigraha clarifies the vision regarding the true nature of the self and, at the same time, to respect the autonomy of the material universe.[84]

A question arises whether it is really possible for embodied beings to be detached from the empirical world? Jain tradition says that it is possible from an absolute, ideal, attitudinal or niścaya point of view. Whereas from an actual, practical or vyavāhāra point of view, one cannot be without the material universe because the embodied being itself is a combination of mind and body, spirit and flesh. And one has an intimate relationship with the material universe. But this relationship could be one of domination or of mutual collaboration and the Jain visionary would prefer the latter. In domination one is a slave to the passions and in collaboration there could be the attitude of detachment and healthy indifference. Thus, Aparigraha helps one to achieve this mental equanimity and allows a sort of ownership achieved not by grabbing the material possession or by fighting for it but through a detached acceptance and use of the same. Any possession out of greed and other passions would come under violence to the material world, in other words, dravya hiṁsā.

Amitagati[85] points out that violence is committed for the sake of accumulation of wealth or possession. Hence a householder should constantly try to limit his activity to obtain possessions. Ownership can have two results: attachment and aversion. The former manifests itself as a tendency to accumulate wealth by possessing, garbing, etc. and the latter in the form of violence. Ownership is in possession of land, house, jewels, money, livestock, servants and other luxury items.[86] Attachment to wealth and a desire to accumulate it are seen when one is found extremely sad at a loss incurred in some transaction, or in hoarding grains and other items to sell them at a higher price or at a later date, overloading animals and extracting more work from servants, etc.[87] Parigraha is evident when one takes things that are not one's own or when not given,[88] when dealing with illicit business,[89] indulging in adulteration, use of false weights and measures[90] and writing false statements or forgery, etc.[91]

Jain ethical literature elaborately deals with the way one has to acquire the means of livelihood. In order to be detached, one has to keep a check on oneself mainly in the way one acquires wealth and other possessions. Firstly, the Jain householder chooses a profession that involves least violence to sub-human beings[92] and he does least violence to his partners in business, his servants, the customers, etc.[93] Secondly, he takes to Dig vrata, literally meaning control of directions. This vow restricts one's movements minimizing greed and violence. It limits one's freedom of movement by climbing, ascending mountains, descending into the well or underground, storehouse etc., entering a cave, etc.[94]

Deśavakaikavrata limits the extent of territory for movements and objects of senses.[95]

Thirdly, the Jain householder takes to Bhogapabhogaparimāṇa vrata, which puts a limit to the use of objects in order to minimize attachment to them. They include meat and honey, intoxicants, ginger, raddish, carrot, butter, unsuitable means of conveyance or unsuitable ornaments, the use of bizarre dresses.[96] The householder should avoid the use of five udumbara fruits[97] and abandon the use of non-sentient but life-substances like roots, fruits, seeds, etc. without boiling them.[98] Finally a Jain householder is expected to fast on aṣṭami, caturdaśi and pūrṇima.[99] Āṣādhara, Vasunandin, Amṛtacandra and others have prescribed the procedure for fasting,[100] meditation, study of scriptures, worship of Jina, saluting and feeding the sādhus, vigilance in conduct and thinking of anuprekṣas or themes of contemplation, etc.[101] Such a means of livelihood according to the tenets of religion not only prepares a Jain householder mentally with attitudes of detachment but also externally curtails him from hoarding.[102]

A significant practice among the Jain householders, which further helps in minimizing attachment to the material universe, is gift offering or Dāna.[103] It is popular among the Buddhists as well. In the absence of this practice no ascetics can survive and consequently there could be no transmission of their sacred doctrine. Ḍāna as understood in its largest sense includes the giving of one's daughter and the transmission of property to one's heirs, the exercise of charity, the construction of temples and community institutions such as common kitchen or poṣadhaśālā, or even the performance of pūja viewed as the giving of flowers, incense, flag staff and similar offerings.

Generally ascetics are given food and drink, clothes, blankets, bedding and other necessary accessories. Āhāra, abhaya, śāṣtra and bhaisājya are the four types of gift offering made to the ascetics. Ācārya Vasunandin says that in any act of gift-offering five factors have to be considered: the recipient (pātra), the giver (dātṛ), the thing given (dātavya, dravya), the manner of giving (dāna vidhi) and the result of giving (dāna phala).[104] Like other meritorious acts, it can contribute to the extinction of karma or to the amassing meritorious karma or may find requital in the present life.

Ācārya Hemachandra proposes a scheme wherein illustrious disciples sow their wealth on the seven fields with compassion for those in great misery.[105] They are:

1. Jain images: wealth is spent on them by setting them up, by performing the eightfold pūja, by taking them in procession through the city, by adorning them with jewels, and fine clothes;
2. Jain temples: wealth is spent on building new domes and for old ones to be restored;
3. Jain scriptures: wealth is spent on copying the sacred texts and giving them to learned monks for writing commentaries;
4. Monks: wealth is spent on alms giving and for taking care of the monks;
5. Nuns: wealth is spent on alms giving and for taking care of the nuns;
6. Laymen: wealth is spent on inviting the co-religionists to birth and marriage festivals, distributing food, betel, clothes and ornaments to them, constructing public poṣadhaśālas and other buildings for them, and encouraging them in religious duties. Charity is to be extended to all those who have fallen into evil circumstances; and,
7. Lay women: all the duties under the last head apply equally to women.

Hemachandra goes on to say that an illustrious householder (mahāśrāvaka) should use his wealth indiscriminately to assist all who are in misery or poverty, or those who are blind, deaf, crippled or sick etc.[106] Such sowing of one's substance is to be made with limitless compassion.

For a Buddhist lay person practice of generosity has been cast in certain routine forms since earliest days of Buddhism. It consists largely in remunerating the monk's services to villagers. Thus a lay person gains merit by giving food, robes, money (often to the head of monasteries for the community's needs) to monks or, sometimes, land or materials or labour for building a new monastery or Vihāra.[107]

Both Jain and Buddhist traditions have given much importance to gift offering, an act of sharing of one's substance or wealth. It only shows the rational understanding of the concept of Jīva as entirely different from the material (Ajīva) and the earnestness of the Jain believer to realize the real self, the ultimate objective of life.

6.1.7. Conclusion

As contemporary India is going through a slow process of development and growth, the land and its people encounter different forms of violence in different spheres of life. Cultural and religious fundamentalism, inequality and social dominance and subjugation between ethnic and linguistic groups, economic imbalance and unequal distribution of wealth, environmental degradation and so on seem to tear the social fabric of India and tarnish the life-style of its people. While different social and political forces are at work to redeem a situation such as this, religious and spiritual resources offer permanent solutions to the contemporary evils in society.

The Śramaṇa religions like Jainism and Buddhism propose their basic ethical principles like non-injury to life and detachment in procuring and use of wealth, etc. as the only source of remedy. The simple life-style and the generous attitude prompted by their sages and spiritual masters is a sure step to meet the challenges of the contemporary world of consumerism and hoarding mentality. Ultimately it is violence done to life out of greed and other passions that causes conflicts among individuals and communities. Even more harm is done to life at the level of attitude. Violence to human and environmental life is prominently seen as life is categorized as high and low, and subsequently treating humans and others as lesser beings. It is the same narrow attitude that prompts people to violence in the use of language, that lodges people in a ghetto world, that refuses to allow changes, accommodations in one's own thinking and behaviour.

Jain and Buddhist attitude to life prompts a dharmic way of life which, in general, promises to preserve and to promote life with dignity and freedom. This prompting could be a happy lead to cross over a life of sorrow and danger in contemporary India, if only the call of the Śramaṇas could be meaningfully heard.

PART - II IS NON-VIOLENCE STILL A MYTH? : THE ŚRAMAṆA VISION OF AHIṀSĀ AS APPLIED TO THE EMERGENCE OF A NON-VIOLENT SOCIETY

6.2.1. The Dilemma and the hope:

Looking at the world today, several critics of Non-violence have almost given up hope. Human history persists in violence. And Non-violence is almost a dream. Some argue that it is the only means left to the weak and the powerless. Behavioural sciences suggest that it is only natural to human beings to be violent. Political bureaucrats and sociologists say that the several dimensions of Non-violence like self-government, self-sufficiency, self-effort, non-cooperative measures, passive resistance, etc., have led individuals and society, state and country to isolation.[108]

This and several other reasons have raised a fundamental question even among its believers whether non-violence is still a myth or a failure. Even Gandhi found his life work of guiding the national political Satyāgraha to be only an illusion of Nonviolence. It succeeded only in part.[109] Non-violence has mostly been a matter of individual practice but not of groups, communities and nations. It is natural for individuals and society to be non-violent toward their family members and relatives, same caste/race and not towards non-relatives and strangers. Usually people are non-violent only temporarily, and even that is one of *controlled violence*. Violence has become a way of life and of achievement. Even the public thinks that violence brings about change in society more easily than by any other means. Media too draws people's attention mostly to violent incidents and events. Even socalist, democratic governments resort to violent, repressive means to ensure law and order. The same can be said of groups, communities, states and even countries. People take to any means in order to achieve their selfish interests.

But generally it is one's spiritual tradition that raises a person to one's human dignity. Humans live for certain ideals and they achieve them in their lives through an acceptable way of life. It is ethical principles that govern one's activities. Hence violence can only be an exception rather than a rule. It is this optimism that keeps principles like Non-violence alive and meaningful. Only a pessimist who is disgusted with this world and who suspects even basic honesty of a human person will regard violence as a general good. People who think that violence is in-built in nature, in sub-human and human life, and who cannot rise from a factual level to an ideal level will approve and defend violence uncritically. It requires effort on the part of man to become moral because moral life is not natural life.[110]

The leaders of the world realize more and more that it is not through forceful means dangers are averted or conflicts resolved but through peaceful means of mediation and dialogue. If changes are taking place in the world today it is not because of forceful submission or violent oppression but because of friendly bilateral relations, peace-commissions, voluntary self-denial, etc. Though the works of peace is not yet complete, the orientation seems to be clear and positive. Nations try to cope with one another and assimilate all that is good and lasting without isolating themselves from one another. These positive steps bring confidence in individuals, groups and nations, shattering the deadly fear that Non-violence is only a myth or a failure.

Human psychology reveals that a person grows in both gentler as well as virile virtues. Gentler virtues like humility, submission, compassion, self-sacrifice, etc., and virile virtues like courage, pride and so on grow in a person simultaneously. Bhagavad Gītā[111] points out that there are certain virtues that are Sāttvic in nature and others, Rājasic and Tāmasic. Fearlessness, active-resistance, non-cooperation with evil structures and individuals, mediation and dialogue, etc. are Sāttvic in nature. Acts that are governed by passions like greed and anger are detrimental to the growth of the individual and they ultimately end up in violence. Such persons are Rājasic by nature. Fear, cowardice, weak submission, etc. would characterize a Tāmasic personality.

Non-violence does not necessarily imply passivity, nor any fear of action. It does not recognize powerlessness or submission as virtues. One who is indifferent to both good and evil is no ethical person. Hence a Non-violent person is knowledgeable about the situation. The power of the opponent does not bother such a person. There is reasonable judgment on what is good and right and the person cannot be bribed by the threat of danger or calamity. A Non-violent person remains fearless even when supports are withdrawn.

6.2.2. Śramaṇa Vision of Ahiṁsā

The Śramaṇa vision of Non-violence is based on the principle of 'reciprocity': As it would be unto thee, so it is with him whom thou intendest to kill. As it would be unto thee, so it is with him whom thou intendest to tyrannize over. As it would be unto thee, so it is with him whom thou intendest to torment. In the same way (it is with him) whom thou intendest to punish, and to drive away.[112] All beings are fond of life, like pleasure, hate pain, shun destruction, like life, long to live. To all life is dear.[113] This is the quintessence of wisdom: not to kill anything. Know this to be the legitimate conclusion from the principle of reciprocity with regard to non-killing.[114]

The special feature in the Śramaṇa vision of Non-violence is that it embraces all life. Chāndogyopaniṣad points out that he who practices Ahiṁsā towards all creatures except in sacrifices at holy places (tirtha) does not return to this world again.[115] 'Holy place' refers to the place of animal sacrifice. According to the Vedic conception, animal sacrifice was not morally wrong. The Law of Manu[116] states that the hiṁsā prescribed in the Vedas should be construed to mean ahiṁsā, because Vedas are the source of moral authority. It is this that led Ācārya Hemachandra to criticize the Law of Manu as 'Hiṁsāśāstra'.[117] The broader understanding of Ahiṁsā by the Śramaṇa sages extends to all living creatures, at all time and in all places. It means not to cause suffering to any living being, at any time, either by mental, vocal or bodily activities.[118] The Buddhist term 'avihiṁsā is defined as that by which another being is not harmed (na vihethyate).[119] According to Vyāsa, Ahiṁsā means absence of oppression (anabhidroha) towards all living beings (sarvabhūta) in all respects (sarvathā) and for all times (sarvadā).[120]

The second characteristic in the Śramana vision of Ahiṁsā is that its meaning is understood from the 'absolute' (Niścaya) point of view and also from the 'relative' or 'practical' (Vyavahāra) point of view. The absolute point of view stresses the ideal of Non-violence and the relative stresses the actual practice of a person, given the situation. It is important to note that the Jaina logic emphasizes the 'truth of seeing'. It is ultimately the 'attitude' that shapes the character of a person. Samayasāra of Ācārya Kundakunda[121] expounds this truth of seeing from both these points of view.

The third aspect in the Śramaṇa vision of Ahiṁsā is that it is proposed as an ethical imperative in the 'negative' form (a-hiṁsā). According to Dr. Bhargava[122] the positive meaning of Non-violence like love, compassion, etc. lead one to certain type of 'attachment' to such sentiments. A negative term suggests 'detachment' and a sense of 'equanimity'. Though love and compassion are important for attaining the final end (Tīrthaṅkarahood) they have to be ultimately given up. The positive dimension of Nonviolence implies 'Love-All-Life' and not merely co-religionists and the like, not even merely human life but also animal and vegetable life.[123] It is finally karuṇā dāna and abhaya dāna, showing compassion and giving protection to all living beings.[124]

Gandhi says: I accept the interpretation of Ahiṁsā, namely, that it is not merely a negative state of harmlessness but it is a positive state of love, of doing good, even to the evil doer. But it does not mean helping the evildoer to continue the wrong or tolerating it by passive acquiescence. On the country, love, the active state of Ahiṁsā requires one to resist the wrong doer by dissociating oneself from him even though it may offend him or injure him physically.[125]

Finally, Śramaṇa vision of Ahiṁsā is 'comprehensive' in its meaning. On the individual plane Ahiṁsā is essential for ethical practice as it leads to individual liberation, mental purity or dispassionate contemplation. On the collective or the social plane, the utility of Ahiṁsā is seen when one speaks of Ahiṁsā by thought, word and deed. The Jaina tradition holds that Ahiṁsā in thought is Anekānta, an attitude of accommodation of the multifarious experiences in reality and life. Ahiṁsā in word or speech is Syādvāda, the acknowledgement that 'truth has two eyes'. Seeing and knowing vary with the person and the context. Lastly, Ahiṁsā in deed is Aparigraha, an attitude of detachment and a willingness to be deprived of possessions.

6.2.3. The Power and the Demands of Ahiṁsā

Such a comprehensive understanding of Śramaṇa vision of Non-violence provides space for a meaningful application in ordinary and in extraordinary, conflicting situations. In times of conflict it requires a great inner power. In such situations Non-violence is observed in order to move the wrong doer to recognize with the victim their common humanity. To bring about this recognition, suffering is necessary.[126]

In any process of Non-violent action one could recognize three stages of demand on a Non-violent person. First, the stage of reasoning in which there is an effort of mutual exchange, dialogue and persuasion through reasoning. Secondly, the stage of suffering in which emotions plays a vital role. There is the emotional persuasion by taking up voluntary suffering like fast, etc. and, thirdly, the stage of Non-violent action. If the first two fail, the person resorts to Non-violent coercion through acts of non-cooperation, civil disobedience, etc.[127]

Of all these, the stage of suffering is that which purifies a person. This suffering may take the form of self-sacrifice, vicarious suffering, etc. The deeper meaning of Non-violence in action is self-suffering, the acceptance of pain within oneself instead of its infliction on the opponent. Such submission to pain, to Gandhi, is of the nature of love, that is, Ahiṁsā.[128] It was the example of Jesus Christ that gave Gandhi an underlying faith in

Non-violence.[129] He saw the necessity of the cross or, what he calls, the suffering-love (Ahiṁsā) for the realization of the self. It is possible to realize self-perfection only at the culminating point of sacrifice.[130] Gandhi elucidated the meaning of non-cooperation, service, etc. in terms of self-denial and self-suffering. Non-violent non-cooperation may mean renunciation of the benefits of a system. We therefore renounce the benefits of schools, courts, titles, legislatures and offices set up under the system.[131] To Gandhi it was a measure of discipline and self-sacrifice. Vicarious suffering suggests that the person feels one with the other who suffers. A social worker may be rich and literate but goes to a poor village adapting himself and his life-style. By doing so, he need not raise the standard of the villagers. It is only a sign that he identifies himself with the conditions of the people. He includes everyone in himself, in his suffering. Vicariousness connotes total inclusiveness extended to the realm of faith.[132]

Jaina tradition may accept vicarious suffering from a practical point of view, like helping the poor, undertaking hardships for the sake of a noble cause, etc. But Jainism believes that everyone has to be responsible for his/her own of karma and bum it by self-effort. But Mahāyāna Buddhism describes the ideal of Bodhisattva as the one who helps others in the process of liberation, undertaking sufferings for the sake of others. He allows others first to enjoy the final liberation. The Bodhisattva suffers in the place of the actual sufferer, transferring his on them. It is an extreme kind of charity. Jainism, on the other hand, does not condemn charity, as they are means for accumulating good karma. For all practical purposes Jainism accepts altruism, as they are only normal and natural to all human beings. Dr. Jesudasan contends that vicarious suffering, an offshoot of Ahiṁsā, imputes a collective meaning to the doctrine of karma in addition to its individualist meaning[133] providing a meeting point between Gandhian and Jaina traditions.

6.2.4. Significance of Ahiṁsā in World-Mission

The power of Non-violence prompted by internal strength and

ability to fight[134] sustains the world of differences. What takes place in oneself is a renewal of spirit or Self-purification. It generates power to withstand evil power in this world. The mission of Non-violence builds and stabilizes common humanity. This does not mean that Ahiṁsā would tolerate unjust and irrational practices such as cooperating with evildoers, bringing dishonour to the country, etc. That would be, in Gandhi's word, demoralizing and cowardice.[135]

6.2.4.1. Plurality and Multiplicity

In a world of dogmatism and absolutism Non-violence implies an attitude of openness or pluralism (Anekānta or multiple perspective)[136], an important Jain contribution to the world of logic. This attitude views a reality from the rational point of view without prejudice or bias. The reason for this is that reality is complex and any of its description has infinite aspects and each aspect can be predicated in infinite ways. Our limited knowledge, grasping one fraction of these infinite aspects, tries to build a system.[137] Such an Ekānta attitude (absolutism or dogmatism) is compelling. Ekānta or one-sided approach or dogmatism is not inherent in the reality but resides in our mind. It is the product of intellectual discrimination. The theory of Anekānta seeks to present a *comprehensive picture of reality.*[138]

Anekānta[139] is the spirit of accommodation, a needed path to end violence in thought, word and deed. Anekānta outlook does not set aside other points of view. All knowledge would be fruitless in the absence of equanimity and no amount of reading of the sacred texts would lead one to any fruitful result. The logical expression of such a comprehensive attitude is further explained in the Jaina theory of Syādvāda and Nayavāda. These are only results of a mental poise, dispassionate outlook and spiritual balance. Anekānta forms the intellectual basis for the ethical doctrine of Non-violence. Persons like Vinobha Bhave stressed the need to understand Syādvāda for the sake of world peace.

Anekānta does not discard any point of view nor does it give exclusive importance to a particular point of view. It is opposed to dogmatism, which gives exclusive importance to a particular point of view. Applying these in the context of peace and Non-violence, first of all the opponent's view is held as equally important; no one's view is side lined and, much less, discarded. Truth in its partiality is seen in both. This is the basis for all types of mediation and arbitration. Reconciliation is possible in peaceful manner and no one side can be dogmatic about its assertions.[140] Finally both the parties seek the truth in what the other claims and both try to accommodate it in one's own programme. In Jain logic any particular assertion as absolute is called 'durnaya'[141] or incorrect.

Incidentally, to the Jains, Ajñānavāda or the theory of 'nescience' is a heresy.[142] Such a theory was preached by the contemporaries of Mahāvīra like Sañjay Velatthiputta. He believed in avyākṛta (unanswerable) problems, neither in affirmation nor in negation and nor in both. Such a view on life led him and others to the doom.

But the Jain Syādvāda and Nayavāda try to solve the problem of uncertainty by a method of assertion from different points of view. From a particular viewpoint the predication is a certainty of expression. Even if it takes an inexpressible form, it is not a doubt. The Jainas do not advocate inexpressibility as the final form of expression as the Buddhists do.[143] All these imply that Anekānta, a mind-set of Ahiṁsā, has a way of solving problems and conflicts.

Anekānta attitude is closely linked to Non-violence and Tolerance.[144] The Jaina teachers usually trace the root cause of violence to ignorance or carelessness.[145] It is ignorance expressed in doubts and uncertainty about what one wants to achieve, carelessness in the process of discernment and decision, etc. that lead an individual or a group to the path of violence. In any communal violence one virtually sees all these happen. But Syād and Naya theories affirm certainty of expressions, possibility of solutions to the problems and winning of peace and understanding through dialogue and meaningful interaction.

6.2.4.2. Dialogue

No one denies the importance of dialogue in the resolution of conflicts.[146] In all human and social interaction dialogue gives a positive meaning to Ahiṁsā as love. The only condition that is required in all dialogue efforts is that one should be free from prejudice. One does not cherish selfishness in oneself and evil thoughts upon the other. Both the parties have equal share in the proceedings and its results. Dialogue trains one in discipline, self-suffering and the acceptance of the other. In today's context, efforts to end war and to restore peace, efforts to avert religious tensions,[147] efforts to serve common humanity, etc. are only glimpses of the world's acceptance of the significance of Non-violence.

6.2.4.3. Non-exploitation

Contemporary Ahiṁsā signifies social, economic and political non-exploitation of all beings.[148] Non-violent activity involves no exploitation.[149] An exploiter commits violence by his 'carelessness' in fulfilling his unjustified desires.[150] Non-violence does not mean non-killing alone. Positively it means protection and non-exploitation of biological life. It disapproves the destruction of property.[151] In Jain terminology, 'property' is an 'external vitality' and hence to destroy it is to engage in violence against a person. Non-violence also means the absence of ill will.[152] 'Active service' is another form of Non-violence.[153]

The twin aspect of Non-violence, namely, non-exploitation/ non-destruction on the one hand, and goodwill/active service on the other, are important in the context of the poor and the social outcastes. In the process of realizing their potentials - money, power and literacy - the poor and the outcastes suffer oppression and torture by structural injustice. It is seen in any political, religious and institutional violence.

Mostly it is the poor and the social outcastes who are victims of exploitation. Social untouchability, rural unemployment, malnutrition, health-hygiene hazards, etc. are but symptoms of a greater evil in the form of injustices done to the poor masses.

6.2.4.4. Active Resistance

The Śramaṇa ascetics were models of non-violent, active resistance in times of hardships and temptations. Jaina scriptures instruct a monk to bear the hardships like a hero,[154] to guard his speech bravely[155] and to cultivate patience, etc. and to continue meditating upon the self.[156] Majjima Nikāya quotes a passage where a monk controls his mind and his tongue: 'undisturbed shall our mind remain, no evil words shall escape our lips, friendly and full of sympathy shall we remain, with heart full of love, free from any hidden malice.'[157] Such passages suggest that the weapons necessary to conquer the battles of life are neither submarines nor airplanes, the dreadful tools of modem war, but such divine qualities are purity, self-reliance, compassion and love.[158]

Active resistance resembles a war of a different type.[159] It is not defeating the enemy by inflicting heavy destruction on his armies, military equipments, transport systems, factories, cities etc. The approach is different. In Prof. Gene Sharp's[160] words, it is to deny the enemy the human assistance and cooperation necessary for exercising control over the population. This approach requires a different view of power in general and political power in particular.

Non-violent active-resistance[161] was a means for Gandhi to achieve Swaraj and it was a unique system of conflict resolution. This approach firmly footed in Satyāgraha with its components of satya, ahiṁsā and tāpasya drew heavily upon the Christian model of contrition, repentance, conversion and reform.[162] Passive resistance was equivalent to Non-violence of the weak and it could be equated side by side with the use of arms.

Prof. Sibley[163] point out that there are different stages in any process of Non-violent, active resistance: In the first stage, all the regular constitutional machinery such as legislative debates, arbitration by third parties, direct negotiations, etc. available are utilized. The second stage is the stage of agitation in which awareness is created through media and a network of communications outside the normal channels. In the third stage the ultimatum is served, documents drawn up and signed and heading towards direct action. The fourth and the last stage is the phase of direct action. It is also the phase of Self-purification: economic boycott, sit-down strikes, non-payment of taxes, mass resignation from public office, deliberate and organized disobedience to certain laws, etc.

Non-violent active resistance is generally used either for changing the attitude of the opponent or for compelling him/her without violence to reach some kind of compromise or resolution of conflict. On the other hand, it has the capacity to dramatize injustice, arouse the sluggish electorate and correct imbalances of power[164] where the constitutional forms have become useless and ordinary democratic methods are no longer available, non-violence assumes the guise of non-violent resistance, even where constitutional forms are preserved, minorities may be exploited and forced to resort to non-violent resistance for the sake, of both justice and self-protection.[165]

The power of non-violent active resistance does not involve any fear because it is built on the power of social truth and moral beauty. Dr. A N. Whitehead says that in human affairs moral power is more basic than economic and political power. Non-violent resistance compels people to make moral choices. It does not suppress reason but frees it from inertia and establishes its sovereignty over prejudice, hatred, anger and greed.[166]

6.2.5. Building a Non-violent Society

Whether a Non-violent society is possible depends on the fulfillment of certain conditions. Under normal circumstances and in actual practice democratic ideals are not followed in most respects. For example, people do not voice forth their grievances against injustice. We fail to receive correct information. Income is distributed unequally. Military and industrial complexes suppress the voice of the ordinary citizens in the name of modernism. In these and other circumstances Non-violent resistance can perform a valuable role.

While referring to the social progress of a nation Dr. Radhakrishnan points out three stages. In the first stage, the law of the jungle prevails, where there is violence and selfishness. In the second, there is rule of law and impartial justice with courts, police and prisons, and in the third, there is Non-violence and non-selfishness, where love and law are one.[167] The last stage is the foundation for a Non-violent society.[168] The reason for the slowness of human progress, according to Gregg,[169] is that we fail to understand and apply this law of Non-violence. He stresses that full understanding of this *law of gentle stimulus* alone can make rapid progress in social and economic realms.[170]

The idea of Non-violent Society and the idea of a New Heaven and a New earth or New Jerusalem in the Christian tradition[171] are parallel in conception. The Christian conception of the New Heaven, New Earth and New Jerusalem is a radical discontinuity from whatever is 'old' and 'destructive'. In it the destructive forces (Satan or Dragon) are punished and eternally confined to give way to the complete victory of creation. There is no more chaos. Old promises are renewed. God will wipe away tears from all faces.[172] Death will be no more.[173] God will give to the thirsty water, wine and milk without price.[174] In the new era the city, its gates and walls are described to represent the transcendent and future reality: 'God dwelling with his people'. The inhabitants in the city have close relationship with God. The realm of the holy is extended to the city and its inhabitants. There is the flowing down of the sacred stream the 'river of life' and the growth of the 'tree of life', which are no longer threatened with destruction because God is reconciled with the nations.

In a similar manner Prof. Sibley[175] describes a Non-violent society in which there is ample social and political freedom, less and less of manipulations, conflicts and wars, discriminate use of physical force, elaboration of machinery that would teach and resolve group conflicts, etc. There will be certain autonomy or right to self-government and a non-authoritarian educational system. In it a large measure of political and economic administration will be decentralized[176] to provide scope for decision-making and implementing such decisions by consensus. In it everybody will enjoy a guarantee of minimum material well being.

6.2.6. Self-realization and Self-governance

Non-violence is called *nirvāṇa,* which consists in peace.[177] Nirvāṇa is generally understood as Self-realization or God-realization. Self-realization is impossible without self-sacrifice. And self-perfection is possible only at the culminating point of sacrifice. Once again. Non-violence in thought, word and deed is inseparable from self-sacrifice. Hence self-sacrifice and self-perfection are the guidelines in the quest for Self-realization or God-realization and they are not possible without Non-violence and Non-attachment (Aparigraha).[178]

To Gandhi, political self-governance is possible by the same means as those required for individual self-governance. One only needs internal strength and ability to fight against the heaviest odds and a continuous striving to sustain the goal once attained.[179] Non-violence should be an indicator of inward freedom to which outer freedom or political independence would be in exact proportion.[180]

Gandhi was aware that one cannot achieve political and economic freedom nor moral and social elevation without Truth and Non-violence or, in concrete terms, without faith in God.[181] The gulf between the rich and the poor is contrary to self-realization and self-governance. One can bring about an economic equality once there is a voluntary surrendering of riches and power. Proper education in Non-violence and Truth precedes such a great sacrifice in personal and collective life. Self-realization and self-governance cannot be achieved at any time if life sails on falsehood and violence[182] and it would be doubly wrong if one indulges in them in the name of Truth and Non-violence.

6.2.7. Conclusion

Is Non-violence still a myth? The answer is yet to be searched. Gandhi believed and he lived.[183] For those who believe in violence as the last resort. Non-violent way of life is a call, a task and a risk.[184] It is a small mass of people who keep struggling with it. For those who prefer to enter into the *broad gate* of the ordinary, violence is often the first means. Though humans are selfish by nature they also have the potential to elevate themselves to the level of ideals. If society is surviving today in spite of all struggles and hazards it is because of hope in the future and overwhelming compassion and love for the living. Generally people give a second thought to resorting to violence because they want peace in themselves and in others. Humanity realizes its strength and worth only in the way it conducts itself especially at the time of tribulations. Hence values such as Non-violence are difficult to follow but a majority of the masses prefer minimal violence.

Adhering to the ideal of Non-violence suppress our lower selves, control the lower levels of our emotions, maturizing them toward a higher level being and living. Several philosophies in Indian history have witnessed to the Non-violent culture, preached and lived their tenets. The Śramaṇa religions, the Jains and the Buddhists, have shown the path of Non-injury to living beings. The lay adherents and monks have tested their inner strength by means of a positive approach to humanity and its surroundings. The way of the Śramaṇas has enlightened several persons like M. K. Gandhi and others and they applied it to other planes of societal living.

Irrespective of its success stories, Non-violence as a value and way of life continues to take momentum especially in the practical aspects of inter-religious and inter-cultural relations. As the dynamics of relationship become more and more complex, Non-violence, in the form of understanding, respect, accommodation, and acceptance seems to be the only way of positive approach. Despite violence of all kinds, especially in political and social milieu, there are groups and organizations that train themselves and others in dialogue and successful negotiations. It is because of this trend, nations build up confidence in one another and engage in smooth and balanced relationship. What nations need today is sensitivity to one another and a pattern of growth and development based on this sensitivity. Unto this effect, Nonviolence is a yardstick and a guiding principle.

Notes

1. Gandhi, M.K., Harijan, 1954, p. 9-10
2. Walter Fernandez, p.93
3. Kappan, S., p. 57-58
4. Seshagiri, N., p. 6-11
5. Walter Fernandez, p. 57
6. Ibid., p 6-68
7. Amaladoss, M., pp. 140-141
8. Williams, R., p 230-231
9. Dasgupta, S.A, P. 100
10. SBE, Vol. XXXVI, Part II, IV. 5.17
11. Samayasāra, 2-3, 38
12. Tathāgataguhya Sūtra, Sikṣāsamuccaya, Vaidhya, p.274
13. Tat Sūtra, 5.2-3; Dulichand Jain mentions that ecoligists, environmentalists and preservationists consider 'life' as sacred and this encourages movements for preservation of animals, etc. realising the fact that every creature has its place in the scheme of nature. See Jain Journal, Vol XXXIV, No.1, July 1999, p.51
14. Ācār Sūtra, 1.1.2.1
15. SBE, Vol.XIII, Vinaya Part, p. 91ff
16. Dasgupta, S.A. Vol I, p. 208
17. Praśnavhyākaraṇa, Pratamaśrutaskandha, Āsravadvāra, Ch. I, Sūtra 2
18. Tat Sūtra, Ibid 7.8
19. SBE, Vol. XIII, Vinaya Part I, p-. 235
20. Dhammapada, 129-130 in SBE, Vol X, Part I
21. Tat Sūtra, ibid. 7.8; Dr. Surendra Verma calls them 'substantive' violence and 'disposiitional' violence. He also enumerated other types of violence, such as by mana, vacana and kāya-mind, speech and body. See 'Meaning and Typology of Violence' in Jain Journal, Vol. XXX, No. 1, July 1995, pp. 16-17
22. Bhattacharya, H., 161-162
23. Jaina Gazette, Vol. 26, p.77
24. Sūt Kr. 2.4.2
25. Ibid., 2.4.9-10
26. Ibid., 2.4.3
27. Narada Thera, p. 81
28. Manu, 5,40, SBE XXV
29. Jaina Gazette, Vol XIV, P.116
30. Hemachandra Biblotheca Indica, No. 172, Calcutta, 1907-21, ii 33-49
31. Pur Sid, 79-89
32. Sikṣāsamuccaya, p.148
33. Sam N, in C..A. F. Rhys Davids and F.L. Woodward, Vol 4, p.60

34. Sikṣāsamuccaya, p. 103
35. The paradox between Ahiṁsā and Sallekhana has been well brought out by Mikal Austin Radford in his paper 'Sallekhanā, Ahiṁsā and the Western Paradox' Indicating the four main categories of suicides according to Durkheim, Radford says Sallekhanā belongs to the second category, namely, the altruistic suicide. It is for the sake of religion that Sallekhanā is undertaken by the Jains. See Jinamañjarī, Vol XI, No. April 1995, pp. 24-25
36. Ācār Sūtra, i.vii.6ff
37. Kalpasūtra, 168, 182 in SBE, Vol XXII
38. Bhagavatīsūtra, p.300
39. Ovavaiya Sutta, 100
40. Buhler, S. Uber das leben Jaina Monches Hemacandra, Vienna, 1889, P.50f
41. For 41 days, 1921 A.D.
42. ERE, Vol I V, P. 484
43. Pur Sid, Ibid. p. 177-178; also see Tat Sūtra, VII, 32
44. Pārājika III in SBE, Vol 13, p. 4
45. Thakkasu, J. Tr., p. 197ff
46. Story fo Siha (Therigatha, 77); of Sappadasa (Theragāthā, 408); of Vakkali (Theragāthā, 350); of Godhika (Kathavathu, 12); also see SBE, Vol XXXV, p. 273 ff
47. Story of the future Sākyamuni giving his body to feed a starving tigress, Jātakamāla, 1, SBB, Vol, I
48. Example of Chandragupta Maurya (4 Cent B.C); Kumārapāla, King of Gujrat (12 Cent. A.D.)., See Jaina Gazette, Vol, 12, p.266
49. Ācar Sūtra, Ibid 1.4.2.6
50. Har Dayal, p.208
51. Ibid., p.202
52. Pur Sid, Ibid.85
53. Ahimsa Voice, January 1990, p.33
54. Eliul Jacques, Ibid., p. 33-34
55. For Gandhi 'to cause pain or wish ill to or take of any being out of anger or a selfish intent is Hiṁsā. On the other hand after a calm and clear Judgement to kill or cause pain to a living being wiht a view to its spiritual or physicsal benefit from a pure, selfless intent may be the purest form of Ahiṁsā.... the final test to its violence or non-violence is after all the intent underlying the act' See Young India, 4.10, 1928; As such, kiling is not hiṁsā when life is destroyed for the sake of those whose life is taken. See Sharma, p.52; Violence is admissible to Gandhi, (i) if non-violence would cause the sacrifice of some other values of great worth like honour of women, freedom and honour of the nation., overall strength and growth of the race, or survival of democracy was at stake. See N.K. Bose, p. 155, 156, 168, 170 (ii) if a sufficient number people

were not ready and could not be persuaded to believe in and practice true Satyāgraha, violent struggles for just causes would be persuaded to believe in and practice true Satyāgraha, violent struggles for just cuses would be justified. Ibid. p. 169, 174 (iii) if there is a little prospect of the conversion of the oppressoer to the course of justice through Satyāgraha, the victims must defend themselves violently. The heart of the doctrine of Non-violence is the principle of 'univerasal convertibility' i.e. belief that all evil-doers, anywhere and in all circumstances, can be persuaded to give up their course of evil if their victims practise Satyāgraha. See N.K. Bose, pp 159, 1765-177)

56. M Bh, Śāntiparvan, 15.48-50
57. Tahtinen Unto, p. 66
58. Dharmakīrti's Verse as quoted in the article "Buddhist Dialectics" by Sankrityayan Rahula (ed): Buddhism–The Marxist Approach, Peoples Publishing House, New Delhi, 1990, p.8
59. Dhammapada, 396-423
60. Vaj Up, 9; Ayyangar, T.R. Srinivasa, p. 422-425
61. M Bh, Ajagaraparvan in Vanaparvan
62. The rivalry between the two great orders or castes: the story of Vaśiṣta and Viśvāmitra in M Bh, Ādiparvan, 6638 f
63. Utt Sūtra, 25.31-32 in SBE, Vol.LV, p. 130-140
64. Ibid., 12
65. Kalpasūtra in SBE, Vol. XXII, Part I, pp.225-226
66. Sutta Nipāta, 3.4 in SBE, Vol X, pp. 74-75
67. Carus Paul, p.92
68. Sankrityayan, Rahula, (ed). pp. 25-29
69. Utt Sūtra, 14.16-17
70. Ibid., 14.12-13
71. Ibid., 14.9
72. Sūt Kr., 1.3.2.13
73. Walter Fernandez, p.18
74. Ācār Sūtra, ibid. 1.2.2.1
75. Sūt Kr. 1.2.1.21-22; 1.9.7
76. Ācār Sūtra, 1.7.3.2
77. Utt. Sūtra, 9.12-16
78. Ibid., 9.20-22
79. Ibid., 9.48
80. Sūt Kr., 1.2.3.16
81. Utt Sūtra, 14.39-40
82. Paul Carus, Ch. 17 Verse 2
83. Ācār Sūtra, 2.1-2, 5-7
84. Parigraha or atachment on the other hand is the root cause of all mental tensions. It does violence to others, their possessions. Aparigraha, detachment or non-possession, resolves economic inequality, maintains

inner peace of the individual and society. See Sagarmal Jain in his paper 'Jaina Concept of Peace' in Jain Journal, XXIX, No. 3, January 1995, pp.107-108; Ahiṁsā and Aparigraha are the twin-virtues that respects the autonomy of the material univese with all thyes of living beings. Integral salvation that embraces the freedom of all creatures form the clutches of the evill demands an attitude of reverence toward life-principle in each being. See Sekhar, Vincent 'Implications of Ahiṁsā on Ecology-A Jaina Perspective 'in Jain Journal, Vol XXVIII, No.2, 1993, p.96; also see the same author in 'Significance of Jain Philosophy for preserving life and Environment'in Thottakara, A (ed.), p.125

85. Das Sūtra, 6.20
86. Cāritrasāra by Cā nundarāya, p.12
87. RKSA, 62
88. Ibid., 57
89. Sar Sid, 7.27
90. Tat Sūtra, 7.22; RKSA, 58
91. Up Das, 1.46
92. Fifteen forbidden trades are listed in Sāgāradharmamṛta of Āṣādhara, see Williams, R., p.117-121
93. There is a general impression that the Jains, being a business community, have an objective of accumulating wealth by any mens. There are several ideas and values in Jaina ethics to show that they are consistent with the spirit of capitalism. See Arvind K.Agarwal's Jaina Ethics and Spirit of Capitalism-A Critical Reappraisal of Weber' in N.K. Singhi, p. 199-202; also see another article in the same book 'Jainism and its perversion in actual practice' by Tarachand Gangwal, p. 124-136); Joharimal Parekh says that Jainism does not believe in materialism and consequently 'human behaviour towards wealth ' has been heavily discounted. He has subscribed to this view in his article 'Jain Economic Thought' See Jain Journal., Vol XXIX, No. 3 January 1995
94. Tat Sūtra, 7.25; Up Das 1.50 See Bhargava, p. 126, Footnote 2
95. Kār AP., 367
96. Sāgāradharmāmṛta, 5.15-17
97. Pur Sid 61
98. Kār Ap 379
99. Siddhasena on Tat Sūtra 7.16
100. Sāgār Dhar, ibid 5.36-38
101. Ibid., 5.36-38
102. 'The ideal of Aparigraha (non-possession of wealth) is an underlying tenet for the simplistic, austere life of a Jain householder which provides ample empirical and logical evidence that the earning of profits is not for the sake of non-productive consumptoin but for reinvestment. This tenet also explains the large scale philanthropic activity doine by such

the miniscule Jaina community in Indian society'. See N.K. Singhi, p.200

103. The giver represents in an imperfect manner the perfect, self-emptying character of the Jina while offering something. See, Lawrence A. Babb, pp. 190-193
104. Śrāvakācāra of Vasunandin, p 200; also see Tat Sūtra, VII. 34
105. Yogaśāstra of Hemacandra, iii, 120
106. It is important to note that Jaina householder pay attention to this aspect of gift offering or Dāna and we could see in any Indian city and elsewhere hospitals, community halls, etc. for public consumption. Social service and welfare has become one of the keynotes of Jaina morality.
107. Anāthapiṇḍaika, a man of unmeasured wealth was called the supporter of orphans and the friend of the poor, offers, Jetavana and Viśākha, a wealthy woman, offers Pubbārama or Eastern Garden, Paul Carus, CH. 24 and 25
108. Tahtinen, Unto, P, 165, 167
109. Ibid., p. 168
110. Atreya, p. 69
111. Bhagabad Gītā, 14.6-18
112. Ācār Sūtra, 1.5.5.4
113. Ibid., 1.2.3.4
114. Sūt Kr I.11.10.. 1.4.10
115. Chānd Up 8.5.1
116. Manu 5.44
117. Yogaśātra, 2.37., also ślokas 33.36
118. Sāṇḍilya Upainṣed. 1.1 This Upaniṣad has leanings towards the Yoga System of Patañjali, See Radhakrishnan, S.
119. Abhidhammakoṣavyākhya p 130, see also Abhidhammadīpa, p.73
120. Yogasūtra: 2.30
121. Samayasāra: 2
122. Dwivedi, R.C., p. 122
123. Ahimsa Voice, Jain '90. p.33. John E. Cort brings out the non-hegemonic character of Medieval Jain kings, supporting all religious communities generously and treating them with impartiality. See, Cort, John E., pp. 85-110.
124. Williams, R., p71
125. Gandhi, M.K. Young India, Jan, as quoted by in Jag Parvesh Chander, p. 412
126. Jesudasan, I. p. 116
127. Bondurant, p viii
128. Gandhi, M.K. Young India, 9 July 1922 as quoted by Chander, J.P. p 352
129. Gandhi, M.K., Harijan, 7 Jan 1939; CW 68:278
130. Gandhi, M.K. Young India, 3 June 1926
131. Ibid., 27 May 1926: CW 30: 486-88

132. Jesudasan, I.: p. 130
133. Ibid.
134. Dasai, Mahadev, p 93
135. Gandhi. M.K. Young India 31, October 1929
136. Anekānta is active indifference, ready to bear or to forego anything for the sake of the end or goal. It is a transcendent spirit of 'detached involvemnet' neither denial of life nor runing away from the world. See Sekhar, Vincent, : 'Ignatian indifference and Jaina Vision of Anekānta,' in Ignis : 3 1994, p.131
137. The Voice of Ahiṁsā, Vol. VII, No. 3-4, p.187.
138. A multi-dimensional outlook and approach to life is neccessay ot understand the issues, problems, etc. Tackling them form different angles will spped up the solutions possible. This has been presented in Sekhar, Vincent, 'Dynamic Pluralism- A Vision toward conflict Resolution and Cosmic integratin'
139. 'Non -violent search for trrth should inspire the inquiries of a thinker and Anekānta demonstrates a spirit of toleration, understanding and respect for the views of others' says Dayanand Bhargava in 'A Few Modern Interpretations of Non-absolutism,' See Nagin, p 115; Ram Jee SIngh has discussed about the relevance of Anekānta in Modern Times, Ibid., pp. 127-134
140. Sūt Kr. 1.102, 21-23
141. Tat Sūtra, 8
142. Sūt Kr. 1.12.1
143. While the Catuṣkoti of the Buddhists says that the nature of the problem is inexpressible in its fundamental aspect, the Jaina concept of inexpressiblity (avaktavya) there is no uncertainty. It only says that words cannot express the nature of the object in its different aspects. In that way, Syādvāda is neither scepticism nor nihilism nor the theory of ignorance. It is a certainty of expression with a certain knowledge from a particular point of view.
144. Amlan Dutta brings out the significance of the attitude of Anekānta in his article "Gandhi and the Contemporary Crisis" to insist that all member of the same class or community must see the truth in the same light is an error that lies at the basis of totalitarianism,' See Gandhian Perspectives, Vol. IV, No. 2, 1991, p. 6
145. Pramāda or Carelessness as the root cause of violence, Bhargava, Dayanand, p. 106; Willams, R: Ibid., pp 230-31; also see Pur Sid 99, SBJ, Vol IV
146. Merchant, M.K. suggests that only through tolerance and Non-violence can conflicts be not only successfully resolved but also can have lasting effect. See "Confict Resolution through Tolerance and Non-violence": Internatioinal Association for the Future of Humanity.
147. In Gandhi's opinion, it is only a prayerful spirit that would bring peace

and goodwill among religions. 'I am convinced that we shall find neither peace nor good will among men through strife among men of different religions, through disputation among them. We shall find truth and peace and good will if we approach the humblest of mankind in a prayerful spirit', CW 64:291

148. 'Ethical Individualism' is the moral basis and an alternate vision of Democracy. It is alternate to 'possessive individualism,' See Ali Ashraf in Gandhian Perspectives, Vol IV, No. 2, 1991. p. 98
149. Gandhi, M.K. Rebuilding our villages. Ahmedabad, 1955, p. 47. 'Root of violence lay in exploitation' See Partha N. Mukherji in Gandhian Perspectives, Vol IX, No. 2., 1996, p.81
150. It is difficult to satisfy a person who has no control over wants. Gandhi's theory of consumption is based on wants. If people could curtail their 'unlimited wants', the desire to exploit others will diminish. See V.T. Patil p. 282
151. Gandhi M.K., Ahmedabad, 1948-49, Vol. II, pp. 1-2
152. Gandhi M.K., Ahmedabad, 1950, p. 186
153. Gandhi M.K., Ahmedabad, 1968, p. 35
154. Ācār Sūtra, 1.65.1; "Non-violent legends in Jainism," by Dr.. Premsuman Jain: The Story of Bharata and Bāhubali; The story of the elephant Meruprabha and Dharmaruci muni in Nāyādhammakahā; the story of Ardakumāra muni in Sūtrakṛtānga; the story of Jinadatta in Avaśyaka Cūrṇi; the story of Cārudatta in Vasudevahindi; the story of Sulusa and Mātaṅga Yamapasa in Āgama Bhāṣya literature. See Ahimsa Voice, Vol II. July 1990
155. Ācār Sūtra, 1.7.2.4
156. Utt Sūtra, II 13.26
157. Maj N 21.1.3-4
158. Jaina Gazette, Vol 12, Lucknow (1915-16), p. 83
159. Non-violent resistance resembles war (i) In having a psychological and moral aim and effort; (ii) In having one similar purpose to win the support of public opinion; (iii) In being a discipline of a parellel emotions and instinct; (iv) In operating against the morale of the opponent; (v) In principles of strategy; (vi) In being a method of settling great disputes and conflicts; (vii) In requiring courage, dynamic energy, capacity to endure failure and suffering, self-sacrifice, self-control, chivalry action; (viii) In being positive and powerful and; (ix) In affording opportunity of serving for a large idea and glory.' See Gregg Richards, p. 127
160. Sharp, Gene: pp 301-2
161. W.E. Muelhlmann discusses the " Problem of passive resistance" in Heimo Rau, pp. 116-128
162. Jesudasan, I, P, 127; For the analysis of Gandhian philosophy of conflict and conflict resolution, see Joan Bondurant, Chapter on 'Gandhi and group conflict'

163. Sibley, Mulford, Q, pp 231-32
164. I'-id., p. 53
165. Ibid., p. 11; In Gandhi 's words..... as an unrepresented and voiceless community, which has been so much misunderstood in the past and which is labouring under curious but storng race prejudice (context of South Africa) it can only defend its honour and status by a process of sacrifice and self-suffering (CW 12:186)
166. Whitehead, A.N., pp 31, 53, .105-106, 205, 213-14 and all of Ch. 5
167. Radhakrishnan, S., P. 238; Partha N. Mukherji says, 'planning for an egalitarian social order is based on love, altruism, spirit of service, dignity of labour, non-vioilence and equality.' See "Sarvodaya and Planning" in Gandhian Perspectives, Vol IX, No. 2, 1996, p. 81
168. See " Building a New World Order on Non -Violence " by Daisaku Ikeda, in Gandhian Perspectives, Vol VIII, No. 1, 1995, pp. 39-55. He says that the ethos of Non-violence has grown out of the spiritual and cultural soil of India and he believes that a vision of a 'Non-war Community' is possible. Ibid., pp. 42-43
169. Gregg, Richard, p 161
170. Dr. S.I. Malhotra points out that creating a higher identity or consciousness that binds everybody together as an integreated whole is the base for buildiing up a nation. It is this identity which must cover the social, political and economic interests of all members. A new political and economic system is to be created in which each region or each community realizes that its development is vitally linked with the rest of the nation. See "Communalism in India: Causes and Cure" in N. Radhakrishnan, pp. 47-48
171. Brown, R, pp. 1015-16
172. Holy Bible, Book of Isaiah, 25:8
173. Ibid., Revelation, 20:13
174. Ibid., Isaiah, 55:1
175. Sibley, pp. 355-57
176. Vijay Ranjan Dutta speaks about the 'participatory democracy' through Panchyati Raj and Gram Sabha for ensuring unity and harmony. See Gandhian Perspectives, Vol. VII, No. 2 1994, pp.76-77. He also points out how some Panchayati Raj Legislations aim at social reform activities. Ibid., p. 81.
177. Sūt Kr. 1.11.11
178. The source of Non-violence is Non-attachment. See "The concept of Morality and Religion in Kant and Gandhi" by Dharm Raj Yadav in Gandhian perspectives, Vol VI, No. 1, 1993, p. 49; Self-realization has to take place in actual life. For Gandhi, Religion is essentially moral or ethical. Hence self-realization or god-realization is synonymous with ethical precepts like Truth and Non-violence. See ibid., pp. 53-55
179. Desai, M: ibid., p.93

180. Gandhi, M.K., Young India, 1 Nov 1928
181. Gandhi, M.K., Harijanbandhu, 3 Jan 1937; CW 64: 191-92
182. Gandhi, M.K., Harijan, 17 Sep. 1938; CW 67: 353; In Gandhi's opinion, it is only a prayerful spirit that would bring peace and good-will among religions: 'I am convinced that we shall find neither peace nor good will among men through strife among men of different religions through disputation among them. We shall find truth and peace and goodwill if we approach the humblest of manking in a prayerful spirit.' CW 64: 291
183. Judith M. Brown narrates the life of Gandhi, especiallhy when Non-violence was on trial. See Ch.9, pp 314-358; Gandhi sought from Kavi Rajachandra answers to questions that disturbed his mind. One of them was about the problem of Ahiṁsā: 'If a snake comes to bite us what should we do? Should we remain calm and silent and allow it to bite or kill it outright to save ourselves?' After a long discourse, Rajachandra says that those who are anxious for their spiritual good, should, when confronted with such situation, offer their body to snake rather than take out its life. See 'Mahatma Gandhi and Kavi Rajachandra on Philosophical Discourse', by Brahmacari Sri Govardhanadasa in Jain Journal, Vol. XXX, No. 2, October, 1995, p.54
184. Jeyaprakash Narayan held that enduring revolutoin in India is possible only through Gandhian Method. See Gandhian Perspectives, Vol IX, No. 2, 1996, pp. 57-67.

CHAPTER VII

INSIGHTS INTO THE ŚRAMAṆIC TRADITIONS

The comparative study of the meaning and understanding of *Dharma* from the points of view of the Vedic, the Brāhmaṇic and the Śramaṇic traditions has shown remarkable insights into the cultural and religious history of ancient India. More particularly it has revealed the dialogical processes of these traditions in assimilating and rejecting ideas and values. The study unfolds a number of aspects of comparison and contrast between these traditions and their overall contribution to Indian life and society.

7.1. *Dharma* is an equivocal term and it refers mainly to the cosmic and the human Order. But this meaning cannot be understood without a context, namely, the thought pattern of society. The historical context of ancient India reveals the encounter of two traditions whose life and ethos were very different from one another. While the Vedic tradition upheld the pravṛtti mārga and the importance of sacrifice to the gods, the śramaṇic traditions followed the path of renunciation in order to achieve the final goal of freedom from the cycle of births. There seems to be a slow conversion from the inadequacy of karma mārga, which rewarded only a better heaven, to jñāna mārga or the way of discriminating wisdom, which would lead people to complete liberation from the saṁsāric existence. This new wisdom seemed to be the possession of the non-āryan tribes, more often discussed by the kṣatriyas of the eastern regions, namely the *Vrātyas,* which later on, was carried to other places by the Brāhmins residing in their courts. The neo-Āryanism preached by these Brāhmins taught the world the karma-saṁsāra and the way of knowledge for the final release of the worldlings from the cycle of births.

7.2. In the second encounter, namely the *class-caste encounter* between the Brāhmaṇas and the Kṣatriyas there developed an anti-Vedic and anti-Brāhmaṇic sentiment. Bhāgavatism (kṛṣṇaism etc.) opposed the Vedic polytheism and religions founded and systematized by ksatriyas like Buddha and Mahāvīra developed atheistic and antivedic tendencies. The inexorable action of karma was enough to explain the world. Other realities like God, grace and the like were extravagant to such thinking. The hierarchy of omniscient teachers substituted the Vedic authority. The attempt to evolve a casteless society in the formation of muni and śrāvaka saṅgha by both the śramaṇa teachers Buddha and Mahāvīra was an open protest against the Brāhmaṇical social order. Their saṅgha admitted all types of people high and low in social category, accepted women priesthood and followed the path of Ahiṁsā as against the sacrificial cult of the Brāhmaṇas. In the attempt to nullify the superiority of the Brāhmins, Buddha and Mahāvīra gave new definitions to Brāhminhood in terms of moral conduct and purity.

7.3. In all such Race-to-Race encounter and Class-to-Class encounter there had been a sort of a slow but gradual assimilations and rejections. The relationship between them had been at first inimical to each other, but later on, the two traditions acknowledged and assimilated the ideas, cults and practices of one another. We cannot say definitely how the race-mingling took place or who possessed such as such an idea first. But history and literature give evidences to the fact of existence of two distinct traditions with distinct life-style and thinking. They also point out to the dissatisfaction of one kind of thinking and the gradual conversion to the other in the process of their self-understanding: for instance, the understanding and acknowledgement of *karma-saṁsāra,* the ideal of *mokṣa* and the path *of renunciation,* etc.

7.4. On the one hand, total renunciation of activities got changed into the renunciation of the fruits of activities as found in the Gītā. Also the *Bhakti cult* propagated by the Gītā and other such religious literature was an attempt to bring about a change in the Brāhmiṇic social stratification. Those who with a surrendering faith in the Divine were equal to those who renounced the world, wealth and children and thereby stood above the social category. Total surrender to the Divine and joining the ascetic order with total renunciation were symbolic protests against Varṇa and Āśrama dharma and an open adherence to casteless society. On the other hand, the *Vedic polytheism* and the general bhakti cult and practices influenced the Śramaṇa traditions in their worship of innumerable gods and goddesses and their performances of rituals for the benefit of worldly ends.

7.5. What is specific to the Śramaṇa traditions is *asceticism* and it is the ascetic ideals that united all of them. These ascetic ideals and practices have their basis on 'Knowledge' opposed to the ritualistic traditions. Knowledge was the key for the attainment of the desired end. The dialogue between the two traditions namely the Brāhmiṇic and the Śramaṇic traditions results in favour of knowledge and in the appreciation and acknowledgement of the *Renouncer tradition.* The acceptance of the fourth Āśrama was an expression to this. While the Brāhmaṇic tradition accepted the first three Āśramas in their order, the Śramaṇic traditions were not particular about their order but contended that the desired end could be achieved in any stage of life. The renunciatory spirit and such practices, which are suitable to attain the End were considered important. In their mutual dialogue there was a slow but gradual change over to ascetic ideals of renunciation and to ascetic practices such as austerity, meditation, etc.

7.6. As the ascetic way of life become means to attain the spiritual ideal even Kṣatriyas embraced mendicant way of life contrary to the prescribed caste duties. The leaders of Śramaṇa religions Buddha and Mahāvīra were Kṣatriya nobles and they took to religious life and gave themselves to severe ascetic practices in order to achieve their goal of life. While the Brāhmiṇic tradition strictly adhered to the *Varṇa* and *Āśrama* dharma, advocated the study of the Vedas only to their Brahmacārins and forbade women from joining religious life. Buddhism and Jainism allowed women priesthood and took them in their religious Order.

7.7. Though *ascetic* ideal and practice are common to all Śramaṇic traditions yet we find differences in their understanding and practice of asceticism. While the *Ājīvikas* and the Jains practice asceticism to the extreme (for instance, practices like *Sallekhana*) the Buddhists chose the middle path between the extremes of pleasure and austerity. Each tradition accepted certain ascetic practices and rejected certain others. But all of them accepted renunciation as their way of life and followed their religious rules and regulations as purifying methods. Their laity to this day voluntarily take up monastic way of life for certain duration of time, and at some stage or other in their life.

7.8. The monastic way of life of the Śramaṇa was a *protest* against the tyranny of caste and also an emphatic '*No*' to the accumulative, consumerist tendency of the world, especially of the rich rulers and landlords. In the formation of sangha the Śramaṇa leaders Buddha and Mahāvīra emulated the model of tribal democracy and thereby stood against the values of State power. The Śramaṇa *Saṅgha* was a revolutionary attempt at building a casteless, democratic society with values like equality, simplicity and brotherliness.

7.9. In the evolution of the understanding of the meaning and nature of dharma, especially in a dialogical context of the Vedic and the Śramaṇic traditions, we find important shifts and stresses. The importance of Vedic gods in maintaining the world Order gets diluted and Sacrifice or Yajña attains a superior status and, along with it, the position of the priestly or sacerdotal class. The simple aim of the Vedic people in their worship and prayer were cattle, long life and strong sons. But in the Brāhmaṇas we see the shift in their objectives. It was mainly *svargakāma* or the desire for heaven. The sacrificial rituals provided a better place in the heavenly regions. But it was in the Āraṇyaka and the Upaniṣadic period we find a definite shift in the objectives of life. It was to know the nature of Ātman, to be absorbed into Brahman through certain ascetic practices like meditation etc. and embrace a life of renunciation. A *new* spirituality was gaining root in the later Vedāntic period.

7.10. As one goes through the sacred literature of India one finds the two distinct trends (complementary and even opposing trends) of the Brāhmaṇic and the Śramaṇic traditions coexisting. The Brāhmaṇic tradition seems to lay stress on Yajña or Sacrificial ceremonies and Varṇāśrama dharma (as evidenced mainly by the Brāhmaṇas, the *Śrauta, Gṛhya* sūtras and the *Dharmaśāstras*). The Śramaṇic traditions emphasize the ideal of *mokṣa* and *sannyāsa* dharma and the practice of meditation and austerity (as evidenced mainly by the Āraṇyakas the Upaniṣads and the Epics, especially, the Mahābhārata).

7.11. Generally in the post Vedic period Dharma assumes different meanings from at both transcendental human levels. They refer more to the world Order, law, ordinances, customary observances etc. But more specifically, it is how one fits in the natural and the social world that becomes the *normative* dimension to Dharma. To ensure the world Order the social classes are supposed to engage in their duties and responsibilities (svadharma).

7.12. On the contrary, the Śramaṇa religions preached a Dharma in keeping with their Śramaṇic ideals, which questioned the traditional Brāhmaṇical trend of thought: Sacrifices are futile in the path of Deliverance. The final objective of man is liberation from the grip of misery produced by the cycle of births. No god is a *saviour* in this process. One has to reap one's Karma, and only the individual is fully responsible in working out his or her salvation. For this one has to take up a life of renunciation and practice asceticism. As these are not easy for the common people to practise, the Śramaṇa religions gave a *two-tier* spirituality, one for the monks and nuns and, the other, for the laity. This is more pronounced in the Jain community where the monks and nuns follow the *mahāvrata* (absolute path of morality) and the laity, the *anuvrata* (practical path of morality).

7.13. Though Buddhism and Jainism have the same Śramaṇic thrust in their ideals and practice, their understanding of *dharma,* its symbolizations and manifestations differ from tradition to tradition. The original teachings of Buddha are interpreted in many ways and several new metaphysical concepts develop in the course of time. Within Buddhism a revolutionary change takes place. *Salvation by faith* and the *Path of Devotion* become prominent due to various reasons. Subsequently later Buddhism abounds in *Buddhas* and *Bodhisattvas,* supernatural beings and other manifestations. In Mahāyāna Buddhism, the Buddhist dharma centres on the one personality, the *universal* Buddha and his manifestations in history like the Brāhmaṇical incarnations.

7.14. The metaphysical dimension of Buddhist dharma in such doctrines as the *Anātman* theory, momentariness, etc. demanded *right* vision, and the wisdom to discriminate the right from the wrong. And to this, meditation became a means. But, later, Mahāyāna Buddhism advocated ideas like heavenly Buddhas who secured places in different paradises for their aspirants and *Nirvāṇa* or Salvation became an easy access to those who tread the path of devotion to and faith in such Buddhas and Bodhisattvas. Instead of being *light* unto themselves the Buddhists had recourse to supernatural beings for securing higher places in the heavenly regions.

7.15. Such an understanding of Buddhist dharma clearly betrays the influence of the Upaniṣadic Universal Soul, the impact of the Bhakti traditions of Hinduism, the idea of the transference of merit, etc. Too much of metaphysical speculations, which become symbolized in too many concepts eventually paved the way to different schools. But the liberal interpretation of their scriptural texts allowed the Buddhists to see their doctrines and practices *inculturated* in different countries in the world and such liberalism implied also glorification of individual liberty and mutual toleration. Whereas in Jain religious history not much change has taken place to this day and newer interpretation of the doctrines are almost nill. Even Ahiṁsā, the cardinal virtue of the Jains, began to be applied to different dimensions of life (Socio-political, etc.) only in recent times. Such strict orthodoxy could be one of the reasons why Jainism remained more confined to the territory of its birth.

7.16. Like Buddhist dharma, Jain dharma too has both metaphysical and ethical dimensions. In the metaphysical realm *dharma* and *adharma* refer to the medium of motion and of rest. They are new concepts not available in any Indian philosophical systems. But they play a very important role in the *salvation-history* of the Soul, i.e., in the process of its Bondage and liberation. The *movement* aspect of dharma enables the Karma particles flow into the Soul as well as get detached from it. The movement and rest of jīva and Pudgala are possible only because of these two substances, *dharma* and *adharma*. But the Buddhist concept of dharma is entirely different from the Jain metaphysical conception. *Dharma* or *dhamma* in Buddhism refers to the ultimate constituent of existence. Everything, both material and non-material is constituted of specific number of dharmas classified in number of ways. Their nature and characteristics, their functions and inter-relations bring about a *dynamism* in life and in the outside world. This *movement dynamics* is very special of dharmas. In this way both the Jain and the Buddhist concept of dharma relate to the movement dynamics of the phenomena of existence.

7.17. Again on the metaphysical level the Buddhist slogan *dhammam caranam gacchāmi* and Jaina *vatthu sabavo dhammo* refer to their respective doctrines and visions concerning life and reality. The implications of the Jain *saptatattva* (seven categories of reality) are many and they are relevant to life. The concept of Jīva implies equality and plurality of souls. It advocates reciprocal love *(as it is to me, so it is to him, etc.)* and respect. The *knowledge* of karma and the necessary *conduct* leads one to liberation. The path is arduous and it involves self-discipline and self-abnegation. One has to pursue the path of the *Enlightened One,* dependent on oneself with self-determination. Mokṣa is immediate in the sense that it is attainable in this very life. It is also eschatological in the sense that karma can be completely annihilated in the future course of events and lives. Both the Buddhist dhamma and the Jain dharma from metaphysical and moral points of view emphasize the nature *of Reality,* the theory of Karma and the way of salvation.

7.18. In the ethical plane both the systems have their own rationale for moral justifications of an act. While the Jains conceive karma as material substance, the Buddhists understand it in moral terms. While the latter emphasize the volition (motivation, intention, etc.) aspect of an act in any moral judgement, the former assign due places to motivations and intentions but look at the very act itself. Jain *Triratna* (Three Jewels *of Right Faith, Right Knowledge and Right Conduct) constitutes the path* of morality and of liberation. Knowledge without conduct and conduct without knowledge and both without vision of Faith are not tenable. In both Buddhist as well as in Jain traditions morality forms part of the religious ideal of Enlightenment. It is not merely a means to attain perfection; it is an integral part of perfection and always associated with Enlightenment or Liberation.

7.19. In Jain dharma, self-realization becomes the goal of moral life and self-realization is not merely for the individual alone. This ideal suggests that the highest good of the self is for the sake of the highest social good. This is how the visionaries and the prophets of Jainism have preached Dharma as they were organically related to their community (Saṅgha). Self-realization is not possible without social institutions because they are instrumental in the process of its attainment self-realization. The Bodhisattva ideal in the Buddhist tradition is somewhat similar to the *suffering servant of Yahweh* in the Christian tradition and this ideal lays stress on the social dimension of liberation.

7.20. The *two-tier spirituality*, prescribed in Buddhist as well as Jain tradition, shows their realistic approach to life. A lesser strict discipline than that of the monks and nuns is prescribed for the laity. Virtues such as kindness, compassion etc. and the practices like meditation, alms-giving, religious conversation, etc. are very much encouraged for the householder. But the ideal of a muni or a monk has always been an inspiration to the lay followers and this is manifested in their eagerness to spend sometime in the monastery along with the religious.

7.21. But, ultimately, it is *Ahiṁsā* or *non-injury* to self and others has become the quintessence of all dharma *(Ahiṁsā paramo dharma)* in these two traditions. It does not mean that the Śramaṇas lay absolute claim over this important virtue but their vision of life and reality has naturally led them to the understanding of this prime value of life. Ahiṁsā is both an intellectual attitude and an ethical conduct. Ahiṁsā at the rational level has contributed to non-absolutist theories like Anekāntavāda and human and natural inter-relatedness though Syādvāda in Jainism. At best these ideals have enhanced the pluralistic culture of India.

7.22. The implications of Ahiṁsā in every day life are seen in the preservation and promotion of life and environment, and in checking violence and its manifestations. The contemporary relevance of Śramaṇa dharma is seen in this prime virtue, which in all its expressions, mediates relationships and helps in promoting and building a cosmic society of love and mutual trust, justice and peace.

BIBLIOGRAPHY

(1) ORIGINAL SOURCES:

1. *Abhidharmadīpa* (Vimalamitra? Isvara?): P. S. Jaini (ed.) 1977; *Abhidhammadīpa with Vibhāsaprabhāvṛtti,* Critically edited with notes and introduction: Ed. P.S. Jaini, Patna, K.P. Jayaswal Research Institute, 1959
2. *Abhidhammakoṣa and Vyākhyā of Vasubandhu:* (ed.) Prhlad Pradhan, Patna, K.P. Jayaswal Research Institute, 1967
3. *Abhidharmakoṣabhāsyam:* La Vallee Poussin (trans.), English translation by Leo M. Pruden, Asian Humanities Press, Berkeley, California, Four Volumes, 1988
4. *Abhidhamma Piṭaka, I Dhammasāṅganī:* Muller, Edward (ed.) Pali Text Society, London, 1885
5. *Abhidhamma Piṭaka, II Vibhaṅga:* Rhys Davids, C.A.F., Pali Text Society, London, 1904
6. *Ācārāṅgasūtra:* (trans.) Jacobi, Hermann, Sacred Books of the East, Vol.22 (Jaina Sutras - Part I)
7. *Aṅguttara Nikāya:* R. Morris (Vols 1-2) and E. Hardy (Vols 3-5) (eds.), 5 Vols. PTS London 1885-1900; (trans.) F.L. Woodward (Vols 1,2 and 5) and E. M. Hare (Vols 3, 4); The Book of the Gradual Sayings, 5 Vols, Pali Text Society, London, 1932-36
8. *Anyayogavyavacched Dvātṛmsikā of Hemacandra:* Dhruva, A. B. (ed.) with introduction, notes and Appendices, Bombay Sanskrit and Prakrit Series, 1933
9. *Āpastambha Dharmasūtra:* (trans.) Buhler, Sacred Books of the East, Vol. II & XIV (Sacred Laws of the Āryas)
10. *Āptamīmāṁsā of Samantabhadra:* Solapura, Sam. Sak. 1826 Comm. Sūri Vidyānandi, Rajnagar, V.S. 1993
11. *Arthaśāstra of Kautilya:* (trans.) by Dr. R. Shamasastry, 3rd edn., Mysore, 1929
12. *Aṣṭādhyāyī of Pāṇini:* (trans.) Katre, Sumitra M., Motilal Banarsidass, Delhi, 1989
13. *Aṣṭāsāhasrikaprajñāpāramitā:* Conze, Edward (trans.), Calcutta,

The Asiatic Society, 1958; E. Conze (trans.), The Perfection of Wisdom in Eight Thousand Lines and its Verse Summary, Four Seasons Foundation, Bolinas, 1973; Sanskrit text in P.L. Vaidya (ed.) with Haribhadra's commentary called Aloka, The Mithila Institute of Post-Graduate Studies and Research in Sanskrit Learning, Darbhanga, 1960

14. *AtharvaVeda:* The Hymns of the Atharvaveda, Sacred Books of the East, Vol. XLII; The Hymns of the Atharva Veda, (trans.) R. T. J. Griffith, (ed.) Satavalakar, S.D. Aundh, 1943
15. *Atthasālinī, Dhammasaṅganīaṭṭhakathā:* (ed.) E. Muller, London, Pali Text Society, 1897
16. *Aupapātika Sūtra:* (ed.) Hema Sagara, Bombay, n.d.
17. *Āvaśyaka Sūtra:* with Cūrṇi of Jinadāsaganī, 2 Vols, Ratlam, 1928-9, V. Abhidhana Rajendra, infra, p. xxvii.
18. *Baudhāyana Dharmasūtra:* (trans.) Buhler, Sacred Books of the East, Vol. II & XIV (Sacred Laws of the Aryas)
19. *Bhagavad Gītā:* The Zaehner, R.C., Oxford University Press, London, 1969; Bhagavadgītā, A verse Translation: Geoffrey Parinder, Sheldon Press, London, 1974
20. *Bhagavatī Sūtra:* with the Commentary of Abhayadeva, India Office MSS., 3 Vols, Bombay, 1918-21 Catalogue Nos. 7444-47 ed. Weber A, Berlin, 1966 (Grammar of the Bhagavatī, Berlin, Koenigl. Akadem. der wissensch. 1866; Commentary of Abhayadeva, Bombay-Ahmedabad, Vik. Sam. 1974-1988
21. *Bhagavatī Ārādhana:* (also Mūlārādhana) Sivakoti Ācārya, Comm. Aparājitasūri, Solapura 1935; Comm. Āṣādhara, Solapura, 1935
22. *Bhāvasaṅgraha:* (ed.) Pannalala Soniti, Bombay, Vik. Sam. 1978
23. *Brahmajāla Sutta:* Sodhi, Bhikkhu (trans.) Buddhist Publication Society, Kandy, 1978; M. Walshe (trans.), Thus Have I Heard: The Long Discourses of the Buddha, Wisdom, London, 1987; Another translation in T. W. Rhys Davids (trans.) (1899-21), Dialogues of the Buddha, Pali Text Society, London, Three Volumes.
24. *Bṛhatkalpasūtra:* Vol. I Brhatkalpabhāṣya, (ed.) Guru Sri Caturvijaya and Puṇyavijaya, Bhavanagar, 1933
25. *Cāritrasāra of Cāmundarāya:* Manikacandra Digambara Jaina Grantamālā, No.9 Bombay, 1917
26. *Civañāna Cittiyar of Arunandi:* with the comm. of Tattuvappirakācar, (ed.) M. Alagappa Mudaliyar, Madras, 1911; (trans.) J.M. Nallaswami Pillai, Sivajñāna Siddhiyar, Madras 1913

27. *Culla Vagga:* (trans.) Rhys Davids, Thomas William and Oldenberg, Sacred Books of the East, Vol. XVII (Vinaya texts, part ii Mahāvagga, Cullavagga); Sacred Books of the East, Vol. XX (Vinaya texts, part iii Cullavagga), Devanagiri Pali Series, Nalanda, 1956

28. *Daśavaikālikasūtra of Ārya Sayyambhava:* (trans.) and notes by Lalwani, K.C. Motilal Banarsidass, Delhi, 1973

29. *Dhammapada:* (trans.) F. Max Muller, Sacred Books of the East, Vol. X; Pali text with English translation in John Ross Carter and M. Palihawadana (trans.), Sacred Writings, Buddhism: The Dhammapada, Quality Paperback Book Club, New York, 1992

30. *Dhammapad-attha-kathā:* (Buddhaghosa's Commentary on Dhammapada) (ed.) H.C. Norman and L.S., 5 Vols, Pali Text Society, London, 1906-1915

31. *Dhammasāṅganī:* (ed.) Muller, Edward, Pali Text Society, 1885 (trans.) Rhys Davids, A Buddhist Manuel of Psychological Ethics, Royal Asiatic Society, London, 1900

32. *Dharmasūtras:* P. Olivelle (trans.). The Law Codes of Ancient India, Oxford University Press, Oxford and New York, 1999

33. *Dīgha Nikāya:* (eds) T. W. Rhys Davids and J. E. Carpenter, 3 Vols, London, Pali Text Society 1890-1911; Dialogues of the Buddha, (trans.) T.W. Rhys Davids and C.A.F. Rhys Davids, 3 Vols, London, PTS, 1899-1921; (ed.) Bhagavata, N.K., Bombay, 1942; (trans.) Sankrtyayana Rahul, Benares, 1963; M. Walshe (trans.). Thus Have I Heard: The Long Discourses of the Buddha, Wisdom, London, 1987

34. *Dīpavaṁśa:* Oldenberg, Hermann (ed. & trans.), London, Williams and Norgate, 1879

35. *Dravyasaṅgraha of Nemichandra:* (ed.) with introduction and translated by Siddhanta Chakravarti Sarat Chandra Ghoshal, The Central Jaina Publishing House, Arrah, 1917; (ed.) S. C. Ghoshal, Motilal Banarsidass Pvt Ltd, Delhi, 1989

36. *Gautama Dharmasūtra:* (trans.) Buhler, Sacred Books of the East, Vols II & XIV (Sacred Laws of the Āryas

37. *Gommaṭasāra (Karmakāṇḍa):* (ed.) Brahmacari, S.P., Lucknow, 1937

38. *Holy Bible, The:* Revised Standard Version, Catholic edition for India, Pub. by Collins for Theological Publications in India, Bangalore, 1973

39. *Iṣṭopadeśa:* Pūjyapāda, Bombay, 1954.

40. *Itivuttaka (as it was said):* (trans.) Woodward, F. L., Minor Anthologies of the Pali, Vol. II (Sacred Books of the Buddhist, Vol. VIII), Oxford University Press, London, 1935
41. *Jātaka, Lomahaṁsa:* (ed.) V. Fausboll, 6 Vols and index, London 1877-1897; (trans.) by various hands, (ed.) E. B. Cowel, 6 Vols and index, Cambridge, 1895-1907
42. *Jātakamālā:* (trans.) Speyer, J. S., Sacred Books of the Buddhist, Vol. I, 1895
43. *Jñānasāra:* Ganin Yasovijaya, Bhavanagar, V.S. 1969
44. *Kalpasūtra:* Jacobi, Hermann, Sacred Books of the East, Vol. XXII, (Jaina Sutras, Part I)
45. *Kārtikeyānuprekṣā of Swami Kārtikeya:* Comm. Subhacandra (ed.) Upadhye, A.N., Agas, 1960
46. *Kathā Vatthu:* (ed.) Taylor, Arnold C., PTS, London, 1894-97, Reprint in 1979; Shwe, Zan Aung, Points of Controversy, or Subjects of Discourse: Being a translation of the Kathā-Vatthu from the Abhidhammapiṭaka, PTS, London, 1915, Reprint in 1969; Commentary by Buddhaghoṣa translated in B.C. Law (trans.), The Debates Commentary, Pali text Society, London, 1989
47. *Kauśiṭaki Brāhmaṇa:* A critical annotated text with introduction Sreekrishna, Sarma, E.R., Wiesbaden Franz Sheiner Verlag, 1968
48. *Kūtadanta Sutta:* T.W. Rhys Davids, Wheel Publication, Ceylon, 1968
49. *Laghīyastrayam of Akalaṅkadeva:* Sanchalaka - Singhi, Jaina Granthamala, Calcutta, 1939
50. *Laṅkāvatāra Sūtra:* (trans.) Suzuki, Daisetz Teitaro, George Routledge and Sons, London, 1932, Reprint in 1973 by Routledge and Kegan Paul, London
51. *Mahābhārata:* (Adi to Bhīṣma Parvans) (ed.) V.S. Sukthankar and others, Pune, 1927; (ed.) T.R. Krishnacharya and T.R. Vyasacharya (Kumbhakonam edn.), 6 Vols, Bombay, 1906; Kamala Subramaniyam, Bharatiya Vidya Bhavan, Bombay, 1965
52. *Mahāparinibbāna Suttānta:* The Book of Great Disease, Sacred Books of the Buddhist, Vol. Ill and Vol. XI; Pali text in T.W. Rhys Davids and J. Estlin Carpenter (eds.), The Dīgha Nikāya, PTS, London, Three Volumes, 1966; M. Walshe (trans.), Thus Have I Heard: The Long Discourses of the Buddha, Wisdom, London, 1987

53. *Mahāpurāṇa of Puṣpadanta:* (ed.) P. L. Vaidya, Manichand Digambara Jaina Granthamālā, Bombay, 1937-41
54. *Mahāvagga in 4 Vols:* T. W. Rhys Davids and Oldenberg, Oxford Clarenden Press, 1881; T. W. Rhys Davids, Thomas William and Oldbenberg, Sacred Books of the East, Vol. XVII, Vol. XIII, Vinaya I
55. *Mahāvaṁśa:* The Great Chronicle of Ceylon, (trans.) William Geiger and Co., Pali Text Society, London, 1912
56. *Majjima Nikāya:* (trans.) I.B. Homer, Middle Length sayings, 3 Vols, London, Pali Text Society, 1954-59; (eds) V. Trenchner and R. Chalmers, 3 Vols, London Pali Text Society, 1887-1901; (trans.) Sankrtyayana Rahula, Saranath, 1933; Bhikku Nanamoli and Bhikku Bodhi (trans.): The Middle Length Discourses of the Buddha: A New Translation of the Majjima Nikāya, Wisdom, Boston, 1995
57. *Manu Dharmasūtra:* (trans.) Buhler, Sacred Books of the East, Vol. (Sacred Laws of the Aryas), (ed.) Maxmuller, 1886
58 *Milindapañhā:* The Questions of King Milinda, T.W. Rhys Davids, Sacred Books of the East, Vols XXXV and XXXVI; V. Trenckner, The Milindapanho: Being Dialogues between King Milinda and the Buddhist Sage Nagasena, PTS, London, 1986
59. *Mūlācāra ofVattakerācārya in 2 parts:* Comm. Vasunandin, Bombay, V.S. 1977-80
60. *Niyamasāra of Kundakundācārya:* Lucknow, 1931, Sacred Books of the Jainas, Vol. IX, (eds) Uggar Sain and Brahmacāri Sital Prasadji, The Central Jain Publishing House, Lucknow, 1931
61. *Pañcādhyayī:* Rajamalla, Indore, Vir. Nir. Sam. 244
62. *Pannavāna Sūtra, Vol. 1-2:* (ed.) Ray Dhanapatisimha Bahadur, Jaina Prabhakara Press, 1884; (eds) Muni Puṇyavijayaji, Dalsukh Malvania and Amritlal M. Bhojak Pārājika; T.W. Rhys Davids and Hermann Oldenberg, Sacred Books of the East, Vol. XIII (Vinaya text, part I), 1881
63. *Paramātma Prakāśa ofYogindudeva:* comm. Brahmadeva, Bombay, 1937
64. *Praśnavyākaraṇa:* see Early Jainism by K.K. Dixit, L.D. Institute of Indology, Ahmedabad, 1978
65. *Pravacanasāra of Kundakunda:* with Comm. Amṛtacandrasūri, English translation by Faddegon Berend, Cambridge at the University Press, 1935
66. *Purusārthasiddhyupāya of Amṛtacandra:* Rayacandra Jain

Śāstramālā, Bombay,1905; Sacred Books of the Jainas, Vol. IV, P.S.V. by Srimat Amṛtacandrasūri; (ed.) Ajit Prasada, The Central Jain Publishing House, Lucknow, 1933

67. *Rāmāyana of Vālmīki:* (trans.) Shastri, Hariprasad, Vols I-III, Shantisadan, London 1962· (trans.) Subramaniyan, Kamala, Bharatiya Vidya Bhavan, Bombay, 1981

68. *Ratnakaraṇḍaka Śrāvakācāra:* Samantabhadra, with commentary of Prabhācandra, Manikacandra Digambara Jaina Granthamālā, no.24, Bombay, 1926

69. *ṚgVeda Saṁhitā:* Together with the commentary of Sāyanācārya, (ed.) F. Max Muller, Vol. VI, London, W.H. Alien, 1849-1874; The Hymns of the Ṛg Veda, Translated with a popular commentary by Ralph T.H. Griffith, Motilal Banarsidass Pvt Ltd., Delhi, 1973

70. *Saddharmapuṇḍarīka:* (trans.) Kem. H, Sacred Books of the East, Vol. XXI, 1889; English in L. Hurvitz (trans.), Scripture of the Lotus Blossom of the Fine Dharma, Translated from the Chinese of Kumārajiva by Leon Hurvitz, Columbia University Press, New York, 1976

71. *Sāgāradharmāmṛta of Āśādhara:* Manikacandra Digambara Jaina Granthamālā, no.2, Bombay, 1917

72. *Samantapāṣādika of Buddhaghoṣa:* (comm. to Vinayapiṭaka), (ed.) J. Takakusu and M. Nagai, 7 Vols in progress, Pali Text Society, London, 1927-47

73. *Samayasāra of Kundakundācārya:* Bhāratīya Jñānāpītha Prakāṣan, vira samvat 2479:1971, (trans.) Prof. A. Chakravarti

74. *Saṁyutta Nikāya:* (trans.) C. A. F. Rhys Davids (Vols 1-2) and F.L. Woodward (Vols 3-5), The Book of Kindred Sayings, 5 Vols, London, 1917-30; (ed.) Bhiksu J. Kasyapa, Nalanda 1959; (trans.) Bhiksu. J. Kasyapa, Benaras, 1954; Pali text in Leon Feer (ed.). The Samyutta-nikāya of the Sutta-piṭaka, PTS, London, 1973-80

75. *Sāmānya Vedānta Upaniṣads:* (trans.) T.R. Srinivasa Ayyangar, (ed.) by S. Subrahmanya Sastri, The Adyar Library, 1941

76. *Sarvārthasiddhi of Pūjyapāda:* with Tattvārtha Sūtra of Umāswami, Sanskrit text with Hindi translation by Phool Chand Siddhānta Śāstri, Varanasi (BJP), 1971

77. *Śatapata Brāhmaṇa:* (trans.) Eggeling Julius, Sacred Books of the East, Vol. XII, XXVI, Oxford, Clarendon Press, 1882-94

78. *Ṣaṭkhaṇḍāgama of Puṣpadanta and Bhūtabali:* comm. Virasenācārya, (ed.) Jaina, H.L., Amaravati, 1939-1959

79. *Sikṣāsamucchaya:* Vaidhya, P.L., edn. The Mithila Institute of Post-Graduate Studies and Research in Sanskrit Learning, Darbhanga, 1961
80. *Śrāvakācāra of Amitagati:* Anantakirti Digambara Jaina Granthamālā, no.2, Bombay, 1922
81. *Śrāvakācāra of Vasuvandin:* (ed.) Hiralal Jain, Jñānapitha Mūrtidevī Jaina Granthamālā, Prakrit Series, no.3
82. *Sthānāṅga Sūtra:* with Abhayadeva's comm., (ed.) Venicandra Suracandra, Bombay, 1918-20; also Ahmedabad, 1937
83. *Sumaṅgalavilāsinī:* Comm. to Dīgha Nikāya by Buddhaghoṣa, (eds.) T.W. Rhys Davids, J. Estlin Carpenter, and W. Stede, 3 Vols, Pali Text Society, London, 1886-1932
84. *Sūtrakṛtāṅga:* Jacobi, Hermann, Sacred Books of the East, Vol. XIV, (comm. Silanka, Bombay, 1917)
85. *Sutta Nipāta:* Discourse Collection, Lord Charlmers (ed.) Buddha's Teachings, Cambridge, Massachusetts, Harvard University Press, London, 1932; Sacred Books of the East, Vol. **X**, Part II; (trans.) Coomarasamy, M., Trubner & Co, London, 1874; Pali text in D. Anderson and H. Smith (eds.), Sutta Nipāta, PTS, London, 1990; K.R. Norman (trans.), The Group of Discourses (Sutta-nipāta), Vol.2, revised translation with introduction and notes by K.R. Norman, PTS, Oxford, 1982; English in Saddhatissa (trans.), Sutta-Nipāta, Curzon, London, 1985
86. *Syādvādamañjarī of Sri Mallisenasūri:* translated and annotated by F. W. Thomas, Motilal Banarsidass, Delhi, 1968
87. *Tattvārthasūtra of Vācaka Umāsvāti:* Comm. by Sanghvi Sukhlala, K.K. Dixit (trans.), L.D.Institute of Indology, Ahmedbad, 1974; Bhatta Akalaṅka on Tat. Sūtra, Calcutta, 1929 (Hindi trans.); Pūjyapāda on Tattvārthasūtra (Sarvārthasiddhi), Reality, Jain, S.A. (trans.), Vīrasasana Saṅgha, Calcutta, 1960; Ganin Siddhasena on Tattvārthasūtra, Surat, 1930
88. *Tevijja Sutta, The:* T.W. Rhys Davids and Debes Paul, Wheel Publication, Ceylon, 1963; English in Walshe (trans.). Thus Have I Heard: The Long Discourses of the Buddha, Wisdom, London, 1987
89. *Thera, Therīgāthā:* (trans.) C. A. F. Rhys Davids, Psalms of the Early Buddhists, 2 Vols, Pali Text Society, London, 1909-13
90. *Udāna:* Buddhist stories and pithy sayings, (ed.) Steinthal, Paul, Pali Text Society, London, 1885
91. *Upaniṣads:* Radhakrishnan, S., The Principal Upaniṣads, George

Allen and Unwin Ltd, London, 1953. (Ref. to Bṛhadāraṇyaka, Chāndogya, Jābāla, Kathā, Kena, Maitreya, Muṇḍaka, Śvetāsvatāra Taittirīya, Sāndilya.Upaniṣads); Vasudev Laxman Shastri, One Hundred and Eight Upaniṣads, pub. Pandurang Jawaji, Bombay, 1925 (ref. to Vajrasuci Upaniṣad); Introduction to Upaniṣads, Max Muller, Sacred Books of the East, Vol. XV, Part II; Ayyangar Srinivasa, T. R., The Samanya Vedanta Upaniṣads, ed. by Subrahmanya Sastri, The Adyar Library, 1941

92. *Upāsakadaśāṅga:* with commentary of Abhayadeva, (ed. with trans.) Hoernle, (Bibliotheca Indica, no. 105), Calcutta, 1890; (ed.) Kankaiyalal, Rajkota, 1961; (ed. and trans.) Hoernle, Rudolf, A. F. Calcutta, The Bibliotheca Indica, 1888
93. *Upāsakādhyayana:* Suri Samadeva, Kasi, 1964
94. *Uttarādhyayana Sūtra:* Jacobi, Hermann, Sacred Books of the East, Vol. XLV (Jaina Sūtras, Part II)
95. *Vaśiṣṭa Dharmasūtra:* (trans.) Buhler, Sacred Books of the East, Vol. II and XLV (Sacred Laws of the Āryas)
96. *Vinaya Texts:* (trans.) T.W. Rhys Davids and H. Oldenberg, Sacred Books of the East, Vols XIII, XVII and XX
97. *Viśuddhimagga of Buddhaghoṣa:* (trans.) Bhikkhu Nyanamoli, The Path of Purification, 1964; (ed.) C. A. F. Rhys Davids, 2 Vols, London, Pali Text Society, 1920-21
98. *Yājñavalkhya Dharmasūtra:* (trans.) Buhler, Sacred Books of the East, Vols II and XIV (Sacred Laws of the Āryas)
99. *Yogaśāstra of Hemacandra:* Sanskrit text with Hindi tr. By Shobhachandra Bharilla, Delhi, 1963; Bibliotheca Indica, No. 172, Calcutta, 1907-21
100. *Yoga-sūtras of Patañjali with Vyāsa-bhāsya:* See Patanjala-Yogadarśanam, (ed.) by R. S. Bhattacharya, Bharatiya Vidya Prakasana, Varanasi, 1963
101. *Yuktianuśāsana of Samantabhadra:* Saharanapura, 1951

(II) MONOGRAPHS:

102. *Amaladoss, M.:* Making all things New (Mission in Dialogue), Gujarat Sahitya Prakash,Anand,1990
103. *Atreya:* Moral and Spiritual foundations of Peace, Banares, International Standard Publications, 1952
104. *Babb, Lawrence, A.:* Ascetics and Kings in a Jain Ritual Culture, Motilal Banarsidass Publishers Pvt. Ltd., Delhi, 1998

105. *Barua, B.M.:* Pre-Buddhist Indian Philosophy, Calcutta, 1921

106. *Basham, A.L.:* History and Doctrines of the Ājivikas, Motilal Banarsidass, Delhi, 1981

107. *Bhagavat, D.N.:* Early Buddhist Jurisprudence, Cosmo Publications

108. *Bhargava, Dayanand:* Jaina Ethics, Motilal Banarsidass, Delhi 1968

109. *Bharucha, Filita:* Role of Space-Time in Jaina's Syādvāda & Quantum Theory, Sri Satguru Publications, 1993

110. *Bhattacharya, Harisatya.:* "Dharma" in Jaina Gazette, Vol. 22, pp. 243-246; "Adharma" in Vol. 23, pp. 290ff., George Town, Madras, 1926; Article in Sri Mahaveer Commemoration Volume I

111. *Bhattacharya, Narendra Nath.:* Jaina Philosophy - Historical Outline, Munshiram Manoharlal Publishers Pvt. Ltd., 1999 (2nd Revised Edition), first published 1975; A Glossary of Indian Religious Terms and Concepts, Manohar Publications, New Delhi, 1990

112. *Bloomfield, Maurice:* The Life and Stories of the Jaina Saviour Parsvanatha, Gian Publishing House, Delhi

113. *Bondurant, Joan:* (ed.) Conquest of Violence, The Gandhian Philosophy of Conflict, University of California Press, Berkeley and Los Angeles, 1965

114. *Bose, N.K.:* Selections from Gandhi, Navajivan Publishing House, Ahmedabad, 1948

115. *Brown, Judith M:* Gandhi - Prisoner of Hope, Yale University Press, New Haven and London, 1989

116. *Carus, Paul:* The Gospel of Buddha, National Book Trust, India, 1971

117. *Chakravarti, A:* A Philosophical Introduction to Pancastikaya

118. *Chander, Jag Parvesh:* Teachings of Mahatma Gandhi, Lahore:, Indian Printing Works, 1945

119. *Chattopadhyaya, Debiprasad:* 'Some Problems of Early Buddhism' in Buddhism: The Marxist Approach, People's Publishing House Ltd, N. Delhi, 1978

120. *Chaudhuri, Sukomal:* Analytical Study of the Abhidharmakoṣa, Firma KLM Pvt Ltd, Calcutta, 1983

121. *Cort, John E :* Open Boundaries - Jain Communities and Cultures in Indian History, State University of New York Press, Albany, 1998

122. *De Bary, Theodore:* Sources of Indian Tradition, Motilal Banarsidass, Delhi, 1963
123. *Desai, Mahadev:* With Gandhi in Ceylon, Madras: Ganesan, 1928
124. *Deussen, P.:* The Philosophy of the Upanisads, Edinburg, 1919
125. *Dutt, Sukumar:* Early Buddhist Monachism, Kegan Paul, Trench, Trubner and Co, London, 1924
126. *Dwivedi, R.C.:* Contribution of Jainism to Indian Culture, Motilal Banarsidass, Varanasi, 1975
127. *Ellul, Jacques:* Violence, SCM Press Ltd., Great Britain, 1920
128. *Fahey, Joseph:* (ed.) A Peace Reader, New York, Paulist Press, 1987
129. *Farquhar. J.N.:* Outline of the Religious Literature of India, oxford, 1920
130. *Gandhi, M.K.:* Hindu Dharma, Ahmedabad, 1950; Sarvodaya, Navajivan Publishing House, Ahmedabad, 1968; Non-violence in Peace and War, Vol. II, Ahmedabad, 1948-49; Rebuilding our Villages, Ahmedabad, 1955; Satyagraha in South Africa, Tr. from Gujarati by V.G,. Desai, Madras, Ganesan, 1928; The Collected works of Mahatma Gandhi (CW) Vols. 1-85 to date; Publication Division of the Ministry of the Information and Broadcasting, Govt. of India, 1958; Young India, Published in books form of Indo Culture, by Tagore and Co., Madras, 1972
131. *Garg, Ganga Ram:* (ed.) Encyclopaedia of the Hindu World, Vols I-III, Concept Publishing Company, New Delhi, 1992
132. *Garrett, John:* Classical Dictionary of India, D.K. Printworld Pvt. Ltd., New Delhi, 1999, first published in 1871
133. *Ghose Narendranath:* Origins of Indo Aryan Literature and Culture, Deep and Deep Publications, Delhi, 1988
134. *Glasenapp, H. V.:* Doctrine of Karman in Jain Philosophy, P. V. Research Institute, Varanasi, 1991; Jainism : An Indian Religion of Salvation, Motilal Banarsidass Publishers Pvt. Ltd., Delhi, 1999
135. *Gopalan, H. V.:* Outlines of Jainism, Wiley Eastern Pvt Ltd, New Delhi, 1973
136. *Green, T.H.:* Prolegomena to Ethics, (ed.) Bradley, Oxford Clarendon Press, 1890
137. *Gregg, Richard, B.:* The Power of Non-Violence, Navajivan Press, Ahmedabad, 1938
138. *Guenther, Herbert, V.:* Philosophy and Psychology in the Abhidharma, Motilal Banarsidass, Delhi, 1974

139. *Guseva, N.R.:* Jainism, Sindhu Publications, Bombay, 1971
140. *Hamilton, Clarence* H.: Buddhism in India, Ceylon, China and Japan (a reading guide), University of Chicaro Press, Illinois, 1931
141. *Handiqui, K.K.:* Yasastilaka and Indian Culture, Jivaraja Jaina Granthamālā, No.2, Solapur, 1949
142. *Har Dayal:* The Boddhisattva Doctrine in Buddhist Sanskrit Literature, Kegan Paul, Trench, Trubner and Co., London, 1932
143. *Hardy, Friedhelm:* The World's Religions, Routledge, London, 1988
144. *Hardy, Spencer, R.:* Eastern Monachism, Williams and Norgate, London, 1860; A Manual of Buddhism, (1st Indian edn., 1967), Williams and Norgate, London, 1860
145. *Hume, David:* A Treatise on Human Nature, Longmans, Green and Co., London 1874
146. *Humphrey, Caroline and James Laidlaw :* The Archetypal Actions of Ritual - A theory of ritual illustrated by the Jain rite of worship, Clardendon Press, Oxford, 1994
147. *Humphreys, Christmas:* A Popular Dictionary of Buddhism, ARCO Publications, London,1962
148. *Iyer Raghvan:* The Moral and Political Writings of Mahatma Gandhi, Vol. 1-3. Clarendon Press, Oxford, 1987
149. *Jain, Jegdishchandra:* Studies in Early Jainism, Navrang, Delhi, 1992; "Metaphysical significance of Dharma and Adharma in Jaina Metaphysics" in Indian Historical Quarterly, Vol.ix, no.3
150. *Jain, N.L.:* Jaina Karmology, English Tr. Ch. VIII of Tattvārtharājavārtika of Akalanka, Pārśvanātha Vidyāpītha, Varanasi, 1998
151. *Jaini.P.S.:* The Jaina Path of Purification, University of California Press, 1979; Gender and Salvation - Jaina Debates on the Spiritual Liberation of Women, Munshiram Manoharlal Publishers Pvt. Ltd., New Delhi, 1991; (ed.) Collected Papers on Jaina Studies, Motilal Banarsidass Publishers Pvt. Ltd., Delhi, 2000
152. *Jain, Surendar, K.:* (ed.) Glimpses of Jainism, Motilal Banarsidass Publishers Pvt. Ltd., Delhi, 1997
153. *Jayasuriya, W. F.:* The Philosophy and Psychology of Buddhism - An Introduction to the Abhidhamma, Y. M. B. A. Press, Colombo, 1963
154. *Jesudasan, Ignatius:* A Gandhian Theology of Liberation, Orbis Books, New York, 1984
155. *Jha, V. N.:* (ed.) Jaina Logic and Epistemology, Sri Satguru Publications Pvt. Ltd., Delhi, 1997

156. *Joshi, L.M.:* Facets of Jaina Religious Consciousness, LD series 85, LD Institute of indology,Ahmedabad, 1981
157. *Kalghatgi, T.G.:* Jainism, The Dr. S. Radhakrishnan Institute for Advanced Study in Philosophy, University of Madras, 1978
158. *Kappen, S.:* Marxian Atheism, Bangalore, 1983
159. *Kern, H.:* Manual of Indian Buddhism, Trassbury, Karl J. Trubner, 1896
160. *Khan, Benjamin:* The Concept of Dharma in Valmiki Ramayana, Munshiram Manoharlal publishers Pvt. Ltd., New Delhi 1965
161. *Krishan, Yuvraj:* The Doctrine of Karma - Its origin and Development in Brahmanical, Buddhist and Jaina Tradition, Motilal Banarsidass Publishers Pvt. Ltd., Delhi, 1997
162. *Kulkarni, Nirmala:* Is there Salvation for Women?, Sri Satguru Publication Pvt. Ltd., Delhi, 1967
163. *Macdonell, A. Arthur:* A History of Sanskrit Literature, London, 1913; with A.B. keith: Vedic Index of Names and Subjects, Vols I-II, Motilal Banarsidass Pvt. Ltd., Delhi, 1995, first published in 1912
164. *Mackenzie, John S.:* A Manual of Ethics, London, 1929
165. *Maduro, Otto:* Religion and social conflicts, (trans) from the Spanish by Rebert R. Barr, Orbis Books, Maryknoll, New York, 1982
166. *Matilal Bimal Krishna:* (ed.) Moral Dilemmas in the Mahabharata, Indian Institute of Advanced Study (Shimla) in association with Motilal Banarsidass, Delhi, 1989
167. *Mcgovern, W.M.:* A Manual of Buddhist Philosophy, Vol. 1, Kegan Paul, London, 1923
168. *Mehta, T. V.:* The Path of Arhat - A Religion of Democracy, Parsvanatha Sodhapitha, Varanasi, 1993
169. *Mishra, Madhusudan:* House Holder's Discipline in Jainism, Eastern Book Linkers, Delhi, 1996
170. *Monier-Williams:* A Sanskrit-English Dictionary, Motilal Banarsidass Pvt. Ltd., Delhi, Reprint 1993, first published by Oxford University Press in 1899
171. *Murti. T. R.V.:* The Central Philosophy of Buddhism, George Allen & Unwin, London, 1955
172. *Narada Thera:* A Manual of Buddhism, A Text book of Buddhism for the SSC, The Associated Newspapers of Ceylon, Columbo, 1951
173. *Nyanatiloka:* Guide through the Abhidhamma Piṭaka, The

Associated Newspapers of Ceylon Ltd, Lake House, Colombo, 1938, (2nd edn. 1957)

174. *Padmarajiah:* Jaina thories of Reality and Knowledge, Jaina Sahitya Vikas Mandal, Bombay, 1963

175. *Patil, V. T.:* (ed.) Studies on Gandhi, Sterling Publishers Pvt Ltd, New Delhi, 1985

176. *Pruden, Leo M:* Abhidharmakoṣabhāṣyam, English translation, Asian Humanities Press, Berkeley, California, Four Volumes, 1988

177. *Radhakrishnan, S.:* Indian Philosophy and Logic, Vol. I, London, 1941; Religion and Society, George Allen and Unwin Ltd, London, 1953; The Principal Upaniṣads, George Allen and Unwin Ltd., London, 1953

178. *Radhakrishnan, N.:* (ed.) Gandhian Perspective of Nation Building For World Peace, Konark Publishers Pvt Ltd in association with Gandhi Smṛti and Darshan Samiti, New Delhi, 1992

179. *Rao, Venkatakrishna, V.:* A Handbook of Classical Sanskrit Literature, Oriental Longmans: Madras, 1961

180. *Rau, Heimo:* (ed.) Mahatma Gandhi as Germans see him, Shakuntala Publishing House, Bombay, 1976

181. *Rhys Davids, T.W.:* Buddhism, Society for promoting Christian knowledge, London, 1925; Buddhist India, Indological Book House, Delhi, 1970; Dialogues of the Buddha, Sacred Books of the Buddhists, Vol. 1-3, Oxford University Press, Ware House, Amen Comer, E.C. London, 1899

182. *Russell, Bertrand:* History of Western Philosophy, London, 1948

183. *Sankrityayan, Rahul (ed.):* Buddhism - A Marxist Approach Peoples Publishing House, New Delhi, 1990

184. *Schubring, Walther:* The Doctrine of the Jainas, Motilal Banarsidass, Delhi, 1962

185. *Sekhar, Vincent:* 'Lord Rṣabhadeva - The First King and the First Tīrthaṅkara' and 'Lord Rṣabhadeva and the Evolution of Human life in various spheres and the contribution of Brahmī and Sundarī', Certificate in Jainology, Paper II, The Ancient Jain History, University of Madras, 1991; Dynamic Pluralism - A Vision toward Conflict Resolution and Cosmic Integration, Interfaith Formation, Madras, 1993; Jain Journal, Vol. XXV, No. 3, January 1991, pp. 110-118; Vol. XXVIII, No. 2, October 1993, pp. 93-100, Jain Bhavan Publication, Calcutta; 'Significance of Jain Philosophy for preserving Life and Environment' in

Thottakara, A. (ed.). Journal of Dharma & Dharmaram Publications, Bangalore, 2000; Jinamañjarī, Vol. V. No. 11, October 1992; Vol. XIV, No. 2, October 1997, Bramhī Society Publication, Ontario, Canada

186. *Seshagiri. N.:* Pollution, National Book Trust, India, 1982
187. *Shanta, N.:* The Unknown Pilgrim: The Voice of the Sadhvis - The History, Spirituality and Life of the Jaina Women Ascetics, Sri Satguru Publications, Delhi, 1997
188. *Sharma:* Gandhi: As a Political thinker, Indian Press, Allahabad 1st impression
189. *Sharma, Binod:* Ethical - Literary values of the two great Epics of India, Crown Publications, Madras, 1990
190. *Shah, Nagin, J.:* (Tr.): Jaina Philosophy and Religion, English Tr. Of Jaina Darsana by Muni Sri Nyayavijayaji, Munshiram Manoharlal Publishers Pvt. Ltd., Delhi, 1998; Jaina theory of Multiple facets of Reality and Truth (Anekāntavāda), Motilal Banarsidass Publishers Pvt. Ltd., Delhi, 2000
191. *Sharp, Gene:* Power and Struggle (Politics of Nonviolent Action, Part 1), Porter Sargent Publishers, May 1974, Methods of Nonviolent Action (Politics of Nonviolent Action, Part 2), Porter Sargent Publishers, June 1973; Dynamics of Nonviolent Action (Politics of Nonviolent Action, Part 3), Porter Sargent Publishers, November 1985
192. *Shivkumar, Muni:* The Doctrine of Liberation in Indian Tradition with Special Reference to Jainism, Munshiram Manoharlal Publishers Pvt. Ltd., Delhi, 2000
193. *Sibley. Mulford,* Q: (Ed.) The Quiet Battle, Bharatiya Vidya Bhavan, Bombay, 1965
194. *Sidgwick, Henry:* Methods of Ethics, Book I. Macmillan & Co., London, 1877
195. *Sikdar, J. C.:* Theory of Reality in Jain Philosophy, P. V. Research Institute, Varanasi, 1991
196. *Singhy N.K.* (ed): Ideal, Ideology and Practice (Studies in Jainism), Printwell Publishers, Jaipur, 1987
197. *Smith, Vincent A.:* Early History of India, Clarenden Press, Oxford, 1914
198. *Stcherbatsky, Th:* Central Conception of Buddhism and the Meaning of the Word 'Dharma', Prize Publication Fund, Vol. VII of the Royal Asiatic Society, London, 1923

199. *Stevenson, Sinclair:* The Heart of Jainism, Munshiram Mansharlal Publishers Pvt. Ltd., New Delhi, Reprinted in 1970
200. *Sugiura, S.:* Hindu logic as preserved in China and Japan, Philadelphia, 1900
201. *Suzuki, D. T.:* Studies in the Laṅkāvatāra Sūtra, 1930; Zen Buddhism and Psychoanalysis, 1960
202. *Tahtinen, Unto:* Nonviolence as an Ethical Principle, Turku 1964,
203. *Tatia, Nathmal:* 'Lectures on Jainism', Annual Lecture series No. 1, Department of Jainology, University of Madras, 1988
204. *Thakkasu, J.* (tr.): A Record of Buddhist Religion, Oxford, 1896
205. *Thottakara, Augustine, CMI:* (ed.) Eco-dynamics of Religion - Thoughts for the Third Millennium, Journal of Dhan a & Dharmaram Publications, Bangalore, 2000
206. *Walker, Benjamin:* Hindu World, in two volumes, George Allen and Unwin Ltd, London,1968
207. *Walter Fernandes* (ed): Inequality, its Base and Search for Solutions, Indian Social Institute, New Delhi, 1986
208. *Warren, H. C.:* Buddhism in Translations, Harvard Oriental Series, Vol. Ill 1896-1900, 1922: Cambridge, Mass., Published by Harvard University, 1906
209. *Wheeler J. Talboys:* The Religious and Cultural History of India, Sanjay Prakashan, Delhi, 1988
210. *Whitehead, A.N.:* Adventures of Ideas, Macmillan, 1933
211. *Williams. R.:* Jaina Yoga., London Oriental Series, London, 1963
212. *Zimmer, H.:* Philosophies of India, Pantheon Books, New York, 1953

(III) REFERENCE BOOKS

213. *Buddhist Dictionary:* Nyanatiloka, Frewin & Co. Columbo, 1972
214. *Classical Dictionary of India:* John Garrett, D.K. Printworld Pvt. Ltd., New Delhi, 1999, first published in 1871
215. *Cultural Heritage of India, The:* The Ramakrishna Mission Institute of Culture, Vols I-V, Calcutta, Reprint 1993
216. *Dictionary of Buddhism - Indian and South-East Asian:* Trevor Ling, K.P. Bagchi & Co., New Delhi, 1981
217. *Encyclopaedia of Indian Culture:* Vols 1-5, R.N. Saletore, Sterling Publishers Pvt. Ltd., Delhi, 1981-1985 (Vol. 1-2,4-5), Humanities Press Inc., 1983 (Vol. 3)

218. *Encyclopaedia of Religion:* (ed.) Mircea Eliade, Macmillan Publishing Company, New York, 1987
219. *Encyclopaedia of Religion and Ethics:* (ed.) Hastings, James, dark T and T (Pub.)
220. *Encyclopaedia of the Hindu World:* Vols I-III, (ed.) Ganga Ram Garg, Concept Publishing Company, New Delhi, 1992
221. *Epigraphica Indica:* 1080 A. C. Government of India, New Delhi
222. *Hindu Classical Dictionary:* Dowson John, Kegan Paul, Trench, Trubner & Co, London,1914
223. *Hindu World - An Encyclopaedic Survey of Hinduism:* Benjamin Walker, Vols I-II, George Allen & Unwin Ltd., London, 1968
224. *Holy Bible. The:* Revised Standard Version, Catholic Edition for India, Theological Publications in India, Bangalore 1973
225. *Mantramañjarī:* The Vedic Experience, Panikkar, University of California Press, 1977
226. *Pali-English Dictionary:* (ed.) T.W. Rhys Davids and Williams Stede, PTS, London,1921-25
227. *Sanskrit-English Dictionary, A:* Sir Monier Monier-Williams, Motilal Banarsidass Pvt. Ltd., Delhi, Reprint 1993, first published by Oxford University Press in 1899
228. *Sources of Indian Tradition:* De Bary, William Theodore, Columbia University Press, New York; Oxford University Press, London, 1958
229. *Vedic Index of Names and Subjects:* Vols I-II, A.A. Macdonell and A.B. Keith, Motilal Banarsidass Pvt. Ltd., Delhi, 1995, first published in 1912
230. *The New Biblical Commentary:* (ed.) Brown, Raymond, E., Theological Publications in India, Bangalore, 1990

(IV) PERIODICALS

231. *Ahimsa Voice,* Jan. 1990, July 1990
232. *Gandhian Perspectives,* Journal of the Gandhian Institute of Studies, Rajghat, Varanasi, Vol. IV, No. 2, 1991; Vol. VI, No. 1, 1993; Vol. VII, No. 2, 1994; Vol. VIII, No. 1, 1995; Vol. IX, No. 2, 1996
233. *Harijan* (English Edition); *Harijanbandhu* (Gujarathi Edition); *Young India* (ed.) (and largely written) by M.K. Gandhi
234. *Ignis:* No. 3, 1994, Gujarat Sahitya Prakash, Anand, 1994;
235. *Indian Historical Quarterly:* Vol. IX, No. 3

236. Jaina Gazette, Vol. 8-10, Allahabad (1912-14); Vol 11-13, Lucknow (1915-16); Vol. 14, 18, Madras (1922); Vol. 20, Madras (1924); Vol. 22-27, Madras (1926-31)

237. *Jain Journal:* Jain Bhavan Publication, Calcutta. Vol. XXV, No. 3, January 1991; Vol. XXVIII, No. 2, October 1993; Vol. XXIX, No. 2, October 1994;; Vol. XXX, No. 1, July 1995; Vol XXX, No. 2, October 1995; Vol. XXIX, No. 3, January 1995; Vol. XXIX, No. 4, April 1995; Vol. XXXIV, No. 1, July 1999

238. *Jinamañjarī:* Bramhi Society Publication, Ontario, Canada, Vol.V, No. 11, October 1992; Vol. XI, No. 1, April 1995; Vol. XIV, No. 2, October 1997

239. *Journal of Dharma:* Vol. XIII, No.3, September 1988; Dharmaram College, Bangalore

240. *Sri Mahāvīra Commemoration Volume I,* Bhattacarya, H., Article on 'Jaina View of Ahiṁsā'

241. *Voice of Ahimsa. The:* Vol. vii, No. 3-4

242. *Vidyajyoti:* Journal of Theological Reflection (VJTR) No.48, 1984, Delhi

Word Index

A

Abhidhamma 61, 64, 126
Active Resistance 184, 192-3
Aghāti Karma 77
Ahiṁsā 15, 105, 121, 161, 172, 185, 186, 187, 188, 190, 212, 214
Ājīvika 36, 38, 39
Ālayavijñana 65
Amitābha 33, 66
Anantacatuṣtaya 104
Anātman 129, 211
Anekānta 109, 111, 121, 187, 189, 190
Anuprekṣas 180
Anuvrata 104
Āpaddharma 60
Aparigraha 176, 178
Āśrama 25, 28, 54, 208
Āraṁbha hiṁsā 116
Arhat 63, 69
Ārta dhyāna 35
Arūpa dhātu 131
Ārya-brāhmans 6, 7
Ārya-kṣatriyas 5
Āryanization 52
Āryans 2, 5
Asceticism 20, 22, 29, 31, 33, 62, 209
Astikāya 145
Asuras 51
Attachment 80
Aśubhopayoga 113
Avidyā 129
Āyatanas 133, 138, 149

B

Bālatapas 35
Bandha 76
Bhāgavatism 51
Bhaikṣācarya 24
Bhauma Sūkta 6
Bhāvana 134
Bhikṣu-sūtra 25
Bhūtavādins 88
Bodhisattva 32, 120, 170, 171, 172
Bodhisattvas 70
Brāhmaṇa 174
Brāhmaṇas 6
Brāhminhood 207

C

Celibacy 117
Compassion 184
Consumerism 182

D

Darśana 89
Dásyus, 3
Deśa vrata 119
Determinism 90
Devaloka. 8
Devayāna 84
Dhamma 129
Dhamma 127, 128, 149, 153
Dharma 46-8, 51, 53-8, 60, 66, 67, 71, 72, 73, 74, 79, 206, 210
Dharma and Adharma 143, 144, 147, 151, 154, 212
Dharma dhyāna 35
Dharmakāya 66, 68
Dhātus 133, 138, 149
Dialogue 165, 191

Dig vrata 119
Discrimination 173
Duhkha 129, 130
Durnaya 190

E

Egotism 166
Eka-vrātya 7
Eka-vrātya. 5
Ekānta 109
Enlightenment 213
Enlightenment 30
Environment 163
Equality 81
Equanimity 175
Eudeamonists 104
Euthanasia 172
Extremism 170

F

Five Vows 115
Fundamentalism 161, 164

G

Ghāti Karma 76

H

Harmony 55
Hedonists 104
Hiṁsā 167
Hiṁsā śāstra 169
Hiṁsāśāstra 185

I

Inequality 162
Intuition 110
īśvaravāda 88

J

Janmāntaravāda 7
Jñāna 52
Jñānamārga 11

K

Kaṣāya 78, 165
Kṣanikavāda 129
Karma 53, 76, 78, 81, 82, 84, 85, 88, 90, 114, 147, 148
Karma 207
Karma-saṁsāra 207
Karmavāda 86
Kṣatriyas, 4
Kriyāvāda 86

L

Law of Violence 169
Leśya 85, 90
Lokākāśa 146

M

Mādhyāmika 64
Maitreya. 71
Māra 30
Mārga, 6
Meditation 21
Meditation 35, 208
Middle path 71
Mithyādṛṣti 172
Mokṣa 55
Monasticism 15
Mukta jīva 152
Muni 176
Muni-sūkta 23
Munidharma 114

N

Nāma 149
Nayavāda 189, 190
Neo-Āryanism 206
Neo-Āryanism 4
Nibbāna 137
Niścaya 104, 105, 186

Niścaya naya 89
Niṣkāma Karma 86
Nirgrantha 34
Nirmāṇakāya 66, 68
Nirvāṇa 83
Nivṛtti mārga, 6
Niyati, 37
Niyativādins 87
Non-attachment 118
Non-exploitation 191
Non-stealing 117
Non-violence 115, 117, 185, 191, 195, 196
Non-violent resistance 193
Non-violent Society 193, 194

O

Omniscient 111, 143
Ordination 114

P

Pañcanamaskāra mantra 107
Pañcaparameṣtin 104
Pañcavratas 115
Parivrājakas 23
Pārśvanātha 3, 11
Passive resistance 192
Pātimokkha 30
Pitṛloka 8
Pitṛyāna 84
Poverty 162
Pradeśa 145
Prajñā 72, 129, 142
Pramāda 78
Promotion 215
Proselytizing 4
Puruṣārtha 59
Puruṣavādins 88
Puruṣārtha 59

R

Raudra dhyāna 35
Ṛṣabhadeva, 10
Ṛta 114
Renunciation 22, 165, 207
Rūpa 149
Ṛūpa dhātu 131

S

Saṅgha 15, 30, 31, 69, 175
Sadācāra 48
Sallekhana 170
Sallekhanā 119
Samādhi 142
Samatā 112
Sāmāyika 112
Sambhogakāya 66, 68
Sannyāsa 26, 27, 28, 55
Sāṁkhya 12
Sāṁkhya-yoga 12
Sṭoma Ritual 4
Saṁvṛtti 6
Saṁyama 74
Saptatattva 79
Saptatattva, 73
Saptatattvas 79
Sarvajña 143
Satyāgraha 192
Self-determination 108
Self-determination 120, 213
Self-governance 195
Self-government 183
Self-help 82
Self-mortification 169, 170
Self-purification 170
Self-realization 103, 195, 214
Self-realization 105
Self-reliance 14
Self-sacrifice 184
Siśnadevas 11
Skandhas 133, 138, 149
Skandhas 132
Sraddha 142
Śrāvakacāra 114
Suchness 65
Śubhopayoga 113

Śuddhopayoga 112
Śukla 90
Śukla dhyāna 36
Svabhāvavādins 87
Svadharma 58, 86
Svargakāma 210
Svasamaya 86
Syādvāda 187, 189, 190

T

Taṇhā 29
Tapas 78, 119
Tilakkhana 66
Tīrtha 106
Triratna 111, 213
True monk 34
Truth 116
Tṛṣṇa 165

U

Udyogami hiṁsā 116
Untouchability 162
Upasaṁpada 30
Ūrdhva gati 152
Utilitarianists 104

V

Vairāgya 165
Varṇa 54
Varna 208
Vijñānavāda 65
Vinaya 31, 67, 69
Violence 166, 167, 173, 183
Virodhi hiṁsā 116
Viveka 165
Vrātya 3, 6
Vrātya-kṣatriyas 5
Vrātyaṣṭoma 5
Vyavahāra 186
Vyavahāra naya 90

W

Wealth 176, 178, 181, 182

Y

Yadṛcchāvādins 87
Yajña 51, 209
Yogācāra 65

Subject Index

Abhidharma
  its contents, 126
  its purpose and end, 126
  the scholastic treatises, 64
Ahiṁsā
  a path to eliminate misery, 121
  against animal sacrifice, 15, 207
  an ethical imperative, 186
  and altruism, 112
  and Anekānta, 186-7, 189, 214
  and conflict-resolution, 190
  and dialogue, 191
  and Gandhi, 187
  and Householder, 171-2
  and Satyāgraha, 192
  and the Law of Manu, 169, 185
  and Vegitarianism, 73
  and world-mission, 188
  as absence of oppression, 186
  contemporary meaning, 191
  controversies about, 172
  from absolute and practical points of view, 186
  hallmark of Śramana way of life, 167, 185, 212
  in its absolute view, 169
  its different planes, 187
  its implications for life, 214
  its implications for society, 161
  its interpretation, 186
  its power and demands, 187-8
  natural ethics, 105
  religion of, 11, 23, 161
  the supreme dharma, 214
  towards all life, 185
Ājīvikas
  and ascetic career, 37
  and extrme asceticism, 36
  and niyati or fatalism, 39
  and the classification of men, 37, 39
  and the practice of nudity, 39
  and the theory of karma, 37
  criticized by buddha, 37
  its meaning, 38
  their penances, 38-9
Ajñānavāda, 91
Akriyāvāda, 91
Ālayavijñāna, 65, 97 (n.72)
Anātma, Anitya and Duhkha, 130
Anatta or Non-substantial Entity, 62
Anekānta, 122 (n.25)
  active indifference, 201 (n.136)
  and absolutism, 111
  and Ahiṁsā, 186, 189, 190, 214
  and dogmatism, 189-90
  and intellectual discrimination, 189
  and Jaina dharma, 73
  and Jaina ethics, 109, 121
  and the spirit of accommodation, 189
  and underlying unity, 46
  plurality and multiplicity, 189-90
Āpaddharma or Situational Ethics, 60
Aparigraha
  ahiṁsā in deed, 187
  an attitude to material universe, 178
  and self-realization, 195
  and the householder, 178, 180
  and truth, 106

in achieving mental equanimity, 179
its definition, 118
its meaning, 176, 178
quintessence of Jain philosophy, 178
Ārya and Anārya, 133
Ārya-kṣatriyas, 5
Asceticism
and abnormality, 22
and Jaina dhyāna or meditation, 35
and śramaṇa traditions, 29
and women, 24
in ājīvikism, 36-40
in Buddhism, 29-33
in India, 22-24
in Jainism, 33-36
its objectives, 20
Āśrama or Order of Life
and Sannyāsa, 24
and Varṇa, 60
gṛhasthāśrama praised and condemned, 26-28
sannyāsa becomes the means of mokṣa, 28
sannyāsa recognized, 26
the four āśramas, 25
to be followed by stages, 26
vanaprastha becomes superfluous, 28
Āsrava or Inflow of Karma, 75
Aṣṭāṅga Mārga or Eight-fold Path, 95 (n.67)
Atharva Veda
and the concept of time or Kāla, 87
and the world of eka-vrātya, 6
and theosophic views, 53
brahman, the Atharvan priest, 50
its brahmacāri, 23
its contents, 50
its literature, 6
its origins, 28
the Vedic Canon, 47
Atheism of the Śramaṇas, 13-4
Ātmavidyā or Knowledge of Self, 8-10
Āyatana, 133

Bālatapas, 35
Bandha or Bondage, 76
Bhagavad Gītā
and Bhakti, 208
and the doctrine of Bhakti, 57
and the synthesis of traditions, 58
and total renunciation, 207-8
dharma as manifestation of god, 57
manifold means of salvation, 58
niskāmakarma, 15-6, 86
sattva, rajas and tamas or tri-guṇa, 184
svadharma, 57-8, 86, 93 (n.26)
Bhakti Cult, 16
Bhikṣu Sūtra or Samaṇa Sūtra, 25
Bhūtavāda, 28
Bodhisattva, 96 (n.70), 100 (n.169)
addressee of the vows in the Mahāyāna, 32
and Ājīvika, 39
and buddhas, 32, 61, 63, 211
and Christianity, 214
and communion of all, 70
and his vows, 33
and salvation by faith, 63
and self-sacrifice, 120, 166, 171
and the ideal of Arhat, 63, 69
and the pāramitas or special vows, 120
and the religious life of buddhists, 16
and violence, 172
as ideal in the Mahāyāna, 166, 188
as the aim of life, 69
Bodhisattva, 96 (n.70)

Brāhmaṇa Literature, 52
Brāhmaṇas and Kṣatriyas, 15, 175
Brahmavādi, 23
Brahmavid or Knower of Brahman, 7
Brāhmin Hegemony, 28
Brāhmin Identity, 174
Brāhmin Priests in Vrātya Land, 6
Brāhminhood, 207
Brāhmins learn from Kṣatriyas, 24
Buddha
a Kṣatriya by caste, 10
and Ājīvikas, 37
and Arhat, 171
and Bimbisāra, 25
and Brahmā, 14
and caste, 175
and dhamma and saṅgha, 61
and ethical purity, 32
and future Buddha, 71
and heretic views, 87
and his austerities, 29
and his First Sermon, 21, 66, 96 (n.68)
and his manifestations, 211
and his original teachings, 64, 68, 167, 211
and his prime vow, 33
and his response to his age, 15-6
and his three bodies or tri-kāya, 68, 96 (n.71)
and Mahāvīra, 15, 37-6, 87, 207
and morality, 152-3
and prayers addressed to Buddha, 32
and renunciation, 11
and the essence of Buddhahood, 31
and the knowledge of dhamma, 128
and the middle-path, 29, 166
and vinaya, 66-7, 69
his personality, 71
moral and intellectual perfection, 69
the Cosmic Buddha, 63
Buddhism
and extreme asceticism, 170
and Jainism, 13
and Marxism, 70
and religious suicide, 171
and Sāṁkhya, 12
its liberal spirit, 71
Buddhist and Brāhmaṇic Morality, 71
Buddhist Monastic-Lay Discipline, 62
Buddhist prayers (austerity measure), 32
Buddhist Psychology, 139-42
Buddhist Religious Literature, 61
Buddhist Social Ideas, 70
Cause of the Universe, Misery, etc., 86-8
Class Encounter, 4-5
Conversion
bondage to release, 148
from karmamārga to jñānamārga, 206
in religious history, 207
of the brāhmins in Vrātya courts, 6
stoma ceremony, 4
Cosmic Buddha, 63

Dāna, 180-1
Determinism and Free Will, 90
Devaloka and Pitṛloka, 8, 27, 53
Dhamma
according to planes of existence, 136
associated and unassociated with the mind, 134
conditioned and unconditioned, 134
defiled and undefiled, 134
directly and indirectly caused, 137
essence of Buddhism, 129
important conclusions, 131

interaction between atoms, 137
its characteristics, 128-9
its classification according to Abhidhammakoṣabhāṣya, 133-5
its classification according to Jayasuria, 135-8
its dynamic conception, 138-9
its general classification, 132-3
its meaning and nature, 127-9
primary and secondary elements, 137
skandha, āyatana and dhātu, 133
units of matter and of the mind, 135
units of thought and of matter, 136

Dharma and Adharma
and ākāśa, 146
astikāya or existence cum extension, 145
differing from dharma in Buddhism, 149-52
establishing the Order in the universe, 143
its implications, 143, 146-9
its nature and significance, 144-6
its relation to guṇasthāna, 148
its relation to jīva and pudgala, 145, 146
its relation to karma, 147-8
its relation to moral discipline, 148
its relation to saṁsāra and mokṣa, 148
its relation with jīva and pudgala, 146
movement and rest, 143, 145
similar to dharma in Buddhism, 153-4

Dharma in Buddhism, 61-72
cosmic and moral law, 66-7
dharma vicāra,127
mahāyāna tradition, 64-6
system of ethics, 67-70
the mādhyāmika school,64-5
the yogācāra school, 65-6

Dharma in Hinduism
a literary survey, 48
brāhmaṇa dharma, 51-2
epic dharma, 56-7
gītā dharma, 57-8
it sources, 47-8
its meaning, 46
nīti dharma, 55-6
pauraṇic dharma, 58-9
puruṣārtha dharma, 59-61
role of śruti and smrti,47-8
sūtra dharma, 54-5
upaniṣadic dharma, 52-4
varṇa and āśrama dharma, 54-5
vedic dharma, 48-51

Dharma in Jainism, 72-83
causes of bondage, 78
system of reality, 74
two levels of meaning, 72
types of karma, 76
view of karma, 88-92
viewed in various ways, 73

Dharma, Law and Religion, 56
Dharmaśāstra, its Nature and Contents, 54
Dhātu, 133
Dhyāna in Jainism, 35
Dialogue between Traditions, 15-6
Dṛṣṭa and Adṛṣṭārtha, 55
Durnaya, 190
Dynamics of Class Structure, 1

Eight-fold Path, 21
Emancipation, 9, 24
Environmental Degradation, 163
Equality and Plurality of Beings, 81

Four Noble Truths and Eight-fold Path, 61
Freedom from Karma, 82
Fundamentalism, 164

Guṇasthāna or Stages of Spiritual Life, 83

Hiṁsā
- *and passion, 168*
- *Buddhist and Jain views, 172*
- *caused by profession, 116*
- *in defense of truth, country, etc., 116*
- *its several meanings, 167*
- *law of Manu as hiṁsā śāstra, 169, 185*
- *life is dear to all, 81*
- *mental and physical, 168*
- *root cause of all evil, 161*
- *unavoidable, 116, 172*
- *violence to life, 166*

Human Personality, 184
- *concentrated and distracted persons, 141-2*
- *healthy and unhealthy attitudes, 139-41*

Idea of God and Doctrine of Karma, 14
Īśvaravāda, 88

Jaina Ethics, 159 (n.135)
- *ascetic and lay morality, 113-4*
- *aticara or violation of a vow, 115*
- *attitude of anekānta, 121*
- *basis and end of morality, 111*
- *celibacy, 117-8*
- *conduct based on knowledge, 107*
- *conscience, the subject of moral judgement, 108*
- *distinct from buddhist ethics, 119*
- *from niścaya and vyavahāra points of view, 105*
- *individual and social ethics, 115*
- *individualistic?, 104*
- *intuition, 110*
- *mahā and anu-vrata, 115*
- *meritorious actions, 112*
- *moral judgement, 109*
- *moral justification, 110*
- *moral worth of an act, 108*
- *motives, 105*
- *non-attachment, 118-9, 200 (n.102)*
- *non-stealing, 117*
- *non-violence, 115-6*
- *right knowledge and belief, 119*
- *self-determinism, 107*
- *self-realization as end of moral life, 104*
- *tri-ratna or three jewels, 111*
- *truth, 116-7*
- *two levels of morality, 112, 113-4*
- *vicarious suffering, 120*
- *virtue and vice, 112*

Jaina Reconciliatory Perspective, 91
Jaina Tattva, its Implications, 79-83
Jaina Tīrtha or Four Holy Orders, 106
Jaina View of Grace, 89, 122 (n.20)
Jaina View of Life, 73, 80
Jainism and Buddhism, 13
- *aspects of violence, 168*
- *dāna or gift-offering, 180-1*
- *euthanesia or mercy-killing, 172*
- *evil and its root cause, 165-7*
- *meaning of violence, 167*
- *self-mortification and compassion, 169*
- *social inequality and caste discrimination, 173-5*
- *wealth and ownership, 176-8, 200 (n.93)*

Jainism and Sāṁkhya, 12
Jambūka, 38
Janmāntaravāda, 7

Jaṭila, 62
Jīva and Ajīva, 74
Jīva from Niścaya and Vyavahāra Perspectives, 79
Jñānamārga or Path of Knowledge, 11-3

Kāla, 87
Karma
and Buddhism, 29, 86
and jñāna, 52
and mokṣa, 79
and passions, 78
and rebirth, 7
and saptatattva, 73
and the idea of God, 14
and tri-gupti, 78
as matter particles, 75
as ritual action, 52
determinant of destiny, 39
freedom from, 21, 33, 35, 36, 74
historical survey, 84-8
in buddhist tradition, 86
in ritualistic tradition, 84
in upaniṣadic tradition, 84
its basic types, 76
its doctrine, 7
its inevitable effects, 37
its origins, 7, 62
materialistic conception, 85
niṣkāma and svadharma of Gītā, 86
re-animation theory, 37
śubha and aśubha karma, 91
Kaṣāya or Passions, 78
Keśī Sūkta, 11, 23
Knowledge - key for realization, 21
Knowledge about Karma, 81
Knowledge and Sacrifices, 10
Kriyāvāda, 91
Kṣanikavāda, 130
Kṣatriyas, 4-5
and asceticism, 25
their theosophical wisdom, 7

Legal Justice, 55
Leśya or Soul-colouring, 90

Mahābhārata and Rāmāyaṇa, 56
Maitreya or the Future Buddha, 71
Makkali Gośāla, 36
Meditation or Dhyāna, 21
Monasticism and Caste-tyranny, 15

Nāgas, 2-3
Names given to Non-āryans, 3
Nami and Śakra, 177
Neo-āryanism, 4, 206
Nirvāṇa, 96 (n.69)
a gradual and tedious path, 83
and dhamma, 153
and non-violence, 195
and suchness, 65-6
and suicide, 170
and the ideal of Arhat, 63
cessation from all pain and suffering, 166
extinction of desire and attachment, 62
freedom from passion, suffering and rebirth, 66
freedom from the cycle of births and deaths, 29
growth towards extinction, 135
immediate and eschatological, 83
mādhyāmika interpretation, 64
self-realization, 21
the aim of Upaniṣads, 9
the fourth real, 137
the supreme dharma, 126, 128
the supreme goal of Buddhist endeavour, 68
Niyati or Fatalism
and Ājīvikas, 37
and the power of karma, 39
comforting the sufferers, 37
its probable sources, 37
its view on life, 87

non-Āryan origin?, 37
Non-violence
a myth?, 195
and active resistance, 192
and anekānta, 186, 189
and conflict resolution, 184, 193
and dialogue, 191
and Gandhi, 186, 187, 192, 198 (n.55)
and inner strength, 195
and inter-religious and inter-cultural dialogue, 196
and manudharmaśāstra, 185
and nirvāṇa, 195
and non-exploitation, 191
and pariṣahājaya or overcoming hardships, 192
and passive resistance, 192, 203 (n.159)
and passivity, 185
and plurality of truth, 189-90
and vicarious suffering, 188
and world-mission, 188
its basis, 185
its critics, 183
its different stages, 192
its meaning in Buddhism, 186
its power and demands, 187-8, 193
natural or unnatural?, 183
positive and negative sense, 186
spiritual traditions, 184
śramaṇa vision, 185
Non-violent Society
building of a non-violent society, 193
its description, 194
new heaven and new earth, 194
Omniscient Teachers, 14

Pañca Skandha, 132, 134, 140, 150
Pañcaparameṣṭi, 107
Parigraha or Attachment, 179, 199 (n.84)
Path of Purification in Buddhism, 31
Poverty and Inequality, 162
Pratītyasamutpāda or Law of Causation, 95 (n.64), 129, 133, 156 (n.39)
Principle of Reciprocity, 81
Pudgala or Matter, 75
Purāṇas, its Contents, 58
Puruṣārtha or Aims of Life, 60
Puruṣavāda, 88

Race to Race Encounter, 2
Rājasūya, 5
Real
in Buddhism, 135
in Jainism, 144
Religion of Ahiṁsā, 11, 23, 161
Religion of Self-help, 82, 120
Religious Encounter, 4
Renouncer and Caste, 208
Renouncer Tradition, 208
Renunciation and Asceticism, 10-1
Renunciation of Pleasures of Life, 81
Ṛg Veda
and keśī sūkta on naked ascetics, 1
and Sāma Veda, 51
and the concept of Ātman, 53
and the gods, 52
and the notion of sin, 9-10
and the word āśrama, 25
and the word Brahmā, 51
and Yajur Veda, 51
its gods, 49, 52
its literature, 48
Right Knowledge, 21
Ṛṣabha, 10
Ṛta
as system of activity, 49
as the Vedic meaning of dharma, 48-9
as world-Order, 46

at celestial and human realms, 49
gods, its offspring, 57
universal Order, 48
Sallekhanā, 119, 170
Salvation by Faith in Buddhism, 66
Saṁvara or Checking the inflow of Karma, 78
Samvṛtti and Nivṛtti Mārga, 6
Saṅgha and Caste, 175
Sānkhya
and Buddhism, 12
and Jainism, 12
and Yoga, 12
Sānskrit Literature, 59-61
Sarvajña or Omniscience, 111
Scholasticism in Buddhism, 64
Sectarianism in the Purāṇas, 59
Self-knowledge, 8-10
Self-realization and Self-governance, 195
Self-reliance, 14
Sin and Reconciliation in Buddhism, 31
Śramaṇa Counter Culture, 182
attachment and dominance, 178
social inequality and discrimination, 173-5
wealth and accumulation, 176-8
Śramaṇa view of Life, 25
Stoma Ritual, 4
Sudharma and Jambusvāmi, 168
Svabhāva, 87
Svadharma or Caste Duty, 58
Syādvāda and Nayavāda, 187, 189, 190, 214

Tandulamatsya, 89
Tāntric Traditions, 22
Tapas, means of Self-knowledge, 27
Tathatā, 95 (n.65)
Tri-kāya, 96 (n.71)
triple-body of the Buddha, 66
Trilakṣaṇa, 95 (n.66)
True Knowledge, 9

Udgatṛ Priests, 51
Upaniṣads
and jñāna mārga, 11, 52
and karma mārga, 10
and kṣatriya teachings, 7
and mokṣa, 28
and neo-āryanism, 4
and nivṛtti mārga, 6
and the āśrama or order of life, 27
and the doctrine of karma, 84-5
and the knowledge of the ātman, 28
and the source of brāhminhood, 174
and the universal Soul, 212
its doctrine, 53
its objectives, 9, 53
its world-view, 48
matter as illusion, 12
realization of brahman, 21
self, karma and renunciation, 53
the theosophical wisdom, 6

Vālmīkiyan Ethics, 57
Varṇa and Āśrama, 60
Veda
and animal sacrifice, 185
as source and authority, 57
brahmacāri of Atharva Veda, 23
brahmacāri of the Vedas, 23
Buddhists and Jains on, 14
its orthodoxy, 14
its source and authority, 173-4
purāṇas as Vedas of the common-folk, 58-9
restriction on Vedic study, 208
ritualism of the Vedas, 24
saving effect of Vedic study, 176
śruti and smṛti, 47
vedānta as their summit,7
vedic view of life, 25

Vijñānavāda, 65
Vinaya and Saṅgha, 31-2, 67
Vinayavāda, 91
Violence
  and accumulation of wealth, 179
  and householder, 179
  and promotion of social good, 173
  and self-mortification, 169
  its aspects, 168
  its counter culture, 173
  its justifications, 169, 171-2
  its meanings, 167
  root of all evil, 165
  the phenomenon, 167
Vows in Hīnayāna Tradition, 32
Vows in Mahāyāna Tradition, 32
Vrātya
  and Atharva Veda, 6
  Brāhmins learning from, 6
  Eka-vrātya, 7
  land of the East, 3
  their wisdom, 6
  vrātya-kṣatriya, 5
  vrātyaṣtoma ritual, 4

Wise and the Fool, 24
Women Disciples of Buddha, 97 (n.80)

Yadṛcchā, 87
Yajur Veda, its New Features, 51
Yati, 24
Yellow hats or Gelug-pa, 97 (n.82)
Yoga and Sāṁkhya, 12